5B

Math in FOCUS®
Singapore Math
by Marshall Cavendish

Consultant and Author
Dr. Fong Ho Kheong

Authors
Gan Kee Soon and Chelvi Ramakrishnan

U.S. Consultants
Dr. Richard Bisk
Andy Clark
Patsy F. Kanter

Marshall Cavendish
Education

US Distributor

HOUGHTON MIFFLIN HARCOURT

COMMON
CORE

© 2013 Marshall Cavendish International (Singapore) Private Limited

Published by Marshall Cavendish Education
An imprint of Marshall Cavendish International (Singapore) Private Limited
Times Centre, 1 New Industrial Road, Singapore 536196
Customer Service Hotline: (65) 6411 0820
E-mail: tmesales@sg.marshallcavendish.com
Website: www.marshallcavendish.com/education

Distributed by
Houghton Mifflin Harcourt
222 Berkeley Street
Boston, MA 02116
Tel: 617-351-5000
Website: www.hmheducation.com/mathinfocus

First published 2013

Math in Focus® Grade 5 Student Book B
ISBN 978-0-547-87534-7

Printed in United States of America

2 3 4 5 6 7 8   1897   18 17 16 15 14 13
4500360944   A B C D E

Contents

8 Decimals

Look for **Practice and Problem Solving**

Student Book A and Student Book B	Workbook A and Workbook B
• **Let's Practice** in every lesson	• **Independent Practice** for every lesson
• **Put on Your Thinking Cap!** in every chapter	• **Put on Your Thinking Cap!** in every chapter

Look for **Assessment Opportunities**

Student Book A and Student Book B	Workbook A and Workbook B
• **Quick Check** at the beginning of every chapter to assess chapter readiness	• **Cumulative Reviews** six times during the year
• **Guided Practice** after every example or two to assess readiness to continue lesson	• **Mid-Year and End-of-Year Reviews** to assess test readiness
• **Chapter Review/Test** in every chapter to review or test chapter material	

9 Multiplying and Dividing Decimals

 **Percent**

11 Graphs and Probability

Fruit Bought at Supermarket

Key
■ Gina
■ Kim

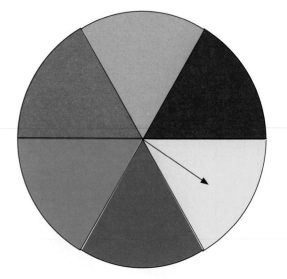

12 Angles

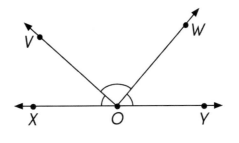

13 Properties of Triangles and Four-sided Figures

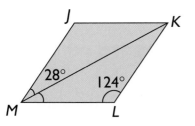

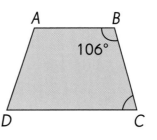

14 Three Dimensional Shapes

15 Surface Area and Volume

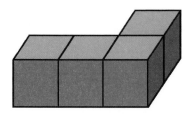

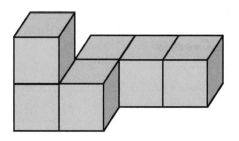

Welcome to

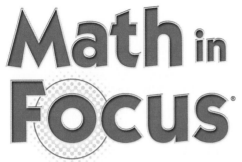

This exciting math program comes to you all the way from the country of Singapore. We are sure you will enjoy learning math with the interesting lessons you'll find in these books.

What makes *Math in Focus*® different?

▶ **Two books** You don't write in the ▢ in this textbook. This book has a matching **Workbook**. When you see the pencil icon , you will write in the **Workbook**.

▶ **Longer lessons** Some lessons may last more than a day, so you can really understand the math.

▶ **Math will make sense** Learn to use bar models to solve word problems with ease.

In this book, look for

Learn	**Guided Practice**	**Let's Practice**	**ON YOUR OWN**
This means you will learn something new.	Your teacher will help you try some sample problems.	You practice what you've learned to solve more problems. You can make sure you really understand.	Now you get to practice with lots of different problems in your own **Workbook**.

Also look forward to *Games, Hands-On Activities, Math Journals, Let's Explore,* and *Put on Your Thinking Cap!*
You will combine logical thinking with math skills and concepts to meet new problem-solving challenges. You will be talking math, thinking math, doing math, and even writing about doing math.

What's in the Workbook?

Math in Focus® will give you time to learn important new concepts and skills and check your understanding. Then you will use the practice pages in the **Workbook** to try:

▶ Solving different problems to practice the new math concept you are learning. In the textbook, keep an eye open for this symbol 🄰 ON YOUR OWN ✎. That will tell you which pages to use for practice.

▶ *Put on Your Thinking Cap!*

   Challenging Practice problems invite you to think in new ways to solve harder problems.

   Problem Solving challenges you to use different strategies to solve problems.

▶ Math Journal activities ask you to think about thinking, and then write about that!

Students in Singapore have been using this kind of math program for many years.
Now you can too — are you ready?

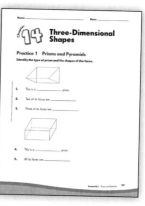

8 Decimals

Lessons

8.1 Understanding Thousandths

8.2 Comparing and Rounding Decimals

8.3 Rewriting Decimals as Fractions and Mixed Numbers

BIG IDEA

▶ Thousandths can be represented with three decimal places or as fractions.

Recall Prior Knowledge

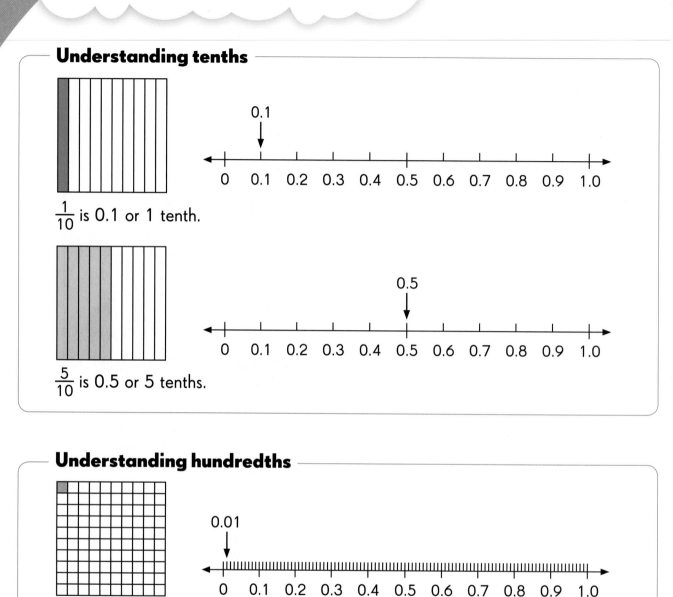

Understanding tenths

$\frac{1}{10}$ is 0.1 or 1 tenth.

$\frac{5}{10}$ is 0.5 or 5 tenths.

Understanding hundredths

$\frac{1}{100}$ is 0.01 or 1 hundredth.

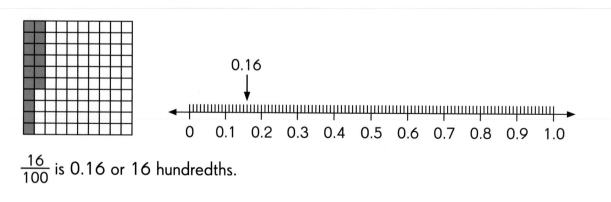

$\frac{16}{100}$ is 0.16 or 16 hundredths.

Understanding tenths and hundredths

10 tenths = 1 one
$$\frac{10}{10} = 1$$

10 hundredths = 1 tenth
$$\frac{10}{100} = \frac{1}{10}$$

0.23 = 23 hundredths
= 2 tenths 3 hundredths
$= \frac{2}{10} + \frac{3}{100}$
$= \frac{23}{100}$

Ones	Tenths	Hundredths
0	2	3

Reading decimals

1.25 = 1 one and 2 tenths 5 hundredths
= 1 one and 25 hundredths
Read 1.25 as one and twenty-five hundredths.

Ones	Tenths	Hundredths
1	2	5

Comparing decimals

Ones	Tenths	Hundredths
2	3	
2	1	3

2.3 is greater than 2.13.

Expressing fractions as decimals

Proper fractions

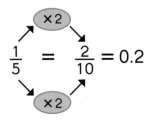

$$\frac{1}{5} = \frac{2}{10} = 0.2$$

Improper fractions

$\frac{5}{4} = \frac{4}{4} + \frac{1}{4}$
$= 1 + \frac{1}{4}$
$= 1 + 0.25$
$= 1.25$

Expressing mixed numbers as decimals

Express $1\frac{3}{20}$ as a decimal.

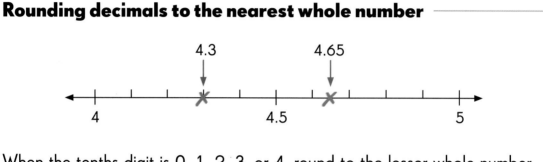

$$\frac{3}{20} = \frac{15}{100} = 0.15$$

$$1\frac{3}{20} = 1 + \frac{3}{20}$$
$$= 1 + \frac{15}{100}$$
$$= 1 + 0.15$$
$$= 1.15$$

Rounding decimals to the nearest whole number

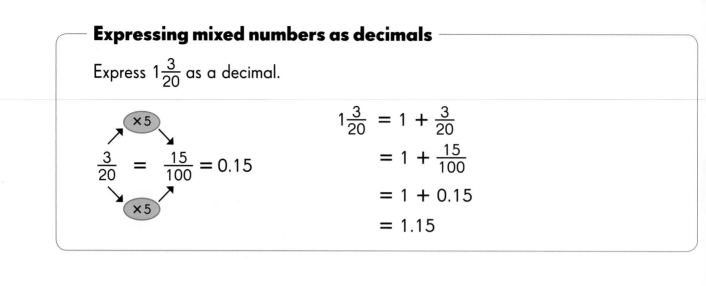

When the tenths digit is 0, 1, 2, 3, or 4, round to the lesser whole number.
4.**3** rounds to 4.

When the tenths digit is 5, 6, 7, 8, or 9, round to the greater whole number.
4.**6**5 rounds to 5.

Rounding decimals to the nearest tenth

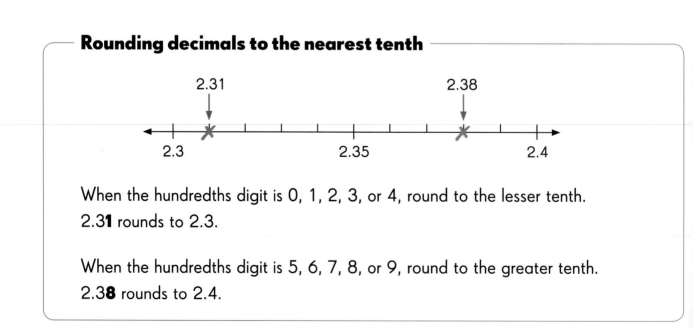

When the hundredths digit is 0, 1, 2, 3, or 4, round to the lesser tenth.
2.3**1** rounds to 2.3.

When the hundredths digit is 5, 6, 7, 8, or 9, round to the greater tenth.
2.3**8** rounds to 2.4.

 **Quick Check**

Find the decimals that the shaded parts represent.

1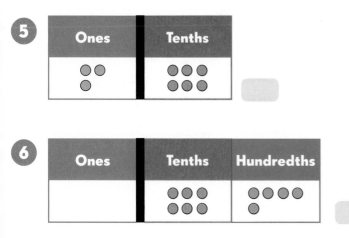

2

Find the decimal that each labeled point represents.

3

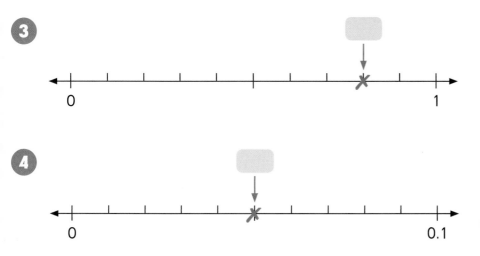

0   1

4

0   0.1

Find the decimal that each place-value chart represents.

5

Ones	Tenths
● ● ●	● ● ● ● ● ●

6

Ones	Tenths	Hundredths
	● ● ● ● ● ●	● ● ● ● ●

Which decimal is greater?

 7 1.28 or 1.5 ☐

Ones		Tenths	Hundredths
1	.	2	8
1	.	5	

8 5.63 or 5.68 ☐

Ones		Tenths	Hundredths
5	.	6	3
5	.	6	8

Express each fraction as a decimal.

9 $\frac{3}{25}$ ☐

10 $\frac{27}{20}$ ☐

Express each mixed number as a decimal.

11 $1\frac{2}{5}$ ☐

12 $2\frac{3}{4}$ ☐

Round to the nearest whole number.

13 3.07 ☐

14 6.5 ☐

15 12.48 ☐

16 88.63 ☐

Round to the nearest tenth.

17 0.92 ☐

18 4.86 ☐

19 28.03 ☐

20 56.34 ☐

Lesson 8.1 Understanding Thousandths

Lesson Objectives

- Read and write thousandths in decimal and fractional forms.
- Represent and interpret thousandths in models or in place-value charts.
- Write a fraction with denominator 1,000 as a decimal.

Vocabulary
thousandth
equivalent

Learn **Show thousandths on a number line, as a part of a model, or in a place-value chart.**

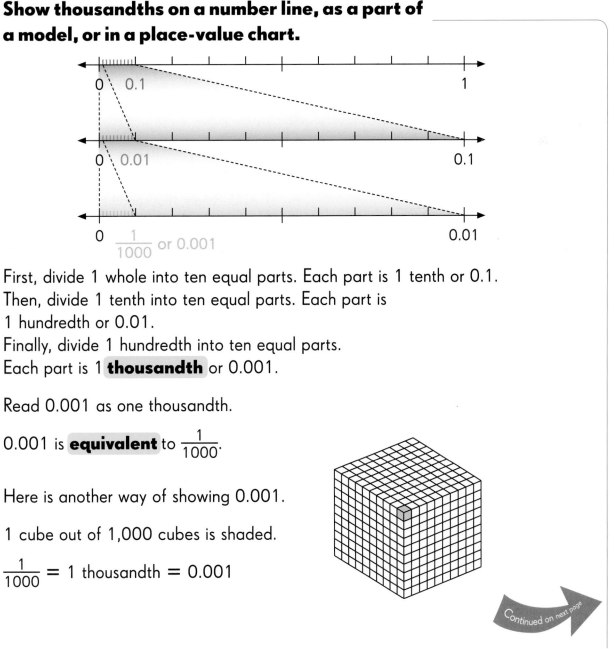

First, divide 1 whole into ten equal parts. Each part is 1 tenth or 0.1.
Then, divide 1 tenth into ten equal parts. Each part is
1 hundredth or 0.01.
Finally, divide 1 hundredth into ten equal parts.
Each part is 1 **thousandth** or 0.001.

Read 0.001 as one thousandth.

0.001 is **equivalent** to $\frac{1}{1000}$.

Here is another way of showing 0.001.

1 cube out of 1,000 cubes is shaded.

$\frac{1}{1000}$ = 1 thousandth = 0.001

Continued on next page

These models show other thousandths.

$\frac{2}{1000}$ = 2 thousandths
= 0.002

$\frac{3}{1000}$ = 3 thousandths
= 0.003

$\frac{4}{1000}$ = 4 thousandths
= 0.004

Thousandths are shown in place-value charts like this.

Ones		Tenths	Hundredths	Thousandths
				○○○ ○○○

6 thousandths = 0.006
3 decimal places

As decimals, thousandths have 3 decimal places.

Ones		Tenths	Hundredths	Thousandths
				○○○○ ○○○○

8 thousandths = 0.008

Guided Practice

Find the decimal that each labeled point represents.

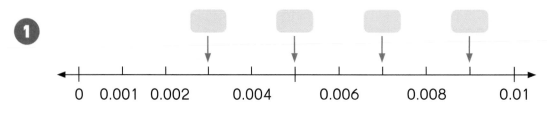

1

0	0.001	0.002		0.004		0.006		0.008		0.01

Find how many cubes should be shaded to show each decimal.

2 $\frac{5}{1000} = 0.005$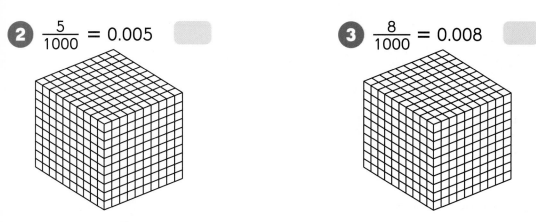

3 $\frac{8}{1000} = 0.008$

Copy and complete each place-value chart to show the decimal.

4

Ones	Tenths	Hundredths	Thousandths

7 thousandths = 0.007

5

Ones	Tenths	Hundredths	Thousandths

9 thousandths = 0.009

Find equivalent hundredths and thousandths.

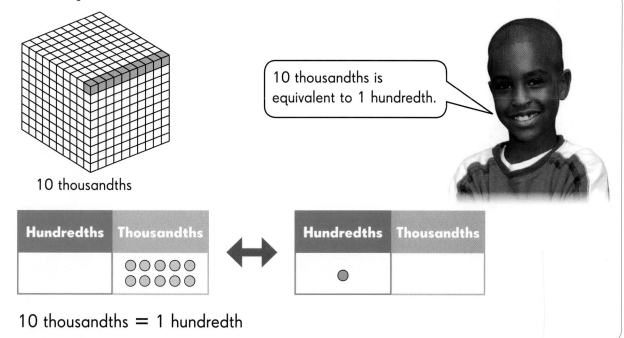

10 thousandths

10 thousandths is equivalent to 1 hundredth.

10 thousandths = 1 hundredth

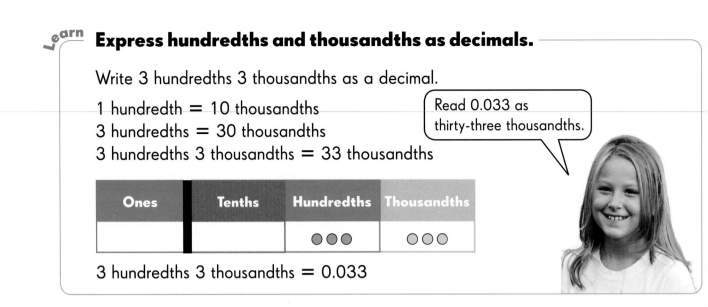

Learn — Express hundredths and thousandths as decimals.

Write 3 hundredths 3 thousandths as a decimal.

1 hundredth = 10 thousandths
3 hundredths = 30 thousandths
3 hundredths 3 thousandths = 33 thousandths

> Read 0.033 as thirty-three thousandths.

Ones	Tenths	Hundredths	Thousandths
		●●●	○○○

3 hundredths 3 thousandths = 0.033

Guided Practice

Find the decimals that the shaded parts represent.

6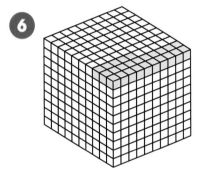

7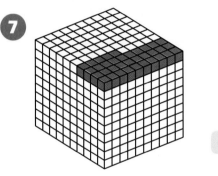

Find the decimal that each place-value chart represents.

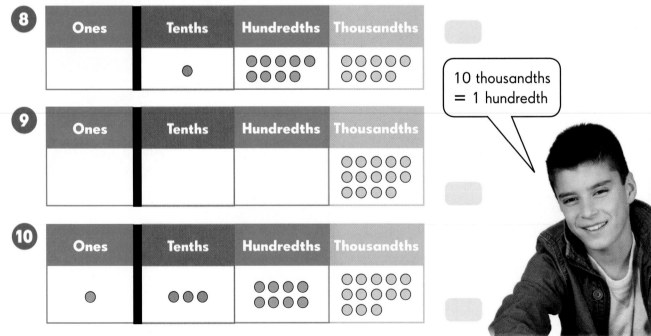

8

Ones	Tenths	Hundredths	Thousandths
	●	●●●●● ●●●●	●●●●● ●●●●

> 10 thousandths = 1 hundredth

9

Ones	Tenths	Hundredths	Thousandths
			○○○○○ ○○○○○ ○○○○

10

Ones	Tenths	Hundredths	Thousandths
●	●●●	●●●● ●●●●	●●●●● ●●●●● ●●●

10   **Chapter 8** Decimals

Express fractions as decimals.

Express $\frac{12}{1000}$ as a decimal.

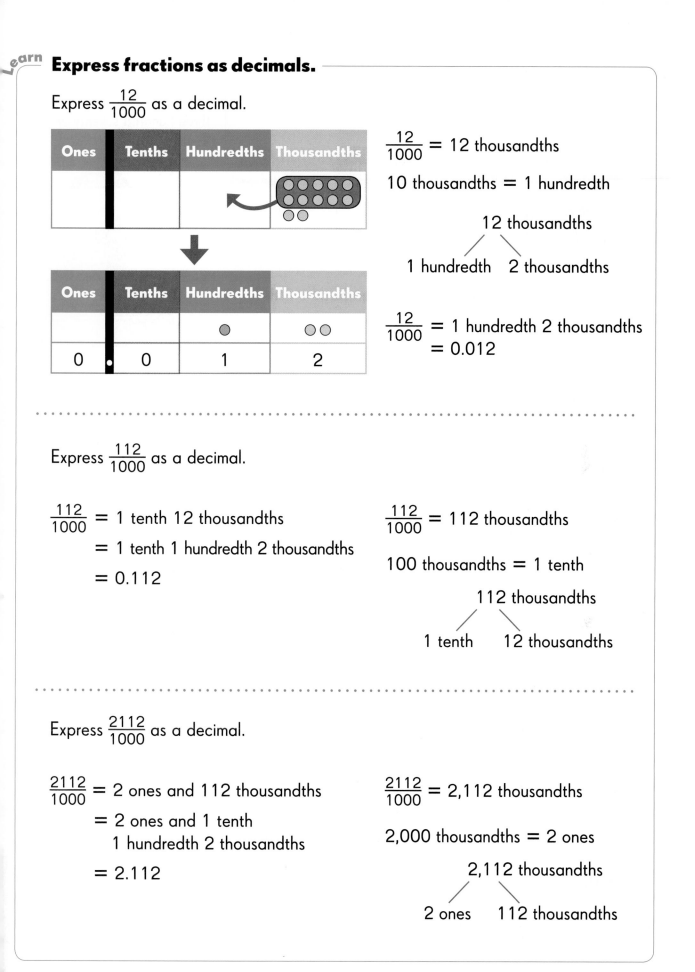

$\frac{12}{1000}$ = 12 thousandths

10 thousandths = 1 hundredth

12 thousandths
1 hundredth   2 thousandths

$\frac{12}{1000}$ = 1 hundredth 2 thousandths
= 0.012

Express $\frac{112}{1000}$ as a decimal.

$\frac{112}{1000}$ = 1 tenth 12 thousandths
= 1 tenth 1 hundredth 2 thousandths
= 0.112

$\frac{112}{1000}$ = 112 thousandths

100 thousandths = 1 tenth

112 thousandths
1 tenth   12 thousandths

Express $\frac{2112}{1000}$ as a decimal.

$\frac{2112}{1000}$ = 2 ones and 112 thousandths
= 2 ones and 1 tenth
1 hundredth 2 thousandths
= 2.112

$\frac{2112}{1000}$ = 2,112 thousandths

2,000 thousandths = 2 ones

2,112 thousandths
2 ones   112 thousandths

Express mixed numbers as decimals.

Express $2\frac{372}{1000}$ as a decimal.

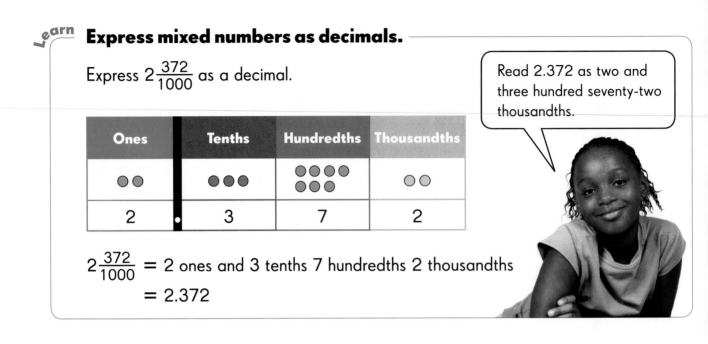

Read 2.372 as two and three hundred seventy-two thousandths.

Ones	Tenths	Hundredths	Thousandths
●●	●●●	●●●● ●●●	●○
2	3	7	2

$2\frac{372}{1000}$ = 2 ones and 3 tenths 7 hundredths 2 thousandths

= 2.372

Guided Practice

Complete.

11. $0.021 =$ ☐ thousandths

12. $0.314 =$ ☐ thousandths

13. $1.81 = 1$ one and ☐ thousandths

14. $3.09 = 3$ ones and ☐ thousandths

Express each fraction or mixed number as a decimal.

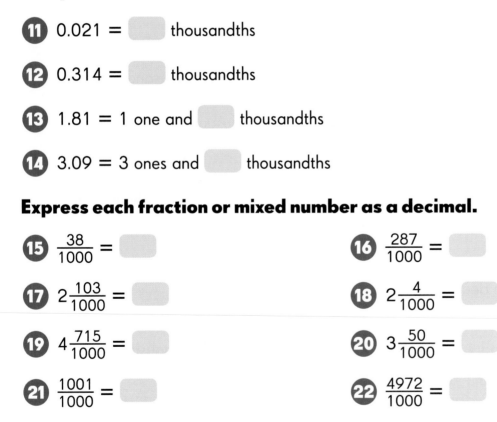

15. $\frac{38}{1000} =$ ☐

16. $\frac{287}{1000} =$ ☐

17. $2\frac{103}{1000} =$ ☐

18. $2\frac{4}{1000} =$ ☐

19. $4\frac{715}{1000} =$ ☐

20. $3\frac{50}{1000} =$ ☐

21. $\frac{1001}{1000} =$ ☐

22. $\frac{4972}{1000} =$ ☐

Explain.

23. Is 0.07 equivalent to 0.070? Explain your answer.

Write decimals in expanded form to show the values of the digits.

Ones		Tenths	Hundredths	Thousandths
8	•	4	0	9

$8.409 = 8$ ones and 4 tenths 9 thousandths

$\qquad = 8 + 0.4 + 0.009$

$\qquad = 8 + \dfrac{4}{10} + \dfrac{9}{1000}$

Guided Practice

Find the missing numbers.

24

Ones		Tenths	Hundredths	Thousandths
7	•	2	5	1

$7.251 = \boxed{}$ ones and $\boxed{}$ tenths $\boxed{}$ hundredths $\boxed{}$ thousandth

$\qquad = 7 + 0.2 + 0.05 + \boxed{}$

$\qquad = 7 + \dfrac{\boxed{}}{10} + \dfrac{\boxed{}}{100} + \dfrac{\boxed{}}{1000}$

25 $6.656 = 6\dfrac{656}{\boxed{}}$

Recognize the place and value of each digit in a decimal.

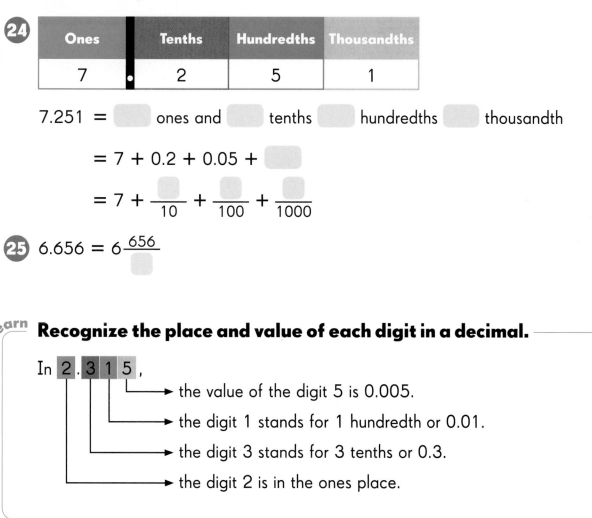

In 2.315,

→ the value of the digit 5 is 0.005.

→ the digit 1 stands for 1 hundredth or 0.01.

→ the digit 3 stands for 3 tenths or 0.3.

→ the digit 2 is in the ones place.

Guided Practice

Complete.

26 In 3.465, the digit 5 is in the ▢ place.

27 In 4.732, the digit 7 stands for ▢.

28 In 26.019, the value of the digit 1 is ▢.

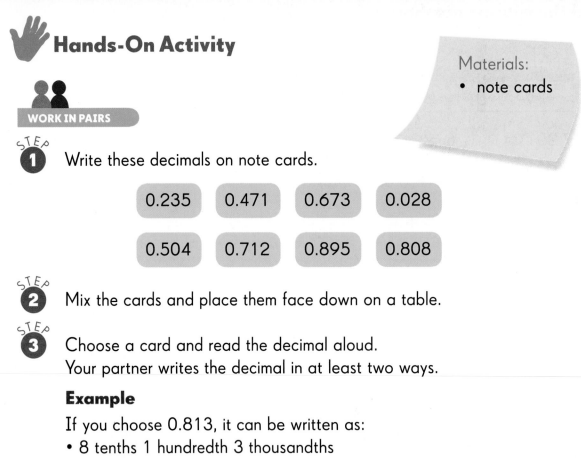

Hands-On Activity

WORK IN PAIRS

Materials:
• note cards

STEP 1 Write these decimals on note cards.

| 0.235 | 0.471 | 0.673 | 0.028 |

| 0.504 | 0.712 | 0.895 | 0.808 |

STEP 2 Mix the cards and place them face down on a table.

STEP 3 Choose a card and read the decimal aloud.
Your partner writes the decimal in at least two ways.

Example

If you choose 0.813, it can be written as:
• 8 tenths 1 hundredth 3 thousandths
• 813 thousandths
• 8 tenths 13 thousandths

STEP 4 Switch roles and repeat **STEP 3**.

Let's Practice

Find the decimals that the shaded parts represent.

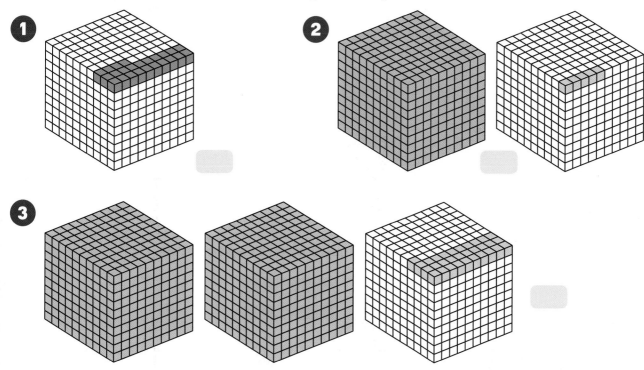

①

②

③

Find the decimal that each labeled point represents.

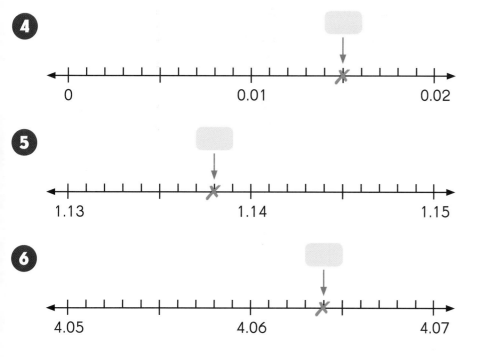

④

⑤

⑥

Copy each number line. Mark ✗ to show where each decimal is located.

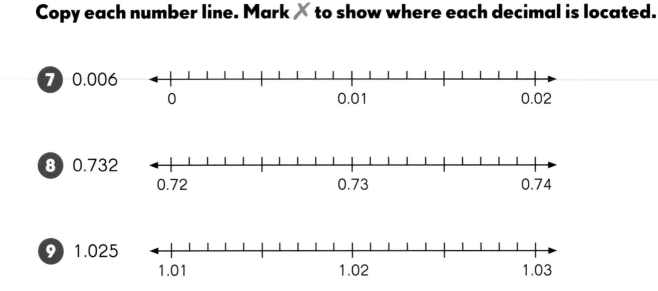

7 0.006

0   0.01   0.02

8 0.732

0.72   0.73   0.74

9 1.025

1.01   1.02   1.03

Find the decimal that each place-value chart represents.

10

Hundredths	Thousandths
	○○○○○ ○○○○○ ○○○○○

↔

Hundredths	Thousandths
●	○○○○

11

Ones	Tenths	Hundredths	Thousandths
	○○	○○○○	○○○○ ○○○

12

Ones	Tenths	Hundredths	Thousandths
○	○○○○ ○○○	○○○ ○○	○○○○○ ○○○○○ ○○

Find the value of the digit 8 in each decimal.

13 0.081 ⬜

14 0.148 ⬜

Express each fraction as a decimal.

15 $\frac{7}{1000}$ ⬜

16 $\frac{13}{1000}$ ⬜

17 $\frac{378}{1000}$ ⬜

18 $\frac{5009}{1000}$ ⬜

Complete.

19 $3.594 = 3 + 0.5 + $ ⬜ $+ 0.004$

20 $6.308 = 6 + 0.3 + $ ⬜

21 $7.281 = 7 + \frac{⬜}{10} + \frac{8}{⬜} + \frac{⬜}{1000}$

22 $40.069 = 40 + \frac{6}{⬜} + \frac{⬜}{1000}$

23 $21.2 = 21 + \frac{⬜}{1000}$

Use the place-value chart to complete.

Ones	Tenths	Hundredths	Thousandths
1	8	4	2

24 The digit ⬜ is in the tenths place.

25 The digit 1 stands for ⬜ .

26 The value of the digit 2 is ⬜ .

ON YOUR OWN

Go to Workbook B:
Practice 1, pages 1–4

Lesson 8.2 Comparing and Rounding Decimals

Lesson Objectives

- Compare and order decimals to 3 decimal places.
- Round decimals to the nearest hundredth.

Learn Use place-value concepts to compare and order decimals.

Order 0.835, 2.641, and 0.329 from least to greatest.

Ones		Tenths	Hundredths	Thousandths
0	.	8	3	5
2	.	6	4	1
0	.	3	2	9

First, compare the ones.

2 ones is greater than 0 ones.

$2.641 > 0.835$

$2.641 > 0.329$

So, 2.641 is the greatest.

Next, compare the tenths in 0.835 and 0.329.

8 tenths is greater than 3 tenths.

$0.835 > 0.329$

So, 0.329 is the least.

The order from least to greatest is
0.329, 0.835, 2.641.

Like comparing whole numbers, you start with the greatest place value.

Order 0.72, 0.273, and 0.7 from greatest to least.

Ones	Tenths	Hundredths	Thousandths
0	7	2	
0	2	7	3
0	7		

First, compare the ones. They are the same.

Next, compare the tenths. 7 tenths is greater than 2 tenths.

So, 0.273 is the least.

Because 0.72 and 0.7 have the same tenths digit, compare the hundredths.

2 hundredths is greater than 0 hundredths.

So, 0.72 is greater than 0.7.

The order from greatest to least is
0.72, 0.7, 0.273.

Guided Practice

Which decimal is greater?

1 0.012 or 0.12

2 0.505 or 0.55

Order the decimals from least to greatest.

3 0.7, 0.18, 0.315

4 0.19, 0.2, 0.185

Use place-value charts to help you compare these decimals.

Order the decimals from greatest to least.

5 1.008, 0.08, 0.108

6 0.505, 0.055, 0.5

Round decimals to the nearest hundredth.

Round 0.014 to the nearest hundredth.

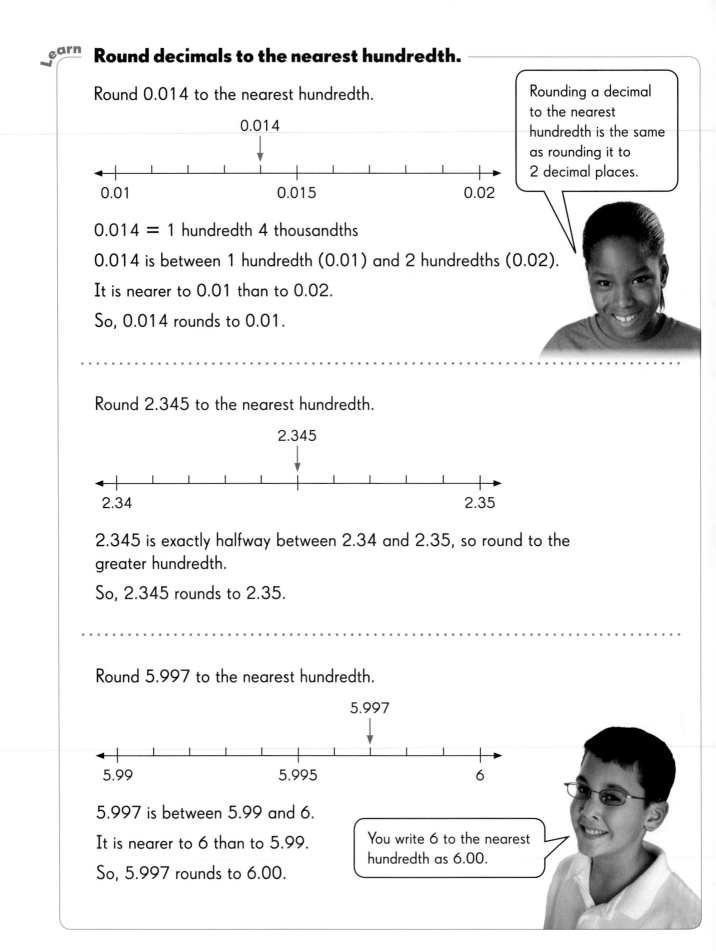

0.014 = 1 hundredth 4 thousandths

0.014 is between 1 hundredth (0.01) and 2 hundredths (0.02).

It is nearer to 0.01 than to 0.02.

So, 0.014 rounds to 0.01.

> Rounding a decimal to the nearest hundredth is the same as rounding it to 2 decimal places.

Round 2.345 to the nearest hundredth.

2.345 is exactly halfway between 2.34 and 2.35, so round to the greater hundredth.

So, 2.345 rounds to 2.35.

Round 5.997 to the nearest hundredth.

5.997 is between 5.99 and 6.

It is nearer to 6 than to 5.99.

So, 5.997 rounds to 6.00.

> You write 6 to the nearest hundredth as 6.00.

Guided Practice

For each decimal, draw a number line. Show the location of each decimal by drawing an ✗ on the number line. Then round the decimal to the nearest hundredth.

Example

0.123

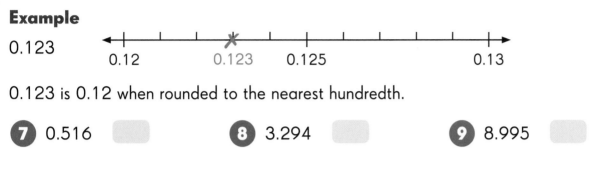

0.123 is 0.12 when rounded to the nearest hundredth.

7 0.516

8 3.294

9 8.995

Round each decimal to the nearest whole number, nearest tenth, and nearest hundredth.

10 2.029

11 25.957

Let's Practice

Compare. Complete with < , >, or =.

1 49.257 ◯ 49.25

2 49.257 ◯ 49.272

3 49.250 ◯ 49.25

Use the place-value chart to compare the decimals. Which is greater? Which is less?

4

	Ones	Tenths	Hundredths	Thousandths
0.809	0	8	0	9
0.832	0	8	3	2

Use the place-value chart to compare the decimals. Which is greater? Which is less?

5

	Ones		Tenths	Hundredths	Thousandths
1.945	1	•	9	4	5
1.954	1	•	9	5	4

Order the decimals from least to greatest.

6 3.06, 3.6, 3.066, 3.006

Order the decimals from greatest to least.

7 3.472, 2.472, 3.274, 2.427

Complete.

8 Rounding to the nearest hundredth is the same as rounding to [ ] decimal places.

9 Round 1.038 to the nearest hundredth.

1.038 is between 1.03 and [ ].

1.038 is nearer to [ ] than to [ ].

So, 1.038 rounds to [ ].

Round each decimal to the nearest whole number, nearest tenth, and nearest hundredth.

10 1.799

11 31.999

ON YOUR OWN

Go to Workbook B: Practice 2, pages 5–8

8.3 Rewriting Decimals as Fractions and Mixed Numbers

Lesson Objective

- Rewrite decimals as fractions and mixed numbers in simplest form.

Learn **Rewrite one- or two-place decimals as fractions or mixed numbers.**

One-place decimals

$0.3 = \frac{3}{10}$

$1.6 = 1\frac{6}{10}$

$= 1\frac{3}{5}$

Two-place decimals

$0.08 = \frac{8}{100}$

$= \frac{2}{25}$

$2.27 = 2\frac{27}{100}$

$\frac{6}{10}$ and $\frac{8}{100}$ can be expressed in simplest form.

$\frac{6}{10} = \frac{6 \div 2}{10 \div 2} = \frac{3}{5}$

$\frac{8}{100} = \frac{8 \div 4}{100 \div 4} = \frac{2}{25}$

Guided Practice

Rewrite each decimal as a fraction or mixed number in simplest form.

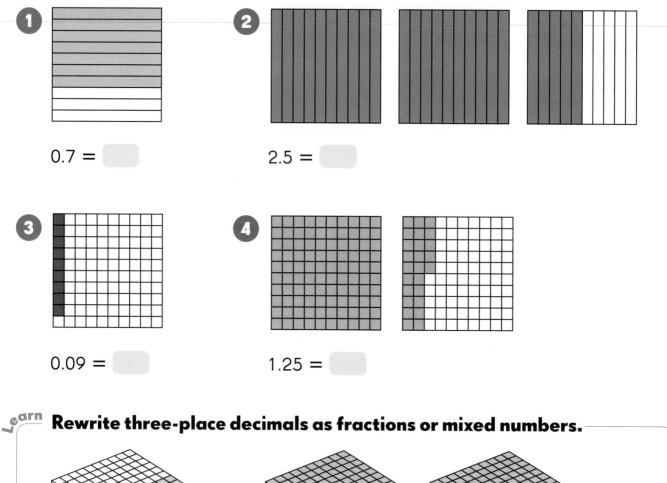

1 0.7 = ☐

2 2.5 = ☐

3 0.09 = ☐

4 1.25 = ☐

Learn **Rewrite three-place decimals as fractions or mixed numbers.**

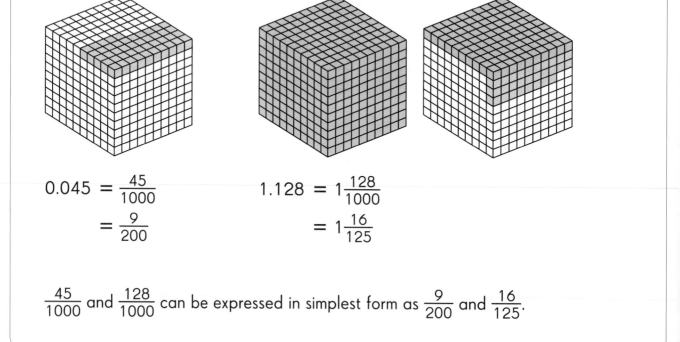

$0.045 = \dfrac{45}{1000}$

$\quad\ \ = \dfrac{9}{200}$

$1.128 = 1\dfrac{128}{1000}$

$\quad\ \ = 1\dfrac{16}{125}$

$\dfrac{45}{1000}$ and $\dfrac{128}{1000}$ can be expressed in simplest form as $\dfrac{9}{200}$ and $\dfrac{16}{125}$.

Guided Practice

Rewrite each decimal as a fraction or mixed number in simplest form.

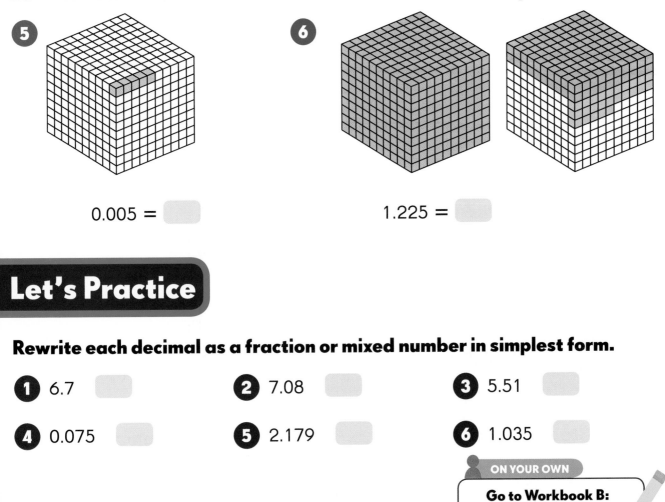

5   0.005 = ▢

6   1.225 = ▢

Let's Practice

Rewrite each decimal as a fraction or mixed number in simplest form.

1 6.7 ▢   **2** 7.08 ▢   **3** 5.51 ▢

4 0.075 ▢   **5** 2.179 ▢   **6** 1.035 ▢

ON YOUR OWN

**Go to Workbook B:
Practice 3, pages 9–12**

CRITICAL THINKING SKILLS
Put On Your Thinking Cap!

PROBLEM SOLVING

The length of a car is measured in meters to 3 decimal places.
The length of the car is 4.26 meters when rounded to the nearest hundredth.
What are the least and greatest possible measurements of its actual length?

ON YOUR OWN

**Go to Workbook B:
Put on Your Thinking Cap!
pages 13–14**

Chapter Wrap Up

Study Guide

You have learned...

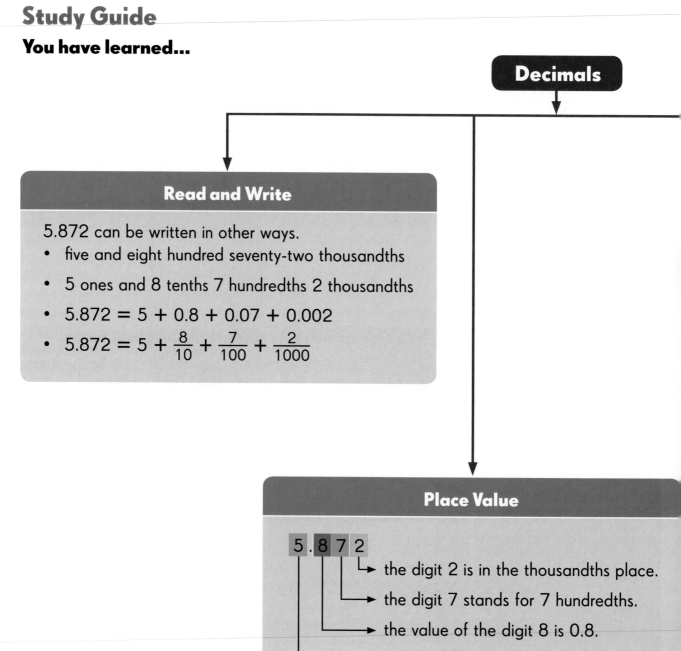

Decimals

Read and Write

5.872 can be written in other ways.
- five and eight hundred seventy-two thousandths
- 5 ones and 8 tenths 7 hundredths 2 thousandths
- $5.872 = 5 + 0.8 + 0.07 + 0.002$
- $5.872 = 5 + \frac{8}{10} + \frac{7}{100} + \frac{2}{1000}$

Place Value

5.872
- the digit 2 is in the thousandths place.
- the digit 7 stands for 7 hundredths.
- the value of the digit 8 is 0.8.
- the digit 5 is in the ones place.

▶ Thousandths can be represented with three decimal places or as fractions.

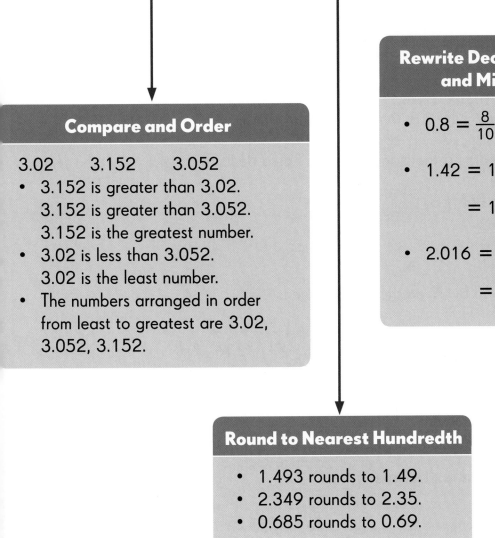

Compare and Order

3.02   3.152   3.052
- 3.152 is greater than 3.02.
  3.152 is greater than 3.052.
  3.152 is the greatest number.
- 3.02 is less than 3.052.
  3.02 is the least number.
- The numbers arranged in order from least to greatest are 3.02, 3.052, 3.152.

Rewrite Decimals as Fractions and Mixed Numbers

- $0.8 = \frac{8}{10} = \frac{4}{5}$

- $1.42 = 1\frac{42}{100}$
  $= 1\frac{21}{50}$

- $2.016 = 2\frac{16}{1000}$
  $= 2\frac{2}{125}$

Round to Nearest Hundredth

- 1.493 rounds to 1.49.
- 2.349 rounds to 2.35.
- 0.685 rounds to 0.69.

Chapter Review/Test

Vocabulary

Choose the correct word.

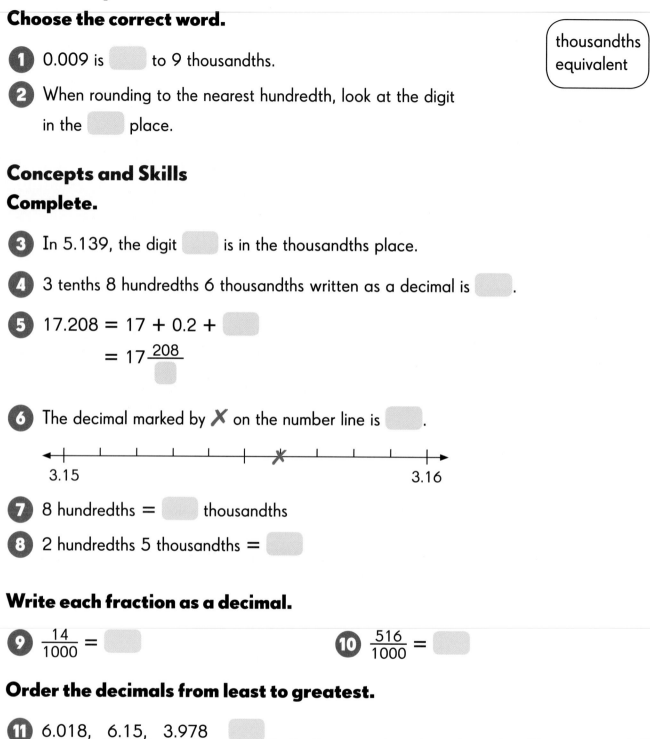

1. 0.009 is _____ to 9 thousandths.

2. When rounding to the nearest hundredth, look at the digit in the _____ place.

> thousandths
> equivalent

Concepts and Skills

Complete.

3. In 5.139, the digit _____ is in the thousandths place.

4. 3 tenths 8 hundredths 6 thousandths written as a decimal is _____.

5. 17.208 = 17 + 0.2 + _____
   = $17\frac{208}{}$

6. The decimal marked by ✗ on the number line is _____.

   3.15 ———————————————✗——————————— 3.16

7. 8 hundredths = _____ thousandths

8. 2 hundredths 5 thousandths = _____

Write each fraction as a decimal.

9. $\frac{14}{1000}$ = _____

10. $\frac{516}{1000}$ = _____

Order the decimals from least to greatest.

11. 6.018, 6.15, 3.978 _____

Round to the nearest hundredth.

12 0.675 [ ]

13 5.099 [ ]

14 35.214 [ ]

Rewrite each decimal as a fraction or mixed number in simplest form.

15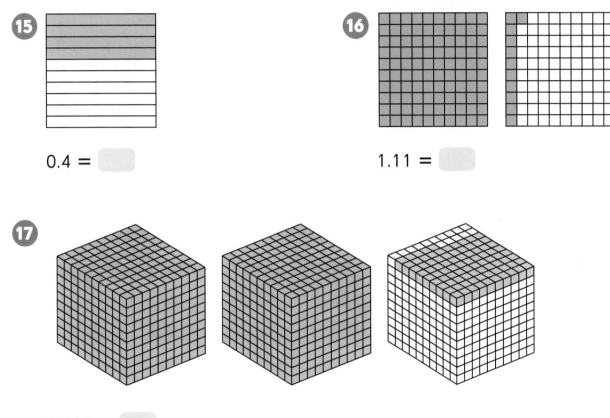

0.4 = [ ]

16

1.11 = [ ]

17

2.085 = [ ]

Rewrite each decimal as a fraction or mixed number in simplest form.

18 6.5 [ ]

19 9.06 [ ]

20 7.10 [ ]

21 3.005 [ ]

22 0.125 [ ]

23 5.258 [ ]

9 Multiplying and Dividing Decimals

Lessons

BIG IDEA

► Decimals can be multiplied and divided in the same way as whole numbers.

Recall Prior Knowledge

Multiplying whole numbers by 10, 100, and 1,000

To multiply a whole number by

- 10, move each digit of the number 1 place to the left.
- 100, move each digit of the number 2 places to the left.
- 1,000, move each digit of the number 3 places to the left.

You can use a place-value chart to show this.

	Ten Thousands	Thousands	Hundreds	Tens	Ones
23				●●	●●●
23 × 10			●●	●●●	
23 × 100		●●	●●●		
23 × 1,000	●●	●●●			

Multiplying whole numbers by tens, hundreds, and thousands

$8 \times 30 = 8 \times (3 \times 10)$
$= (8 \times 3) \times 10$
$= 24 \times 10$
$= 240$

$6 \times 500 = 6 \times (5 \times 100)$
$= (6 \times 5) \times 100$
$= 30 \times 100$
$= 3,000$

$12 \times 4,000 = 12 \times (4 \times 1,000)$
$= (12 \times 4) \times 1,000$
$= 48 \times 1,000$
$= 48,000$

Dividing whole numbers by 10, 100, and 1,000

To divide a whole number by

- 10, move each digit of the number 1 place to the right.
- 100, move each digit of the number 2 places to the right.
- 1,000, move each digit of the number 3 places to the right.

You can use a place-value chart to show this.

	Ten Thousands	Thousands	Hundreds	Tens	Ones
13,000	●	●●●			
13,000 ÷ 10		●	●●●		
13,000 ÷ 100			●	●●●	
13,000 ÷ 1,000				●	●●●

Dividing whole numbers by tens, hundreds, and thousands

$$90 \div 30 = (90 \div 3) \div 10$$
$$= 30 \div 10$$
$$= 3$$

$$600 \div 200 = (600 \div 2) \div 100$$
$$= 300 \div 100$$
$$= 3$$

$$12,000 \div 6,000 = (12,000 \div 6) \div 1,000$$
$$= 2,000 \div 1,000$$
$$= 2$$

Estimating products

Estimate the product of 238 and 28.
238 × 28 is about 200 × 30.
$$200 \times 30 = (200 \times 3) \times 10$$
$$= 600 \times 10$$
$$= 6,000$$
The estimated product of 238 and 28 is 6,000.

238 rounds to 200.
28 rounds to 30.

Estimating quotients

Estimate the quotient of 186 ÷ 12.
186 ÷ 12 is about 190 ÷ 10.
190 ÷ 10 = 19
The estimated quotient of 186 ÷ 12 is 19.

12 rounds to 10.
Choose a number close to
186 that can be evenly
divided by 10.
186 is about 190.

Adding decimals

When you add decimals, write the numbers so that the decimal points line up.

Add decimals with one decimal place without regrouping.
Add 3.2 and 1.4.

Step 1
Add the tenths.

```
    3 . 2
 +  1 . 4
 ─────────
        6
```

Step 2
Add the ones.

```
    3 . 2
 +  1 . 4
 ─────────
    4 . 6
```

So, 3.2 + 1.4 = 4.6.

Add decimals with two decimal places with regrouping.
Add 2.93 and 3.58.

Step 1
Add the hundredths.

```
        1
    2 . 9 3
 +  3 . 5 8
 ──────────
          1
```

Step 2
Add the tenths.

```
    1   1
    2 . 9 3
 +  3 . 5 8
 ──────────
        5 1
```

Step 3
Add the ones.

```
    1   1
    2 . 9 3
 +  3 . 5 8
 ──────────
    6 . 5 1
```

So, 2.93 + 3.58 = 6.51.

Subtracting decimals

When you subtract decimals, write the numbers so that the decimal points line up.

Subtract decimals with one decimal place without regrouping.
Subtract 0.3 from 1.6.

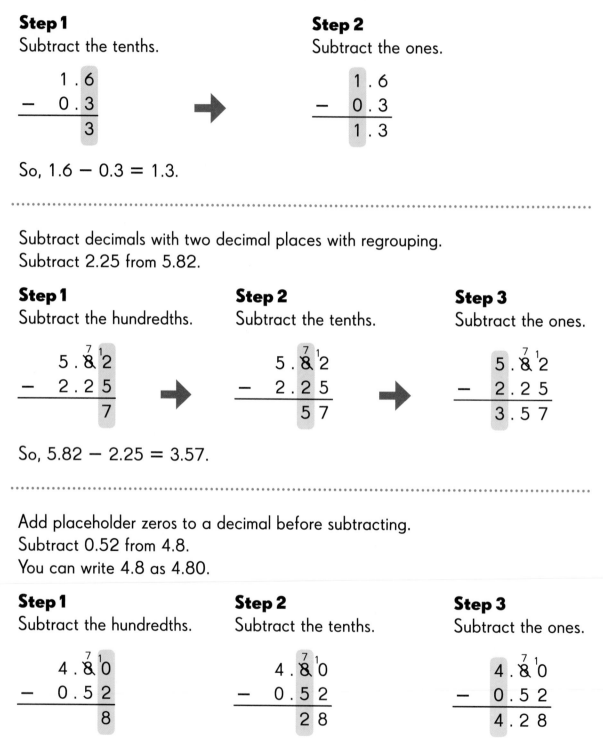

Step 1
Subtract the tenths.

$$
\begin{array}{r}
1\ .\ 6 \\
-\ \ 0\ .\ 3 \\
\hline
3
\end{array}
$$

Step 2
Subtract the ones.

$$
\begin{array}{r}
1\ .\ 6 \\
-\ \ 0\ .\ 3 \\
\hline
1\ .\ 3
\end{array}
$$

So, 1.6 − 0.3 = 1.3.

Subtract decimals with two decimal places with regrouping.
Subtract 2.25 from 5.82.

Step 1
Subtract the hundredths.

$$
\begin{array}{r}
5\ .\ 8^{7}\ 2^{1} \\
-\ \ 2\ .\ 2\ 5 \\
\hline
7
\end{array}
$$

Step 2
Subtract the tenths.

$$
\begin{array}{r}
5\ .\ 8^{7}\ 2^{1} \\
-\ \ 2\ .\ 2\ 5 \\
\hline
5\ 7
\end{array}
$$

Step 3
Subtract the ones.

$$
\begin{array}{r}
5\ .\ 8^{7}\ 2^{1} \\
-\ \ 2\ .\ 2\ 5 \\
\hline
3\ .\ 5\ 7
\end{array}
$$

So, 5.82 − 2.25 = 3.57.

Add placeholder zeros to a decimal before subtracting.
Subtract 0.52 from 4.8.
You can write 4.8 as 4.80.

Step 1
Subtract the hundredths.

$$
\begin{array}{r}
4\ .\ 8^{7}\ 0^{1} \\
-\ \ 0\ .\ 5\ 2 \\
\hline
8
\end{array}
$$

Step 2
Subtract the tenths.

$$
\begin{array}{r}
4\ .\ 8^{7}\ 0^{1} \\
-\ \ 0\ .\ 5\ 2 \\
\hline
2\ 8
\end{array}
$$

Step 3
Subtract the ones.

$$
\begin{array}{r}
4\ .\ 8^{7}\ 0^{1} \\
-\ \ 0\ .\ 5\ 2 \\
\hline
4\ .\ 2\ 8
\end{array}
$$

So, 4.8 − 0.52 = 4.28.

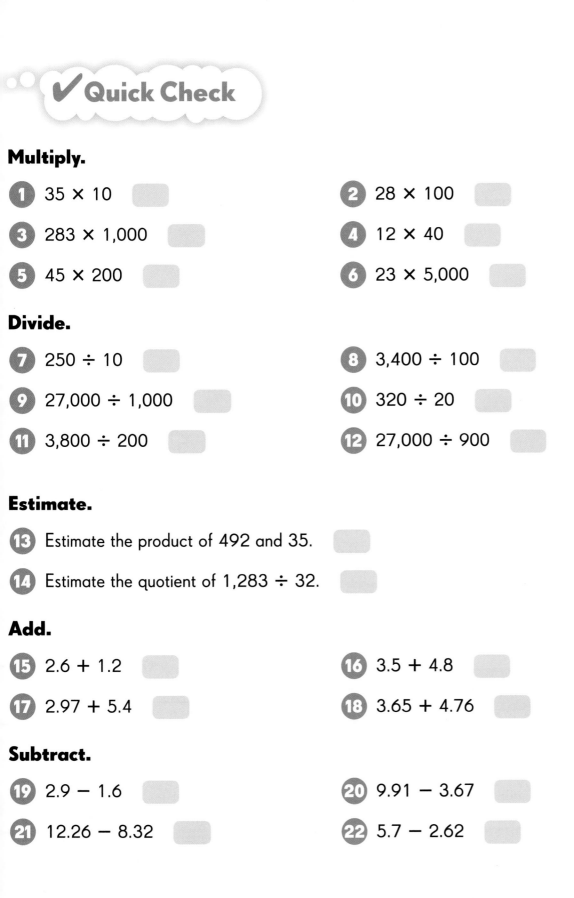

✔ Quick Check

Multiply.

1 35 × 10

2 28 × 100

3 283 × 1,000

4 12 × 40

5 45 × 200

6 23 × 5,000

Divide.

7 250 ÷ 10

8 3,400 ÷ 100

9 27,000 ÷ 1,000

10 320 ÷ 20

11 3,800 ÷ 200

12 27,000 ÷ 900

Estimate.

13 Estimate the product of 492 and 35.

14 Estimate the quotient of 1,283 ÷ 32.

Add.

15 2.6 + 1.2

16 3.5 + 4.8

17 2.97 + 5.4

18 3.65 + 4.76

Subtract.

19 2.9 − 1.6

20 9.91 − 3.67

21 12.26 − 8.32

22 5.7 − 2.62

Lesson 9.1 Multiplying Decimals

Lesson Objective

• Multiply tenths and hundredths by a 1-digit whole number.

Learn **Multiply tenths by a whole number.**

Multiply 0.2 by 4.

Method 1

A number line can help you multiply. Starting at 0, move 0.2 for each step. Where will you be on the number line after 4 steps?

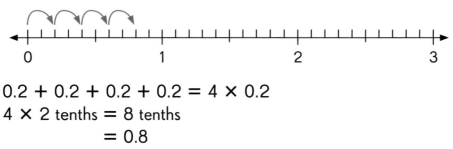

0.2 + 0.2 + 0.2 + 0.2 = 4 × 0.2
4 × 2 tenths = 8 tenths
             = 0.8

After 4 steps, you will be at 0.8 on the number line.

Method 2

A place-value chart can help you multiply. It is easier to use when multiplying greater numbers.

Multiply the tenths by 4.

$$\begin{array}{r} 0.\mathbf{2} \\ \times \quad \mathbf{4} \\ \hline 0.\mathbf{8} \end{array}$$

4 × 2 tenths = 8 tenths

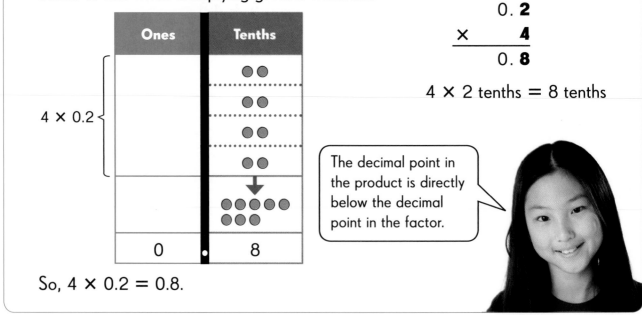

The decimal point in the product is directly below the decimal point in the factor.

So, 4 × 0.2 = 0.8.

Learn Multiply decimals with one decimal place by a whole number.

Multiply 2.4 by 3.

Ones	Tenths
●●	●●●●
●●	●●●●
●●	●●●●

3×2.4

Ones	Tenths
●●●●●●	●●●●●●●● ●

Ones	Tenths
● ●● ●● ●●	●●
7	2

Step 1 Multiply the tenths by 3.

$$\begin{array}{r} \overset{1}{2}.\mathbf{4} \\ \times \mathbf{3} \\ \hline \mathbf{2} \end{array}$$

3×4 tenths $= 12$ tenths

Regroup the tenths.
12 tenths $=$ 1 one and 2 tenths

Step 2 Multiply the ones by 3.

$$\begin{array}{r} \overset{1}{\mathbf{2}}.4 \\ \times \mathbf{3} \\ \hline \mathbf{7}.2 \end{array}$$

3×2 ones $= 6$ ones

Add the ones.
6 ones $+$ 1 one $=$ 7 ones

So, $3 \times 2.4 = 7.2$.

Guided Practice

Multiply. Write the product as a decimal.

1

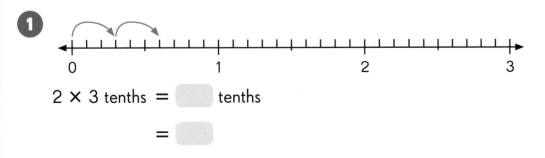

2×3 tenths $=$ ⬚ tenths

$=$ ⬚

Multiply. Write the product as a decimal.

2

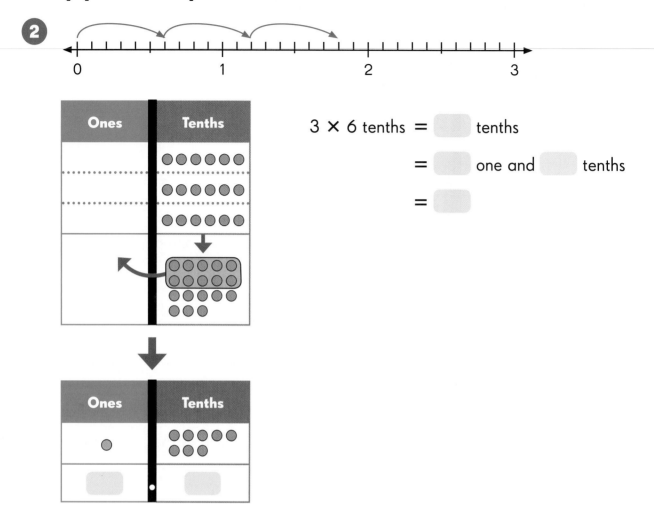

3×6 tenths = ⬜ tenths

= ⬜ one and ⬜ tenths

= ⬜

Multiply.

3

$$\begin{array}{r} 0\,.\,2 \\ \times \quad 3 \\ \hline \end{array}$$

4

$$\begin{array}{r} 0\,.\,6 \\ \times \quad 8 \\ \hline \end{array}$$

5

$$\begin{array}{r} 4\,.\,9 \\ \times \quad 2 \\ \hline \end{array}$$

6

$$\begin{array}{r} 3\,.\,7 \\ \times \quad 7 \\ \hline \end{array}$$

Multiply hundredths by a whole number.

Karen bought 3 apples at $0.45 each. How much did she pay in all?

3 × $0.45 = ?

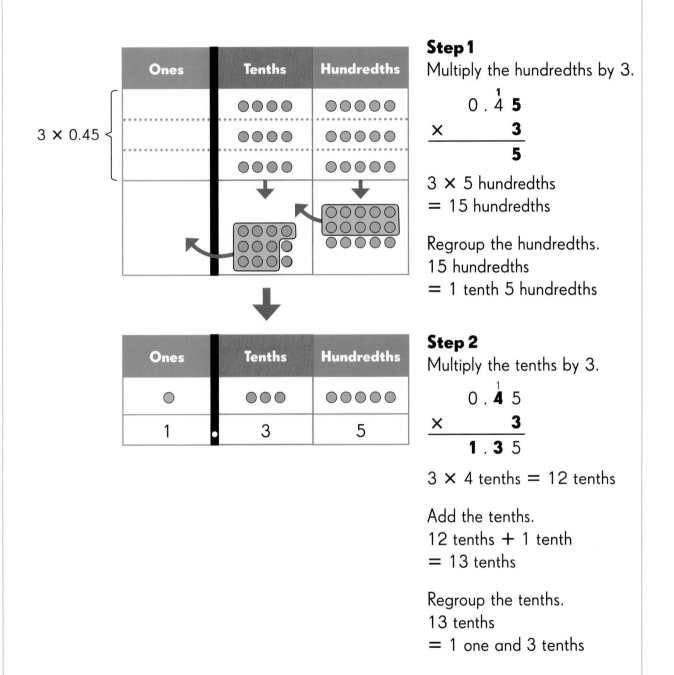

Step 1
Multiply the hundredths by 3.

$$\begin{array}{r} 0.4\overset{1}{5} \\ \times \quad 3 \\ \hline 5 \end{array}$$

3 × 5 hundredths
= 15 hundredths

Regroup the hundredths.
15 hundredths
= 1 tenth 5 hundredths

Step 2
Multiply the tenths by 3.

$$\begin{array}{r} 0.\overset{1}{4}5 \\ \times \quad 3 \\ \hline 1.35 \end{array}$$

3 × 4 tenths = 12 tenths

Add the tenths.
12 tenths + 1 tenth
= 13 tenths

Regroup the tenths.
13 tenths
= 1 one and 3 tenths

So, 3 × $0.45 = $1.35.

She paid $1.35 in all.

Multiply decimals with two decimal places by a whole number.

Marcus bought 3 DVDs for $15.45 each. How much did he pay in all?

3 × $15.45 = ?

Step 1

$$
\begin{array}{r}
1\ 5\ .\ 4\ \overset{1}{4}\ \mathbf{5} \\
\times \qquad \mathbf{3} \\
\hline
\mathbf{5}
\end{array}
$$

⬇

Multiply the hundredths by 3.
3 × 5 hundredths = 15 hundredths

Regroup the hundredths.
15 hundredths = 1 tenth 5 hundredths

Step 2

$$
\begin{array}{r}
1\ \overset{1}{5}\ .\ \overset{1}{\mathbf{4}}\ 5 \\
\times \qquad \mathbf{3} \\
\hline
\mathbf{3}\ 5
\end{array}
$$

⬇

Multiply the tenths by 3.
3 × 4 tenths = 12 tenths

Add the tenths.
12 tenths + 1 tenth = 13 tenths

Regroup the tenths.
13 tenths = 1 one and 3 tenths

Step 3

$$
\begin{array}{r}
\overset{1}{1}\ \overset{1}{\mathbf{5}}\ .\ \overset{1}{4}\ 5 \\
\times \qquad \mathbf{3} \\
\hline
\mathbf{6}\ .\ 3\ 5
\end{array}
$$

⬇

Multiply the ones by 3.
3 × 5 ones = 15 ones

Add the ones.
15 ones + 1 one = 16 ones

Regroup the ones.
16 ones = 1 ten 6 ones

> You can multiply other units of measurements just as you multiply decimals, using this method.

Step 4

$$
\begin{array}{r}
\overset{1}{\mathbf{1}}\ \overset{1}{5}\ .\ \overset{1}{4}\ 5 \\
\times \qquad \mathbf{3} \\
\hline
\mathbf{4}\ 6\ .\ 3\ 5
\end{array}
$$

Multiply the tens by 3.
3 × 1 ten = 3 tens

Add the tens.
3 tens + 1 ten = 4 tens

So, 3 × $15.45 = $46.35.
He paid $46.35 in all.

Guided Practice

Multiply. Write the product as a decimal.

7 4 × 6 hundredths = ☐ hundredths

                    = ☐ tenths ☐ hundredths

                    = ☐

8 3 × 7 hundredths = ☐ hundredths

                    = ☐ tenths ☐ hundredth

                    = ☐

Multiply.

9
```
    0.03
×      2
───────
```

10
```
    0.07
×      5
───────
```

11
```
    0.65
×      5
───────
```

12
```
    2.08
×      4
───────
```

13
```
    2.16
×      4
───────
```

14
```
    3.14
×      6
───────
```

15
```
    1.05
×      5
───────
```

16
```
    6.95
×      8
───────
```

17
```
   31.78
×      5
───────
```

Write in vertical form. Then multiply.

18 6 × $15.35 ☐

19 4 × 26.45 cm ☐

20 5 × 1.76 kg ☐

21 3 × 18.25 m ☐

22 7 × 3.45 L ☐

23 4 × $17.45 ☐

Let's Practice

Multiply. Write the product as a decimal.

1 2 × 4 tenths = [ ] tenths

= [ ]

2 2 × 2 hundredths = [ ] hundredths

= [ ]

3 5 × 7 tenths = [ ] tenths

= [ ] ones and [ ] tenths

= [ ]

4 6 × 4 hundredths = [ ] hundredths

= [ ] tenths [ ] hundredths

= [ ]

Multiply.

5
```
    0 . 3
×       3
```
[ ]

6
```
   0 . 0 4
×        2
```
[ ]

7
```
  1 0 . 1 2
×         4
```
[ ]

Write in vertical form. Then multiply.

8 4 × 2.6 mi [ ]

9 7 × 5.8 oz [ ]

10 5 × 2.15 lb [ ]

11 7 × 6.08 ft [ ]

12 3 × 11.82 yd [ ]

13 4 × 5.36 gal [ ]

ON YOUR OWN

**Go to Workbook B:
Practice 1, pages 15–20**

9.2 Multiplying by Tens, Hundreds, and Thousands

Lesson Objectives

- Multiply tenths and hundredths by 10, 100, and 1,000.
- Multiply tenths and hundredths by multiples of 10, 100, and 1,000.

Learn **Multiply decimals by 10.**

Look at these examples.

	Hundreds	Tens	Ones	Tenths	Hundredths
12		●	●●		
12 × 10	●	●●			
1			●		
1 × 10		●			
0.1				●	
0.1 × 10			●		
0.12				●	●●
0.12 × 10			●	●●	

	Hundreds	Tens	Ones	Tenths	Hundredths
12		1	2		
12 × 10	1	2	0		
1			1		
1 × 10		1	0		
0.1			0	1	
0.1 × 10			1		
0.12			0	1	2
0.12 × 10			1	2	

What happens to the digits of the decimal when it is multiplied by 10?
Each digit moves 1 place to the left in the place-value chart.

Hands-On Activity

Materials:
• place-value chips
• place-value chart

WORK IN PAIRS

STEP 1 Take turns to put and move the chips on the place-value chart to show how to multiply each number by 10.

STEP 2 Take turns to complete the place-value chart. Draw arrows to show how each digit has moved.

	Hundreds	Tens	Ones	Tenths	Hundredths	Thousandths
16.8						
16.8 × 10						
1.68						
1.68 × 10						
1.608						
1.608 × 10						

STEP 3 Look at the decimal point in these examples.
How does the decimal point move when multiplying by 10? What can you say about the products? Discuss with your partner.

$16.8 \times 10 =$ ⬚ $1.68 \times 10 =$ ⬚ $1.608 \times 10 =$ ⬚

Guided Practice

Multiply.

1 $4.5 \times 10 =$ ⬚

2 $0.56 \times 10 =$ ⬚

3 $12.6 \times 10 =$ ⬚

4 $0.027 \times 10 =$ ⬚

5 $3.082 \times 10 =$ ⬚

6 $25.078 \times 10 =$ ⬚

Guided Practice

Complete.

7 $0.03 \times \boxed{} = 0.3$

8 $57.3 \times \boxed{} = 573$

9 $\boxed{} \times 10 = 264.7$

10 $10 \times \boxed{} = 81.45$

Learn

Multiply decimals by tens.

You can break apart numbers to multiply whole numbers.

Multiply 3 by 20.
$$3 \times 20 = (3 \times 2) \times 10$$
$$= 6 \times 10$$
$$= 60$$
So, $3 \times 20 = 60$.

> To multiply decimals by multiples of 10, use the same rule as multiplying whole numbers by multiples of 10.

Use the same method to multiply decimals.

$$0.3 \times 20 = (0.3 \times 2) \times 10$$
$$= 0.6 \times 10$$
$$= 6$$
So, $0.3 \times 20 = 6$.

$$0.33 \times 20 = (0.33 \times 2) \times 10$$
$$= 0.66 \times 10$$
$$= 6.6$$
So, $0.33 \times 20 = 6.6$.

Guided Practice

Complete.

11 $0.4 \times 30 = (0.4 \times \boxed{}) \times 10$
$= \boxed{} \times 10$
$= \boxed{}$
So, $0.4 \times 30 = \boxed{}$.

12 $0.44 \times 30 = (0.44 \times 3) \times \boxed{}$
$= \boxed{} \times 10$
$= \boxed{}$
So, $0.44 \times 30 = \boxed{}$.

Multiply decimals by 100 and 1,000.

Think about the rules you learned for multiplying whole numbers by 100 and 1,000. You can use these rules to help you multiply decimals by 100 and 1,000.

Look at these examples.

	Thousands	Hundreds	Tens	Ones	Tenths	Hundredths	Thousandths
3				000			
3 × 100		000					
3 × 1,000	000						
0.003							000
0.003 × 100					000		
0.003 × 1,000				000			

	Thousands	Hundreds	Tens	Ones	Tenths	Hundredths	Thousandths
3				3			
3 × 100		3	0	0			
3 × 1,000	3	0	0	0			
0.003				0	0	0	3
0.003 × 100		0	0	0	3		
0.003 × 1,000	0	0	0	3			

What happens to the digits of the decimal when it is multiplied by 100?
Each digit moves 2 places to the left in the place-value chart.

What happens to the digits of the decimal when it is multiplied by 1,000?
Each digit moves 3 places to the left in the place-value chart.

 **Hands-On Activity**

Materials:
- place-value chips
- place-value chart

WORK IN PAIRS

1 Take turns to put and move the chips on the place-value chart to show how to multiply each number by 100 and 1,000.

STEP
2 Take turns to complete the place-value chart. Draw arrows to show how each digit has moved.

	Thousands	Hundreds	Tens	Ones	Tenths	Hundredths	Thousandths
12.03							
12.03 × 100							
3.009							
3.009 × 100							
4.19							
4.19 × 1,000							
0.013							
0.013 × 1,000							

STEP
3 Look at the decimal point in these examples.
How does the decimal point move when multiplying by 100 and 1,000? What can you say about the product?
Discuss with your partner.

12.03 × 100 = ☐   3.009 × 100 = ☐

4.19 × 1,000 = ☐   0.013 × 1,000 = ☐

> Sometimes, I have to write a zero at the end of the product.

Guided Practice

Multiply.

13 $2.9 \times 100 = $ ▢

14 $3.09 \times 100 = $ ▢

15 $1.259 \times 100 = $ ▢

16 $4.7 \times 1,000 = $ ▢

17 $4.75 \times 1,000 = $ ▢

18 $0.475 \times 1,000 = $ ▢

Complete.

19 $3.1 \times $ ▢ $= 310$

20 $5.029 \times $ ▢ $= 502.9$

21 $14.03 \times $ ▢ $= 14,030$

22 ▢ $\times 0.045 = 45$

23 ▢ $\times 100 = 23$

24 $1,000 \times $ ▢ $= 1,302$

Learn Multiply decimals by hundreds and thousands.

Multiply 0.8 by 200.
$$0.8 \times 200 = (0.8 \times 2) \times 100$$
$$= 1.6 \times 100$$
$$= 160$$
So, $0.8 \times 200 = 160$.

Multiply 0.14 by 3,000.
$$0.14 \times 3,000 = (0.14 \times 3) \times 1,000$$
$$= 0.42 \times 1,000$$
$$= 420$$
So, $0.14 \times 3,000 = 420$.

> To multiply decimals by multiples of 100 and 1,000, use the same rules as multiplying whole numbers.

Guided Practice

Complete.

㉕ 0.7 × 400 = (0.7 × ⬚) × 100

             = ⬚ × 100

             = ⬚

So, 0.7 × 400 = ⬚.

㉖ 0.19 × 4,000 = (0.19 × 4) × ⬚

                 = ⬚ × 1,000

                 = ⬚

So, 0.19 × 4,000 = ⬚.

㉗ 0.143 × 3,000 = (0.143 × ⬚) × 1,000

                   = ⬚ × 1,000

                   = ⬚

So, 0.143 × 3,000 = ⬚.

Hands-On Activity

Materials:
- ruler
- measuring tape

WORK IN PAIRS

1 Use a ruler to measure your handspan in centimeters, correct to one decimal place. Then find the length of 10 and 50 of your handspans in centimeters.

2 Use a measuring tape to measure your pace in meters, correct to two decimal places. Then find how far you will walk if you take 100 paces and 1,000 paces.

Let's Practice

Copy and complete the table.

1

Number	24.5	3.54	0.136	2.079	42.05
Number × 10					
Number × 100					
Number × 1,000					

Multiply.

2 0.5 × 30

3 1.5 × 50

4 0.04 × 40

5 0.44 × 60

6 0.027 × 70

7 0.127 × 80

8 0.2 × 300

9 1.6 × 400

10 2.6 × 500

11 0.24 × 600

12 2.36 × 700

13 0.018 × 800

14 0.3 × 2,000

15 8.7 × 3,000

16 0.46 × 6,000

17 1.05 × 4,000

18 0.021 × 7,000

19 2.019 × 5,000

Complete.

Example 168.9 = 16.89 × 10
= 1.689 × 100

20 35.6 = 3.56 × ☐
= 0.356 × ☐

21 58 = 5.8 × ☐
= 0.58 × ☐
= 0.058 × ☐

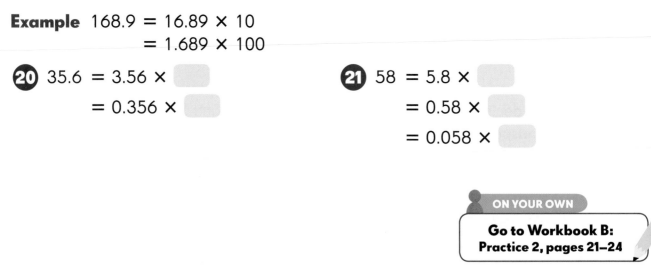

ON YOUR OWN

**Go to Workbook B:
Practice 2, pages 21–24**

9.3 Dividing Decimals

Lesson Objectives

Vocabulary
dividend
___
per unit

- Divide tenths and hundredths by a 1-digit whole number.
- Round quotients to the nearest tenth or hundredth.

ᴸᵉᵃʳⁿ **Divide tenths by a whole number without regrouping.**

A ribbon, 0.8 meter long, is cut into 2 equal pieces. How long is each piece?

$0.8 \div 2 = ?$

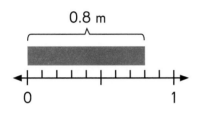

0.8 m

0   1

Line up the decimal point in the quotient with the decimal point in the **dividend**.

Step 1
Divide the ones by 2.
0 ones ÷ 2 = 0 ones

```
        0
   2 ) 0 . 8
        0
```

Step 2
Divide the tenths by 2.
8 tenths ÷ 2 = 4 tenths

```
      0 . 4
 2 ) 0 . 8
      0
      8
      8
      0
```

Ones	Tenths
	⚪⚪⚪⚪
	⚪⚪⚪⚪

Ones	Tenths
	⚪⚪⚪⚪
	⚪⚪⚪⚪

So, $0.8 \div 2 = 0.4$.
Each piece is 0.4 meter long.

Guided Practice

Divide.

1

$$2 \overline{\smash{)}\ 0.4}$$

2

$$3 \overline{\smash{)}\ 0.9}$$

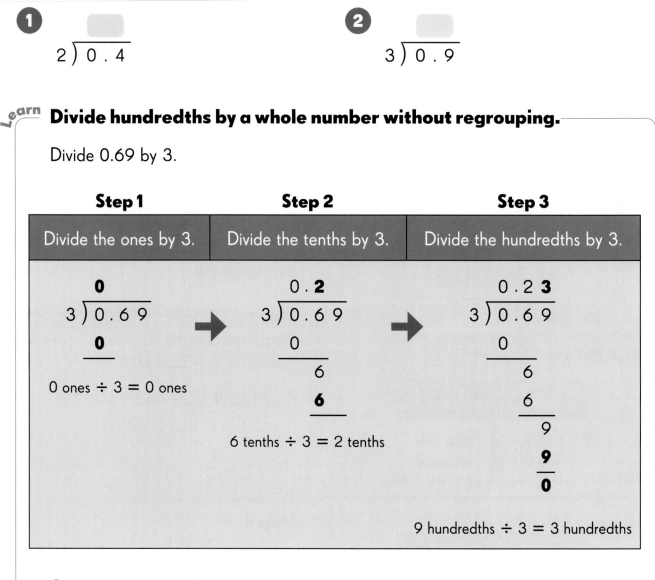

Learn **Divide hundredths by a whole number without regrouping.**

Divide 0.69 by 3.

Step 1	Step 2	Step 3
Divide the ones by 3.	Divide the tenths by 3.	Divide the hundredths by 3.

So, 0.69 ÷ 3 = 0.23.

Guided Practice

Divide.

3

$$2 \overline{\smash{)}\ 0.26}$$

4

$$3 \overline{\smash{)}\ 0.93}$$

Divide decimals with one decimal place by a whole number with regrouping.

Divide 0.8 by 5.

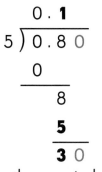

Step 1
Divide the ones by 5.
0 ones ÷ 5 = 0 ones

$$
\begin{array}{r}
0 \\
5\overline{)0.8} \\
\underline{0}
\end{array}
$$

Step 2
Divide the tenths by 5.
8 tenths ÷ 5 = 1 tenth R 3 tenths

$$
\begin{array}{r}
0.\mathbf{1} \\
5\overline{)0.8\,0} \\
\underline{0} \\
8 \\
\mathbf{5} \\
\overline{\mathbf{3}\,0}
\end{array}
$$

Regroup the remainder 3 tenths.
3 tenths = 30 hundredths

Step 3
Divide the hundredths by 5.
30 hundredths ÷ 5 = 6 hundredths

$$
\begin{array}{r}
0.1\,\mathbf{6} \\
5\overline{)0.8\,0} \\
\underline{0} \\
8 \\
5 \\
\overline{3\,0} \\
\mathbf{3\,0} \\
\overline{0}
\end{array}
$$

So, 0.8 ÷ 5 = 0.16.

Guided Practice

Complete.

5 7 tenths ÷ 4 = [ ] tenth R [ ] tenths

6 2 tenths ÷ 4 = [ ] hundredths ÷ 4

= [ ] hundredths

Divide.

7 [ ]

2) 0 . 9

8 [ ]

5) 2 7 . 5

9 [ ]

8) 0 . 4

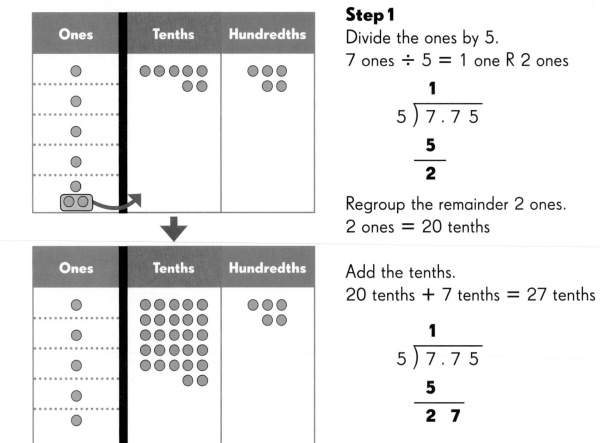

Divide decimals with two decimal places by a whole number with regrouping.

A vegetable pizza costs $7.75. The cost is shared equally by 5 students. How much will each student pay?

$7.75 ÷ 5 = ?

Step 1
Divide the ones by 5.
7 ones ÷ 5 = 1 one R 2 ones

```
       1
5 ) 7 . 7 5
    5
    ‾
    2
```

Regroup the remainder 2 ones.
2 ones = 20 tenths

Add the tenths.
20 tenths + 7 tenths = 27 tenths

```
       1
5 ) 7 . 7 5
    5
    ‾
    2 7
```

Ones	Tenths	Hundredths

Ones	Tenths	Hundredths

Ones	Tenths	Hundredths

So, $7.75 \div 5 = \$1.55$.
Each student will pay $1.55.

Step 2
Divide the tenths by 5.
27 tenths ÷ 5 = 5 tenths R 2 tenths

$$
\begin{array}{r}
1\,.\,\mathbf{5} \\
5\,\overline{)\,7\,.\,7\,5} \\
5 \\
\hline
2\ 7 \\
\mathbf{2\ 5} \\
\hline
2
\end{array}
$$

Regroup the remainder 2 tenths.
2 tenths = 20 hundredths

Add the hundredths.
20 hundredths + 5 hundredths
= 25 hundredths

$$
\begin{array}{r}
1\,.\,\mathbf{5} \\
5\,\overline{)\,7\,.\,7\,5} \\
5 \\
\hline
2\ 7 \\
\mathbf{2\ 5} \\
\hline
\mathbf{2\ 5}
\end{array}
$$

Step 3
Divide the hundredths by 5.

$$
\begin{array}{r}
1\,.\,5\,\mathbf{5} \\
5\,\overline{)\,7\,.\,7\,5} \\
5 \\
\hline
2\ 7 \\
2\ 5 \\
\hline
2\ 5 \\
\mathbf{2\ 5} \\
\hline
0
\end{array}
$$

Guided Practice

Regroup into hundredths. Then divide.

10 3 tenths 5 hundredths ÷ 7 = ☐ hundredths ÷ 7

= ☐ hundredths

= ☐

11 4 tenths 2 hundredths ÷ 6 = ☐ hundredths ÷ 6

= ☐ hundredths

= ☐

Divide.

12 ☐

2)‾0‾.‾9‾2‾

13 ☐

5)‾6‾.‾0‾5‾

14 ☐

3)‾2‾.‾2‾5‾

15 $7.40 ÷ 4 ☐

16 $64.25 ÷ 5 ☐

17 $26.95 ÷ 5 ☐

Learn **Find quotients to the nearest tenth.**

Find the value of 5 ÷ 8 to the nearest tenth.

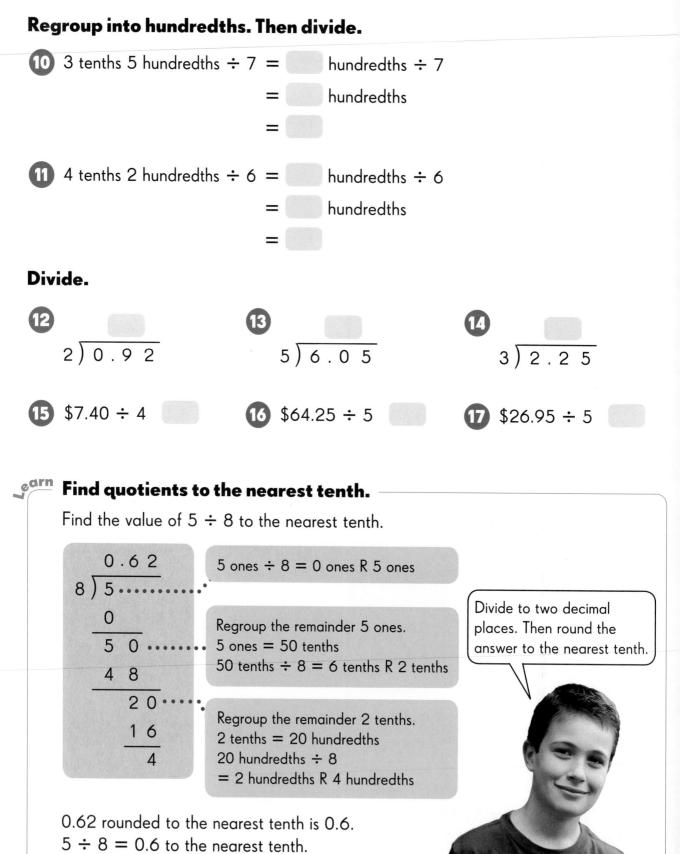

```
      0 . 6 2
  8 )‾5‾
      0
    ‾‾‾‾‾
      5 0
      4 8
    ‾‾‾‾‾
        2 0
        1 6
      ‾‾‾‾‾
          4
```

5 ones ÷ 8 = 0 ones R 5 ones

Regroup the remainder 5 ones.
5 ones = 50 tenths
50 tenths ÷ 8 = 6 tenths R 2 tenths

Regroup the remainder 2 tenths.
2 tenths = 20 hundredths
20 hundredths ÷ 8
= 2 hundredths R 4 hundredths

Divide to two decimal places. Then round the answer to the nearest tenth.

0.62 rounded to the nearest tenth is 0.6.
5 ÷ 8 = 0.6 to the nearest tenth.

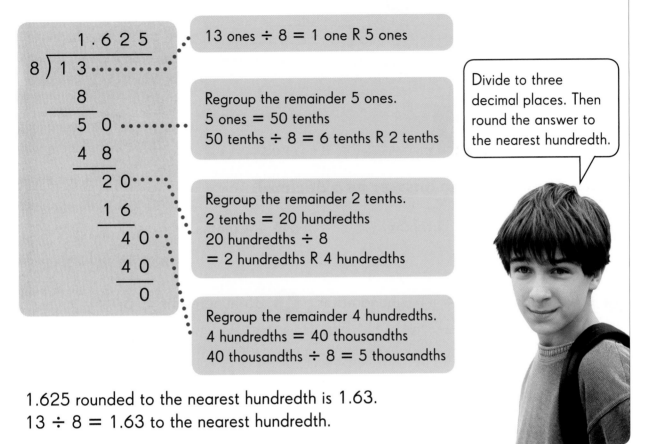

Find quotients to the nearest hundredth.

Find the value of 13 ÷ 8 to the nearest hundredth.

```
        1 . 6 2 5
  8 ) 1 3
        8
        5 0
        4 8
          2 0
          1 6
            4 0
            4 0
              0
```

13 ones ÷ 8 = 1 one R 5 ones

Regroup the remainder 5 ones.
5 ones = 50 tenths
50 tenths ÷ 8 = 6 tenths R 2 tenths

Regroup the remainder 2 tenths.
2 tenths = 20 hundredths
20 hundredths ÷ 8
= 2 hundredths R 4 hundredths

Regroup the remainder 4 hundredths.
4 hundredths = 40 thousandths
40 thousandths ÷ 8 = 5 thousandths

Divide to three decimal places. Then round the answer to the nearest hundredth.

1.625 rounded to the nearest hundredth is 1.63.
13 ÷ 8 = 1.63 to the nearest hundredth.

Guided Practice

Regroup into tenths. Then divide.

18 2 ones ÷ 3 = ⬚ tenths ÷ 3

= ⬚ tenths R ⬚ tenths

19 4 ones ÷ 7 = ⬚ tenths ÷ 7

= ⬚ tenths R ⬚ tenths

Divide. Round each quotient to the nearest tenth.

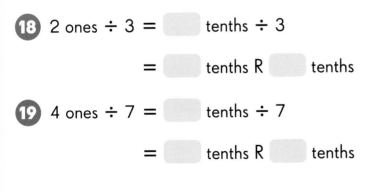

20
```
      ___
  4 ) 0 . 7 2
```

21
```
      ___
  8 ) 7 . 5 6
```

22
```
      ___
  4 ) 9
```

Lesson 9.3 Dividing Decimals   **57**

Divide. Round each quotient to the nearest hundredth.

(23) ☐
6)0.79

(24) ☐
5)1.27

(25) ☐
7)27.06

Let's Practice

Divide. Then write the answer as a decimal.

1 9 tenths ÷ 3 = ☐ tenths
= ☐

2 24 tenths ÷ 4 = ☐ tenths
= ☐

3 6 hundredths ÷ 2 = ☐ hundredths
= ☐

4 35 hundredths ÷ 5 = ☐ hundredths
= ☐

Divide.

5 8 tenths ÷ 3 = ☐ tenths R ☐ tenths

6 9 tenths ÷ 4 = ☐ tenths R ☐ tenth

Divide.

7 0.6 ÷ 3 ☐

8 2.7 ÷ 9 ☐

9 4 ÷ 8 ☐

10 0.4 ÷ 5 ☐

11 0.08 ÷ 4 ☐

12 0.51 ÷ 3 ☐

13 2.48 kg ÷ 4 ☐

14 $81.63 ÷ 9 ☐

15 5 cm ÷ 8 ☐

Divide. Round each quotient to the nearest tenth.

16 0.8 ÷ 5 ☐

17 2.68 ÷ 4 ☐

18 27.38 ÷ 9 ☐

Divide. Round each quotient to the nearest hundredth.

19 3.39 ÷ 6 ☐

20 0.79 ÷ 2 ☐

21 8 ÷ 7 ☐

Find the price **per unit** of each item below. Then find out which brand is a better buy.

Example

A
$14 for 10 feet

B
$10.80 for 8 feet

Price per foot of jump rope means the price of 1 foot of jump rope.

Jump rope
Brand A: Price per foot = $14 ÷ 10 = $1.40
Brand B: Price per foot = $10.80 ÷ 8 = $1.35
Brand B is a better buy.

22

4 pounds
A
$3.60

5 pounds
B
$3

Plastic clay
Brand A: Price per pound = ☐
Brand B: Price per pound = ☐
Brand ☐ is a better buy.

23

A
$5.40 for 3 yards

B
$8.50 for 5 yards

Ribbon
Brand A: Price per yard = ☐
Brand B: Price per yard = ☐
Brand ☐ is a better buy.

24

400 mL
A
$5.60

500 mL
B
$7.50

Craft paint
Brand A: Price per 100 mL = ☐
Brand B: Price per 100 mL = ☐
Brand ☐ is a better buy.

25

7 oz
A
$10.85

4 oz
B
$6.40

Glass beads
Brand A: Price per ounce = ☐
Brand B: Price per ounce = ☐
Brand ☐ is a better buy.

ON YOUR OWN

Go to Workbook B:
Practice 3, pages 25–32

Dividing by Tens, Hundreds, and Thousands

Lesson Objectives

- Divide tenths and hundredths by 10, 100, and 1,000.
- Divide tenths and hundredths by multiples of 10, 100, and 1,000.

Learn Divide decimals by 10.

Look at these examples.

	Hundreds	Tens	Ones	Tenths	Hundredths
120					
120 ÷ 10					
10					
10 ÷ 10					
1					
1 ÷ 10					
0.1					
0.1 ÷ 10					

	Hundreds	Tens	Ones	Tenths	Hundredths
120	1	2	0		
120 ÷ 10		1	2	0	
10		1	0		
10 ÷ 10			1	0	
1			1		
1 ÷ 10			0	1	
0.1			0	1	
0.1 ÷ 10			0	0	1

You can write 12.0 as 12 and 1.0 as 1.
What happens to the digits of the decimal when it is divided by 10?
Each digit moves 1 place to the right in the place-value chart.

Hands-On Activity

Materials:
• place-value chips
• place-value chart

STEP 1 Take turns to put and move the chips on the place-value chart to show how to divide each number by 10.

STEP 2 Take turns to complete the place-value chart. Draw arrows to show how each digit has moved.

	Hundreds	Tens	Ones	Tenths	Hundredths	Thousandths
163						
163 ÷ 10						
72.6						
72.6 ÷ 10						
0.29						
0.29 ÷ 10						

STEP 3 Look at the decimal point in these examples.
How does the decimal point move when dividing by 10? What can you say about the quotient? Discuss with your partner.

163 ÷ 10 = ☐   72.6 ÷ 10 = ☐   0.29 ÷ 10 = ☐

Guided Practice

Divide.

1 291 ÷ 10 = ☐

2 49.1 ÷ 10 = ☐

3 6.31 ÷ 10 = ☐

4 4.07 ÷ 10 = ☐

5 6.78 ÷ 10 = ☐

6 89.02 ÷ 10 = ☐

Complete.

7 $45.6 \div \boxed{} = 4.56$

8 $0.55 \div \boxed{} = 0.055$

9 $\boxed{} \div 10 = 39.14$

10 $\boxed{} \div 10 = 1.008$

Learn Divide decimals by tens.

You can break apart numbers to divide whole numbers.

Divide 60 by 20.
$$60 \div 20 = (60 \div 2) \div 10$$
$$= 30 \div 10$$
$$= 3$$
So, $60 \div 20 = 3$.

Use the same method to divide decimals.

$$6 \div 20 = (6 \div 2) \div 10$$
$$= 3 \div 10$$
$$= 0.3$$
So, $6 \div 20 = 0.3$.

$$0.6 \div 20 = (0.6 \div 2) \div 10$$
$$= 0.3 \div 10$$
$$= 0.03$$
So, $0.6 \div 20 = 0.03$.

$$0.06 \div 20 = (0.06 \div 2) \div 10$$
$$= 0.03 \div 10$$
$$= 0.003$$
So, $0.06 \div 20 = 0.003$.

To divide decimals by multiples of 10, use the same rule as dividing whole numbers by multiples of 10.

Guided Practice

Complete.

11 $8 \div 40 = (8 \div \boxed{}) \div 10$
$$= \boxed{} \div 10$$
$$= \boxed{}$$
So, $8 \div 40 = \boxed{}$.

12 $0.8 \div 40 = (0.8 \div \boxed{}) \div 10$
$$= \boxed{} \div 10$$
$$= \boxed{}$$
So, $0.8 \div 40 = \boxed{}$.

13 $0.08 \div 40 = (0.08 \div 4) \div \boxed{}$

$\qquad = \boxed{} \div 10$

$\qquad = \boxed{}$

So, $0.08 \div 40 = \boxed{}$.

$_{\mathrm{Learn}}$ Divide decimals by 100 and 1,000.

Think about the rules you learned for dividing whole numbers by 100 and 1,000. You can use these rules to help you divide decimals by 100 and 1,000.

Look at these examples.

	Thousands	Hundreds	Tens	Ones	Tenths	Hundredths	Thousandths
3,000	●●●						
3,000 ÷ 100			●●●				
3,000 ÷ 1,000				●●●			
3				●●●			
3 ÷ 100						●●●	
3 ÷ 1,000							●●●

⬇

	Thousands	Hundreds	Tens	Ones	Tenths	Hundredths	Thousandths
3,000	3	0	0	0			
3,000 ÷ 100			3	0	0	0	
3,000 ÷ 1,000				3	0	0	0
3				3			
3 ÷ 100				0	0	3	
3 ÷ 1,000				0	0	0	3

If all the digits to the right of the decimal point are zeros, you do not have to write them. You write 30.00 as 30 and 3.000 as 3.

What happens to the digits of the decimal when it is divided by 100?
Each digit moves 2 places to the right in the place-value chart.

What happens to the digits of the decimal when it is divided by 1,000?
Each digit moves 3 places to the right in the place-value chart.

Hands-On Activity

WORK IN PAIRS

STEP 1 Take turns to put and move the chips on the place-value chart to show how to divide each number by 100 and 1,000.

STEP 2 Take turns to complete the place-value chart. Draw arrows to show how each digit has moved.

	Thousands	Hundreds	Tens	Ones	Tenths	Hundredths	Thousandths
235							
235 ÷ 100							
53.2							
53.2 ÷ 100							
64							
64 ÷ 1,000							
4,061							
4,061 ÷ 1,000							

STEP 3 Look at the decimal point in these examples.
How does the decimal point move when dividing by 100 and 1,000?
What can you say about the quotient? Discuss with your partner.

235 ÷ 100 =   53.2 ÷ 100 =

64 ÷ 1,000 =   4,061 ÷ 1,000 =

Guided Practice

Divide.

14 $308 \div 100 = $ ☐

15 $3.8 \div 100 = $ ☐

16 $30.8 \div 100 = $ ☐

17 $2{,}016 \div 1{,}000 = $ ☐

18 $201 \div 1{,}000 = $ ☐

19 $26 \div 1{,}000 = $ ☐

Complete.

20 $420 \div $ ☐ $= 4.2$

21 $70.5 \div $ ☐ $= 0.705$

22 $1{,}061 \div $ ☐ $= 1.061$

23 $890 \div $ ☐ $= 0.89$

24 ☐ $\div 100 = 3.01$

25 ☐ $\div 1{,}000 = 67.25$

Learn Divide decimals by hundreds and thousands.

Divide 28 by 200.
$$28 \div 200 = (28 \div 2) \div 100$$
$$= 14 \div 100$$
$$= 0.14$$
So, $28 \div 200 = 0.14$.

Divide 2.8 by 200.
$$2.8 \div 200 = (2.8 \div 2) \div 100$$
$$= 1.4 \div 100$$
$$= 0.014$$
So, $2.8 \div 200 = 0.014$.

Divide 69 by 3,000.
$$69 \div 3{,}000 = (69 \div 3) \div 1{,}000$$
$$= 23 \div 1{,}000$$
$$= 0.023$$
So, $69 \div 3{,}000 = 0.023$.

To divide decimals by multiples of 100 and 1,000, use the same rules as dividing whole numbers.

Guided Practice

Complete.

26 $16 \div 400 = (16 \div \boxed{}) \div 100$

$\qquad = \boxed{} \div 100$

$\qquad = \boxed{}$

So, $16 \div 400 = \boxed{}$.

27 $1.6 \div 400 = (1.6 \div \boxed{}) \div 100$

$\qquad = \boxed{} \div 100$

$\qquad = \boxed{}$

So, $1.6 \div 400 = \boxed{}$.

28 $36 \div 4,000 = (36 \div \boxed{}) \div 1,000$

$\qquad = \boxed{} \div 1,000$

$\qquad = \boxed{}$

So, $36 \div 4,000 = \boxed{}$.

Let's Explore!

You know that $9 \times 7 = 63$.

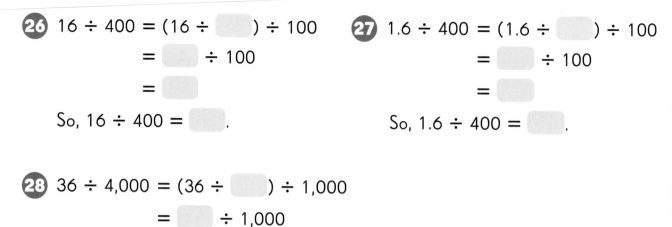

Look at these problems.
Suppose you know that $23 \times 8 = 184$. Solve these problems using mental math.

1 2.3×8

2 0.23×8

Let's Practice

Copy and complete the table.

1

Number	4,078	407	47.8	4.7	4.78
Number ÷ 10					
Number	4,078	407.8	407	47.8	4.7
Number ÷ 100					
Number	4,078	4,780	4,070	408	480
Number ÷ 1,000					

Divide.

2 18 ÷ 30

3 1.6 ÷ 40

4 24 ÷ 60

5 2.05 ÷ 50

6 0.14 ÷ 70

7 1.68 ÷ 80

8 93 ÷ 300

9 19.2 ÷ 600

10 49.7 ÷ 700

11 164 ÷ 2,000

12 75 ÷ 5,000

13 2,164 ÷ 4,000

Complete.

Example 0.23 = 2.3 ÷ 10
= 23 ÷ 100
= 230 ÷ 1,000

14 0.68 = 6.8 ÷
= 68 ÷
= 680 ÷

15 4.165 = ÷ 10
= ÷ 100
= ÷ 1,000

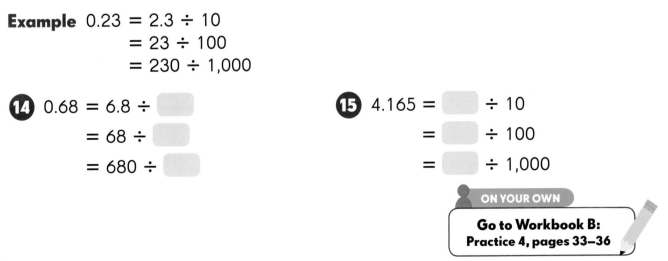

ON YOUR OWN

Go to Workbook B:
Practice 4, pages 33–36

Lesson 9.5 Estimating Decimals

Lesson Objective

- Estimate decimal sums, differences, products, and quotients.

Vocabulary
estimate
divisor

Learn Estimate sums by rounding to the nearest whole number.

Just as you did with whole numbers, you can **estimate** the answers to problems involving decimals.

Estimate $6.75 + $15.45 by rounding to the nearest dollar.

To the nearest dollar, $6.75 rounds to $7.
To the nearest dollar, $15.45 rounds to $15.
$7 + $15 = $22
$6.75 + $15.45 is about $22.

Add 31.65 and 8.02. Then estimate to check if your answer is reasonable.

Add:

```
  3 1 . 6 5
+    8 . 0 2
  3 9 . 6 7
```

Estimate:
31.65 is about 32.
8.02 is about 8.
32 + 8 = 40

How close is your estimated answer to the actual answer?

39.67 is close to 40. The answer is reasonable.

Guided Practice

Add. Then estimate to check if your answer is reasonable.

1 3.78 + 5.2 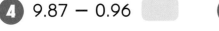 **2** 12.9 + 3.26 **3** 14.9 + 25.23

Learn **Estimate differences by rounding to the nearest whole number.**

Estimate the value of 7.13 − 5.7 by rounding to the nearest whole number.

To the nearest whole number, 7.13 rounds to 7.
To the nearest whole number, 5.7 rounds to 6.
7 − 6 = 1
7.13 − 5.7 is about 1.

··

Subtract 1.86 from 11.09. Then estimate to check if the answer is reasonable.

Subtract:

$$
\begin{array}{r}
1\ \overset{0}{\cancel{1}}.\overset{1}{0}\ 9 \\
-\quad 1\ .\ 8\ 6 \\
\hline
9\ .\ 2\ 3
\end{array}
$$

Estimate:
11.09 is about 11.
1.86 is about 2.
11 − 2 = 9

How close is your estimated answer to the actual answer?

9.23 is close to 9. The answer is reasonable.

Guided Practice

Subtract. Then estimate to check if your answer is reasonable.

4 9.87 − 0.96 **5** 5.75 − 5.05 **6** 24.59 − 19.68

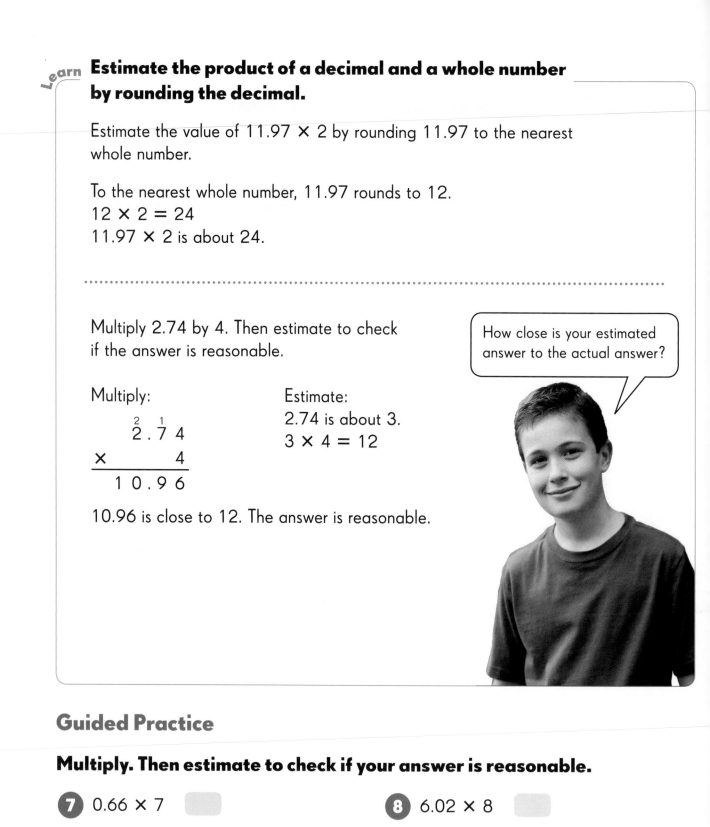

Learn

Estimate the product of a decimal and a whole number by rounding the decimal.

Estimate the value of 11.97 × 2 by rounding 11.97 to the nearest whole number.

To the nearest whole number, 11.97 rounds to 12.
12 × 2 = 24
11.97 × 2 is about 24.

....

Multiply 2.74 by 4. Then estimate to check if the answer is reasonable.

How close is your estimated answer to the actual answer?

Multiply:

$$\begin{array}{r} {\overset{2}{}\overset{1}{}} \\ 2.7\,4 \\ \times \qquad 4 \\ \hline 1\,0.9\,6 \end{array}$$

Estimate:
2.74 is about 3.
3 × 4 = 12

10.96 is close to 12. The answer is reasonable.

Guided Practice

Multiply. Then estimate to check if your answer is reasonable.

7 0.66 × 7

8 6.02 × 8

9 0.98 × 3

10 3.15 × 9

ᵉᵃʳⁿ Estimate quotients of a decimal and a whole number.

Estimate the value of 23.64 ÷ 3.
Just as in whole number division, to estimate the quotient,
choose a number close to the dividend that can be evenly
divided by the **divisor**.
Change 23.64 to the nearest whole number that can be evenly divided by 3.

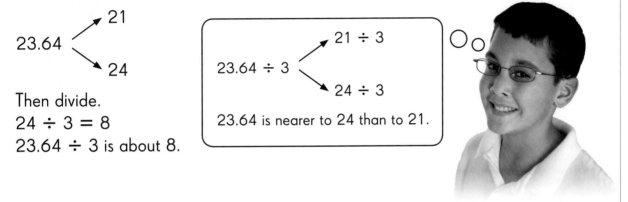

```
          21
23.64  <
          24
```

Then divide.
24 ÷ 3 = 8
23.64 ÷ 3 is about 8.

```
              21 ÷ 3
23.64 ÷ 3  <
              24 ÷ 3
23.64 is nearer to 24 than to 21.
```

Divide 40.4 by 5. Then estimate to check if the answer is reasonable.

Divide:

```
      8 . 0 8
5 ) 4 0 . 4
    4 0
    ___
        4
        0
        ___
        4 0
        4 0
        ___
          0
```

Estimate:
40.4 is about 40.
40 ÷ 5 = 8

8.08 is close to 8.
The answer is reasonable.

How close is your estimated
answer to the actual answer?

Guided Practice

Divide. Then estimate to check if your answer is reasonable.

11 12.3 ÷ 3

12 17.73 ÷ 9

13 20.93 ÷ 7

Lesson 9.5 Estimating Decimals   **71**

Estimate sums by rounding to the nearest tenth.

Estimate the value of 2.49 + 6.54 by rounding to the nearest tenth.

To the nearest tenth, 2.49 rounds to 2.5.
To the nearest tenth, 6.54 rounds to 6.5.
2.5 + 6.5 = 9
2.49 + 6.54 is about 9.

> You can estimate differences and products similarly by rounding to the nearest tenth.

Guided Practice

Complete each estimate.

14 10.46 − 3.52
10.46 is 10.5 when rounded to the nearest tenth.
3.52 is 3.5 when rounded to the nearest tenth.
10.5 − 3.5 = ▢
So, 10.46 − 3.52 is about ▢.

15 0.47 × 4
0.47 is 0.5 when rounded to the nearest tenth.
0.5 × 4 = ▢
So, 0.47 × 4 is about ▢.

> 5 tenths × 4 = 20 tenths
> = 2

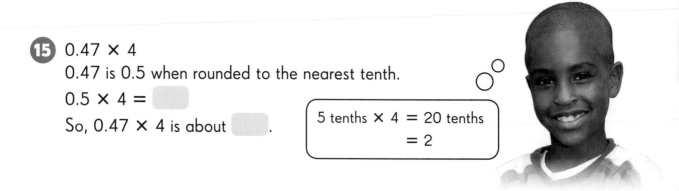

Complete each estimate.

16 3.46 ÷ 4

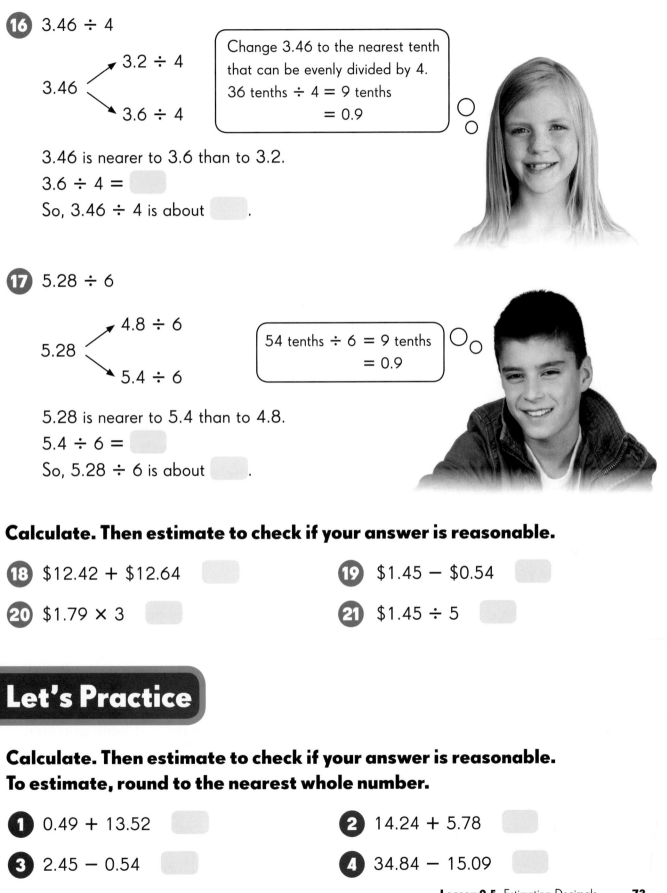

3.46
- 3.2 ÷ 4
- 3.6 ÷ 4

> Change 3.46 to the nearest tenth that can be evenly divided by 4.
> 36 tenths ÷ 4 = 9 tenths
> = 0.9

3.46 is nearer to 3.6 than to 3.2.

3.6 ÷ 4 = ⬜

So, 3.46 ÷ 4 is about ⬜.

17 5.28 ÷ 6

5.28
- 4.8 ÷ 6
- 5.4 ÷ 6

> 54 tenths ÷ 6 = 9 tenths
> = 0.9

5.28 is nearer to 5.4 than to 4.8.

5.4 ÷ 6 = ⬜

So, 5.28 ÷ 6 is about ⬜.

Calculate. Then estimate to check if your answer is reasonable.

18 $12.42 + $12.64 ⬜

19 $1.45 − $0.54 ⬜

20 $1.79 × 3 ⬜

21 $1.45 ÷ 5 ⬜

Let's Practice

Calculate. Then estimate to check if your answer is reasonable. To estimate, round to the nearest whole number.

1 0.49 + 13.52 ⬜

2 14.24 + 5.78 ⬜

3 2.45 − 0.54 ⬜

4 34.84 − 15.09 ⬜

Calculate. Then estimate to check if your answer is reasonable. To estimate, round the decimal to the nearest whole number.

5 6.47 × 8

6 14.97 × 6

Calculate. Then estimate the quotient by choosing a whole number close to the dividend that can be evenly divided by the divisor.

7 6.49 ÷ 5

8 14.78 ÷ 5

Calculate. Then estimate to check if your answer is reasonable. To estimate, round to the nearest tenth.

9 25.09 + 4.92

10 6.49 + 23.86

11 76.84 − 24.18

12 7.51 − 3.48

13 0.54 × 7

14 7.28 × 9

Calculate. Then estimate the quotient by choosing a tenth close to the dividend that can be evenly divided by the divisor.

15 11.68 ÷ 4

16 63.72 ÷ 6

Solve. Show your work.

17 The mass of an envelope is 2.2 grams. Round the mass to the nearest gram. Then estimate the total mass of 275 envelopes. Will your estimate be more or less than the actual total?

18 Bottle A contains 2.75 liters of orange juice. Bottle B contains 1.28 liters of apple juice. Round the volume of juice in the bottles to the nearest tenth of a liter. Then estimate the total volume of juice. Will your estimate be more or less than the actual total?

ON YOUR OWN

Go to Workbook B:
Practice 5, pages 37–40

Lesson 9.6 Real-World Problems: Decimals

Lesson Objective

- Solve real-world problems involving decimals.

Learn **Solve one-step real-world problems.**

9 nickels are placed in a row touching one another. Each coin measures 2.12 centimeters across. What is the total length of the row of coins?

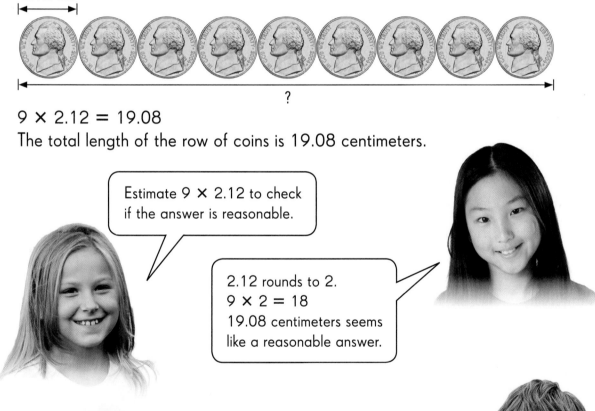

2.12 cm

?

$9 \times 2.12 = 19.08$
The total length of the row of coins is 19.08 centimeters.

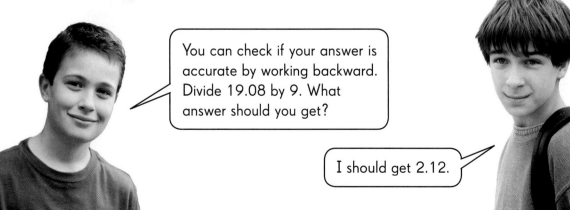

Estimate 9 × 2.12 to check if the answer is reasonable.

2.12 rounds to 2.
9 × 2 = 18
19.08 centimeters seems like a reasonable answer.

You can check if your answer is accurate by working backward. Divide 19.08 by 9. What answer should you get?

I should get 2.12.

Guided Practice

Solve.

1 The mass of a half-dollar is about 11.34 grams. Find the total mass of 8 half-dollars.

$8 \times 11.34 = $ ⬜

The total mass of the coins is ⬜ grams.

Learn Solve two-step real-world problems using models.

A piece of metal 6.54 yards long is cut into two pieces. One piece is twice as long as the other. What is the length of the longer piece? Give your answer correct to the nearest tenth of a yard.

From the model,

3 units → 6.54 yd

1 unit → 6.54 ÷ 3 = 2.18 yd

2 units → 2 × 2.18 = 4.36 yd

4.36 is 4.4 when rounded to the nearest tenth.

The length of the longer piece of metal is about 4.4 yards.

I can estimate to check the answer.
4.36 rounds to 4.
4 ÷ 2 = 2
The shorter piece is about 2 yards.

2 + 4 = 6
6 is close to 6.54.
So, 4.36 yards is a reasonable answer.

A row of 7 boxes of spaghetti is 24.64 centimeters wide.
Find the width of 9 boxes. Round your answer to the nearest
tenth of a centimeter.

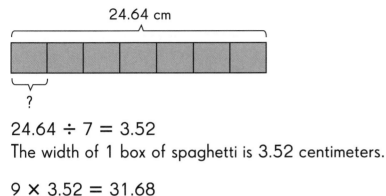

24.64 cm

?

$24.64 \div 7 = 3.52$
The width of 1 box of spaghetti is 3.52 centimeters.

$9 \times 3.52 = 31.68$
31.68 is 31.7 when rounded to the nearest tenth.
The width of 9 boxes of spaghetti is about 31.7 centimeters.

Guided Practice

Solve. Use models to help you.

2 Heather saved $12.15. Zach saved 3 times as much as Heather. Serena
saved $24.50 more than Zach. How much money did Serena save?

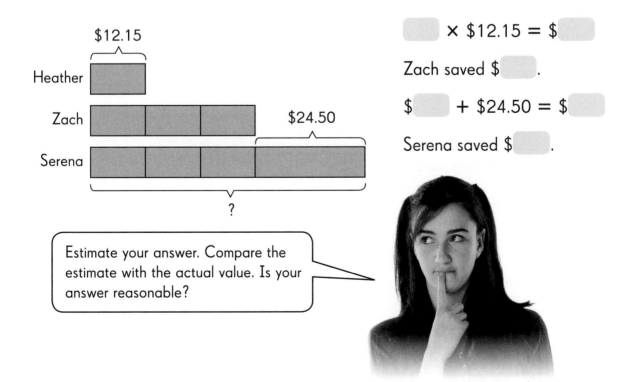

$12.15

Heather

Zach

$24.50

Serena

?

Estimate your answer. Compare the
estimate with the actual value. Is your
answer reasonable?

[ ] × $12.15 = $[ ]

Zach saved $[ ].

$[ ] + $24.50 = $[ ]

Serena saved $[ ].

Solve. Use models to help you.

 3 Ms. Gonzales wants to buy 3 watches at a cost of $69.65 each. Estimate the least number of $5 bills she needs to buy the watches.

$69.65 is about $ ☐ .

3 × $ ☐ = $ ☐

The total cost of 3 watches is about $ ☐ .

☐ ÷ 5 = ☐

She needs at least ☐ $5 bills to buy the watches.

4 A wooden vase and 4 glass vases have a total weight of 21.6 pounds. The weight of the wooden vase is 3.3 pounds. What is the weight of each glass vase? Round your answer to the nearest hundredth of a pound.

21.6 − 3.3 = ☐

The total weight of 4 glass vases is ☐ pounds.

☐ ÷ 4 = ☐

The weight of each glass vase is about ☐ pounds.

5 A sports shop sells 3 light bowling balls and 3 heavy bowling balls for Ten-pin bowling. The weight of a heavy bowling ball is twice that of a light bowling ball. The total weight of the 6 bowling balls is 52.65 pounds. Find the total weight of the 3 heavy bowling balls to the nearest pound.

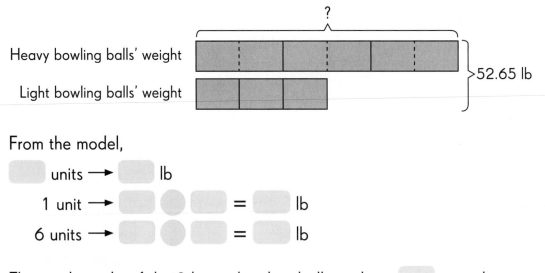

From the model,

☐ units ⟶ ☐ lb

1 unit ⟶ ☐ ● ☐ = ☐ lb

6 units ⟶ ☐ ● ☐ = ☐ lb

The total weight of the 3 heavy bowling balls is about ☐ pounds.

 **Hands-On Activity**

Bring an advertisement from a supermarket or grocery store to class. One partner will act as a customer, and the other will act as the cashier.

STEP 1
Pick 3 items from the advertisement and write the number of each item you want to buy. Then estimate the total cost.

Example
2 pounds of grapes at $2.49 per pound
4 packets of tea at $4.15 per packet
3 muffins at $0.69 per muffin.

STEP 2
Your partner calculates the total cost. Compare the actual cost with the estimated cost.

STEP 3
Switch roles and pick another 3 items.

Let's Explore!

Kevin wants to go to the supermarket to buy some bread. He has some quarters and dimes. He has $1.15 in all. How many quarters and how many dimes could he possibly have?

Let's Practice

Solve. Show your work.

1 Yani has 9 half-dollars. How much money does she have?

2 Carol measures a whiteboard with her handspan and finds that it is 20 handspans long. Her handspan is 18.4 centimeters long. What is the length of the whiteboard?

3 The school nurse buys 8 bottles of hand lotion. The cost of each bottle is $7.65. He gives the cashier $80. How much change does he get?

4 The sum of two numbers is 70.4. One of the numbers is 9 times the other. What are the two numbers?

5 The perimeter of a rectangle is 35.54 inches longer than the perimeter of a square of side 6.75 inches. Find the perimeter of the rectangle to the nearest tenth of an inch.

6 A studio is buying 4 MP3 players for $129.55 each. Estimate the least number of $100 bills needed to buy the MP3 players.

7 A pound of regular nails cost $8.75 and a pound of finishing nails cost $9.45. A contractor bought 7 pounds of regular nails and 30 pounds of finishing nails. How much did she pay altogether?

8 Kiki's family drank a total of 42.5 gallons of milk in January and February. Her family drank 5.3 gallons more milk in February than in January. How many gallons of milk did Kiki's family drink in February?

9 Two pails of different sizes contain 34.5 liters of water altogether. When 0.68 liter of water is poured from the bigger pail into the smaller pail, the amount of water in the bigger pail is 9 times that in the smaller pail. How much water was there in each pail at first?

ON YOUR OWN

Go to Workbook B:
Practice 6 and 7, pages 41–50

Put On Your Thinking Cap!

PROBLEM SOLVING

Solve these problems.

1. The number in the square is the product of the numbers in the two circles next to it. Find the numbers in the circles.

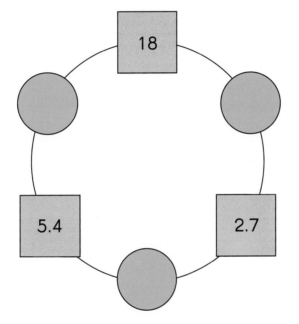

2. Simone bought a total of 10 birthday hats and noisemakers.
Each birthday hat cost $1.50 and each noisemaker cost $2.50.
The noisemakers cost $13 more than the birthday hats.
How many of each item did she buy?

ON YOUR OWN

**Go to Workbook B:
Put on Your Thinking Cap!
pages 51 – 54**

Chapter Wrap Up

Study Guide

You have learned...

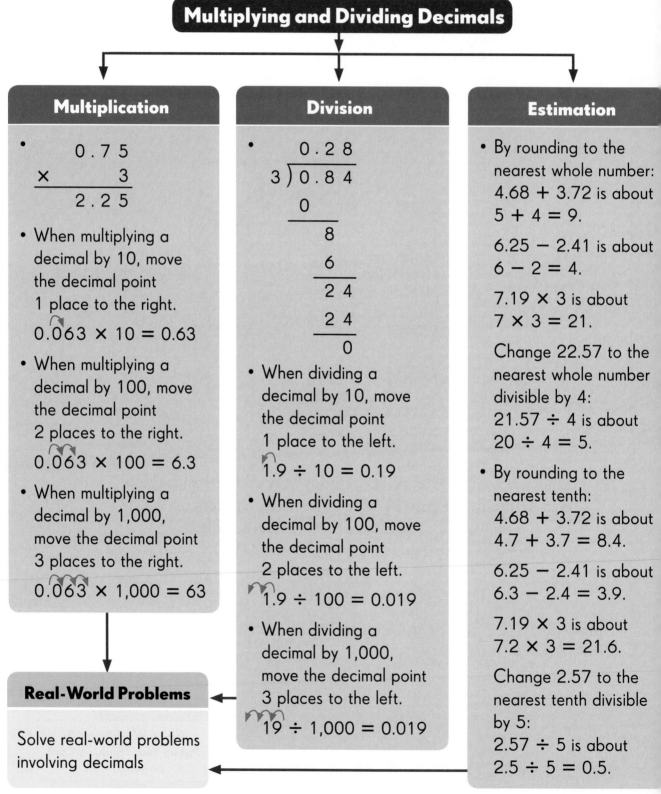

Multiplying and Dividing Decimals

Multiplication

- $$\begin{array}{r} 0.75 \\ \times\ \ \ \ 3 \\ \hline 2.25 \end{array}$$

- When multiplying a decimal by 10, move the decimal point 1 place to the right.
  $0.063 \times 10 = 0.63$

- When multiplying a decimal by 100, move the decimal point 2 places to the right.
  $0.063 \times 100 = 6.3$

- When multiplying a decimal by 1,000, move the decimal point 3 places to the right.
  $0.063 \times 1,000 = 63$

Division

- $$\begin{array}{r} 0.28 \\ 3\overline{)0.84} \\ 0 \\ \hline 8 \\ 6 \\ \hline 24 \\ 24 \\ \hline 0 \end{array}$$

- When dividing a decimal by 10, move the decimal point 1 place to the left.
  $1.9 \div 10 = 0.19$

- When dividing a decimal by 100, move the decimal point 2 places to the left.
  $1.9 \div 100 = 0.019$

- When dividing a decimal by 1,000, move the decimal point 3 places to the left.
  $19 \div 1,000 = 0.019$

Estimation

- By rounding to the nearest whole number:
  $4.68 + 3.72$ is about $5 + 4 = 9$.

  $6.25 - 2.41$ is about $6 - 2 = 4$.

  7.19×3 is about $7 \times 3 = 21$.

  Change 22.57 to the nearest whole number divisible by 4:
  $21.57 \div 4$ is about $20 \div 4 = 5$.

- By rounding to the nearest tenth:
  $4.68 + 3.72$ is about $4.7 + 3.7 = 8.4$.

  $6.25 - 2.41$ is about $6.3 - 2.4 = 3.9$.

  7.19×3 is about $7.2 \times 3 = 21.6$.

  Change 2.57 to the nearest tenth divisible by 5:
  $2.57 \div 5$ is about $2.5 \div 5 = 0.5$.

Real-World Problems

Solve real-world problems involving decimals

Chapter Review/Test

Vocabulary

1 Rounding can be used to ▢ sums, differences, products and quotients.

2 In 20 ÷ 5 = 4, 20 is the ▢ and 5 is the ▢.

Concepts and Skills
Multiply.

3 3.7 × 4 ▢

4 6.08 × 9 ▢

5 8.562 × 20 ▢

6 0.128 × 300 ▢

7 2.6 × 1,000 ▢

8 8.712 × 9,000 ▢

Complete.

9 2.156 × ▢ = 215.6

10 ▢ ÷ 10 = 67.05

Divide. Round each answer to the nearest tenth.

11 1.35 ÷ 9 ▢

12 4.1 ÷ 5 ▢

Divide.

13 24.3 ÷ 30 ▢

14 1.6 ÷ 100 ▢

15 59 ÷ 500 ▢

16 318 ÷ 3,000 ▢

Calculate. Then estimate to check if your answer is reasonable.

17 4.15 + 5.38 ▢

18 9.74 − 3.86 ▢

19 2.07 × 9 ▢

20 22.18 ÷ 4 ▢

Problem Solving

Solve. Estimate to check if your answer is reasonable.

21 A pitcher contains 4.32 pints of lemon syrup. 12.6 pints of water are added to the syrup to make lemonade. How much lemonade is made?

22 A ribbon is 12.3 feet long. Another ribbon is 3.12 feet shorter than it. What is the total length of the two ribbons?

23 A piece of wood is 1.75 meter long. A carpenter saws off 0.8 meter from it. Then he saws the remaining piece into 2 pieces of equal length. How long is each of the equal pieces?

24 A fifth-grade class painted pieces of cardboard for an art project. Each piece of cardboard had an area of 6.25 square inches. The students painted 200 pieces of cardboard each day.

a What is the total area of cardboard that they have painted by the end of the third days?

b At the end of the third day, the students glued together all their pieces of painted cardboard to form a large square mural. Then, they cut the mural into 40 strips of equal sizes so they could move the mural. What is the area of each smaller strip of cardboard? Express your answer as a decimal.

Chapter

10 Percent

Regular price: $25.50
Trivia Games
45% Discount!

Regular price: $38.00
Word Games
50% Discount!

Regular price: $25.50
Checkers & Chess
65% Discount!

How much are the checkers after the discount?

What fraction of the checkerboard is shaded green? What is this fraction expressed as a percent?

Lessons

10.1 Percent
10.2 Expressing Fractions as Percents
10.3 Percent of a Number
10.4 Real-World Problems: Percent

BIG IDEAS

▶ Percent is another way of expressing a part of a whole.
▶ Percent means 'out of 100'.

Recall Prior Knowledge

Writing fractions with a denominator of 100 as a decimal

$\frac{37}{100}$ of the square is shaded.

$\frac{37}{100}$ can be written as 0.37.

0.37 is the same as $\frac{37}{100}$ or 37 out of 100.

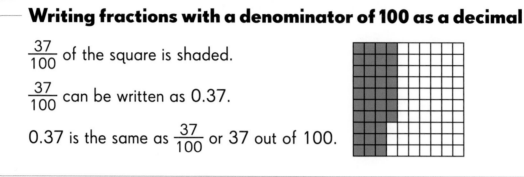

Finding equivalent fractions by multiplying the numerator and denominator by the same number

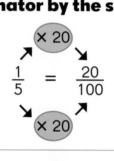

Simplifying fractions by dividing the numerator and denominator by the same number

$$\frac{15}{100} = \frac{3}{20}$$

Finding equivalent fractions and decimals

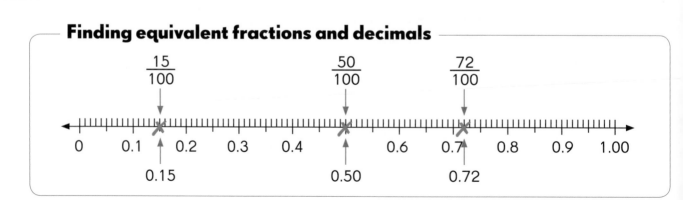

Express as a decimal.

1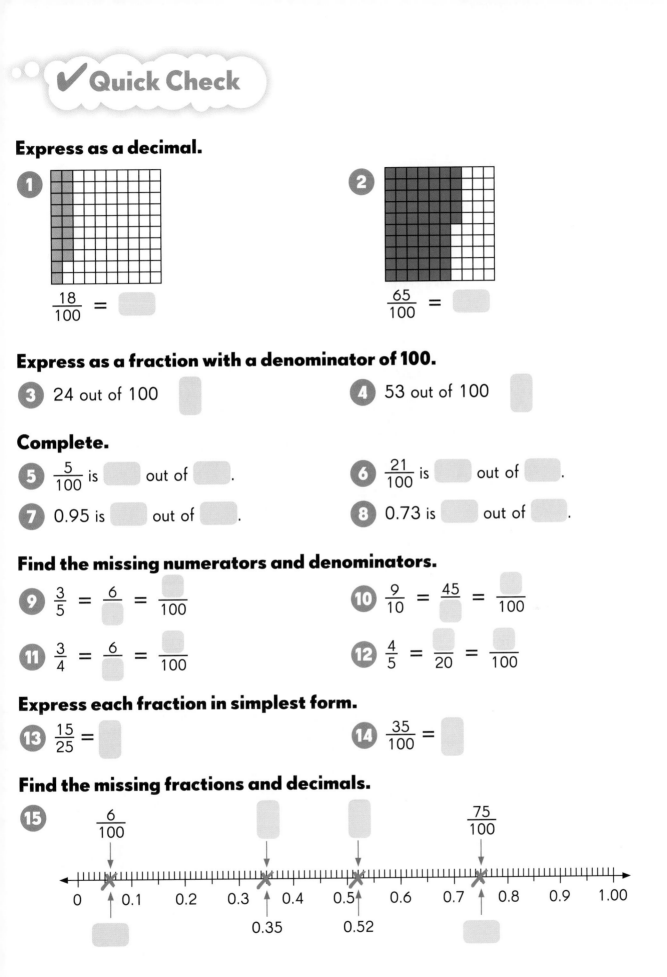

$\frac{18}{100}$ = ☐

2 $\frac{65}{100}$ = ☐

Express as a fraction with a denominator of 100.

3 24 out of 100 ☐

4 53 out of 100 ☐

Complete.

5 $\frac{5}{100}$ is ☐ out of ☐.

6 $\frac{21}{100}$ is ☐ out of ☐.

7 0.95 is ☐ out of ☐.

8 0.73 is ☐ out of ☐.

Find the missing numerators and denominators.

9 $\frac{3}{5} = \frac{6}{☐} = \frac{☐}{100}$

10 $\frac{9}{10} = \frac{45}{☐} = \frac{☐}{100}$

11 $\frac{3}{4} = \frac{6}{☐} = \frac{☐}{100}$

12 $\frac{4}{5} = \frac{☐}{20} = \frac{☐}{100}$

Express each fraction in simplest form.

13 $\frac{15}{25}$ = ☐

14 $\frac{35}{100}$ = ☐

Find the missing fractions and decimals.

15

$\frac{6}{100}$ ☐   ☐ $\frac{75}{100}$

0   0.1   0.2   0.3   0.4   0.5   0.6   0.7   0.8   0.9   1.00

☐   0.35   0.52   ☐

Lesson 10.1 Percent

Lesson Objective

- Relate and compare percents, decimals, and fractions.

Vocabulary
percent

Learn **Percent is another way of writing a part of a whole.**

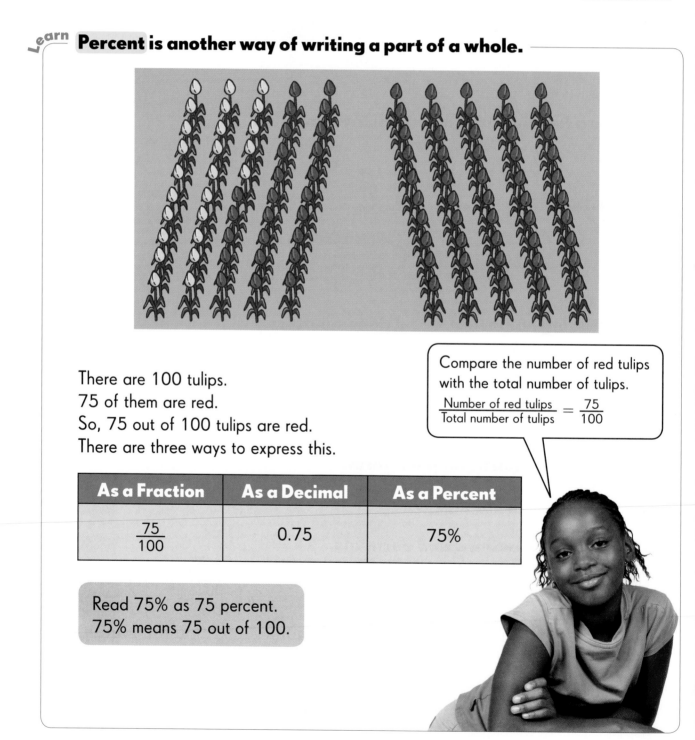

There are 100 tulips.
75 of them are red.
So, 75 out of 100 tulips are red.
There are three ways to express this.

Compare the number of red tulips with the total number of tulips.

$$\frac{\text{Number of red tulips}}{\text{Total number of tulips}} = \frac{75}{100}$$

As a Fraction	As a Decimal	As a Percent
$\frac{75}{100}$	0.75	75%

Read 75% as 75 percent.
75% means 75 out of 100.

Guided Practice

Complete the table.

1 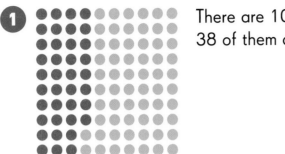 There are 100 beads.
38 of them are red.

Express 38 out of 100 as a fraction, a decimal, and a percent.

As a Fraction	As a Decimal	As a Percent

Learn Express a part of a whole as a fraction and a percent.

The large square is divided into 100 parts.
25 parts are shaded.
So, 25 out of 100 equal parts are shaded.
$\frac{25}{100}$ of the large square is shaded.

> What percent of the whole is shaded? What percent of the whole is not shaded?

25% of the large square is shaded.
75% of the large square is not shaded.

Guided Practice

Complete.

2 [ ] parts out of 100 equal parts are shaded.

$\frac{\boxed{}}{100}$ of the large square is shaded.

[ ] % of the large square is shaded.

$\frac{\boxed{}}{100}$ of the large square is not shaded.

[ ] % of the large square is not shaded.

Express as a percent.

3 72 out of 100 [ ]

4 28 out of 100 [ ]

5 39 out of 100 [ ]

6 61 out of 100 [ ]

Express each fraction as a percent.

7 $\frac{17}{100} = \boxed{} \%$

8 $\frac{53}{100} = \boxed{} \%$

9 $\frac{68}{100} = \boxed{} \%$

10 $\frac{82}{100} = \boxed{} \%$

Express each fraction as an equivalent fraction and a percent.

11 $\frac{7}{10} = \frac{70}{100} = \boxed{} \%$

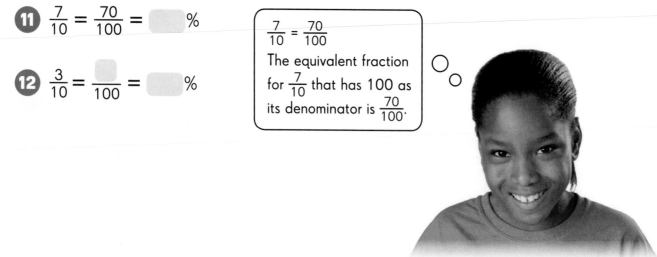

$\frac{7}{10} = \frac{70}{100}$
The equivalent fraction for $\frac{7}{10}$ that has 100 as its denominator is $\frac{70}{100}$.

12 $\frac{3}{10} = \frac{\boxed{}}{100} = \boxed{} \%$

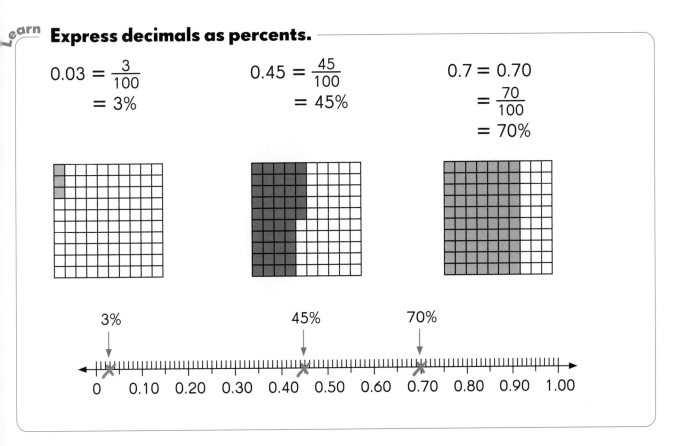

Learn

Express decimals as percents.

$$0.03 = \frac{3}{100}$$
$$ = 3\%$$

$$0.45 = \frac{45}{100}$$
$$ = 45\%$$

$$0.7 = 0.70$$
$$ = \frac{70}{100}$$
$$ = 70\%$$

Guided Practice

Express each decimal as a percent.

13 $0.56 = \dfrac{\boxed{}}{100}$

$ = \boxed{}\%$

14 $0.08 = \boxed{}$

$ = \boxed{}\%$

15 $0.9 = \dfrac{\boxed{}}{10}$

$ = \dfrac{\boxed{}}{100}$

$ = \boxed{}\%$

16 $0.4 = \boxed{}$

$ = \boxed{}\%$

Express percents as fractions.

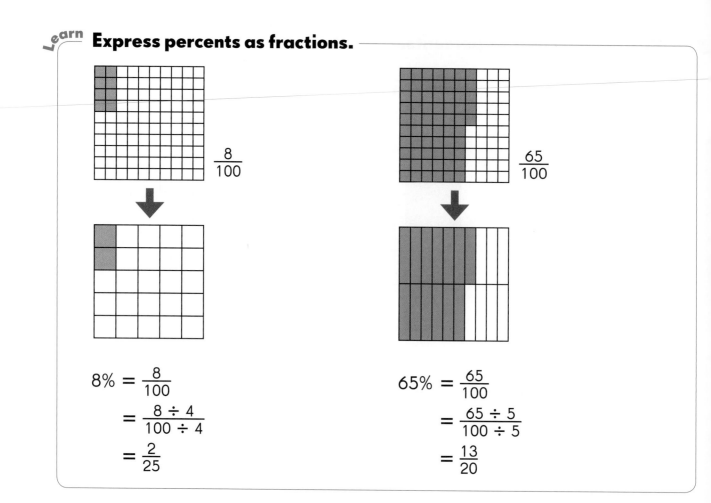

$$8\% = \frac{8}{100}$$
$$= \frac{8 \div 4}{100 \div 4}$$
$$= \frac{2}{25}$$

$$65\% = \frac{65}{100}$$
$$= \frac{65 \div 5}{100 \div 5}$$
$$= \frac{13}{20}$$

Guided Practice

Express each percent as a fraction in simplest form.

17 $94\% = \dfrac{}{100}$

$= $

18 $88\% = \dfrac{}{100}$

$= $

19 $42\% = $

20 $56\% = $

21 $12\% = $

22 $78\% = $

Express percents as decimals.

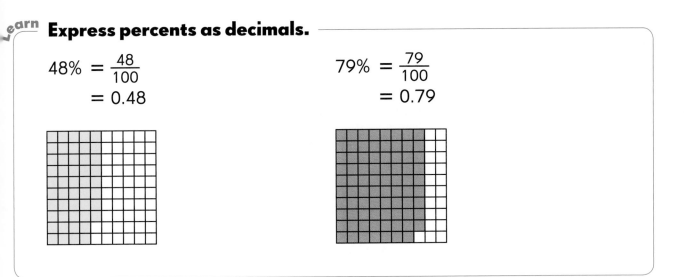

$$48\% = \frac{48}{100}$$
$$= 0.48$$

$$79\% = \frac{79}{100}$$
$$= 0.79$$

Guided Practice

Express each percent as a decimal.

23 $38\% = \dfrac{\boxed{}}{100}$

  $= \boxed{}$

24 $4\% = \dfrac{\boxed{}}{100}$

  $= \boxed{}$

25 $97\% = \dfrac{\boxed{}}{100}$

  $= \boxed{}$

26 $60\% = \dfrac{\boxed{}}{100}$

  $= \boxed{}$

Find the missing fractions, decimals, and percents.

27

Fraction	$\boxed{}$	$\frac{22}{100}$	$\boxed{}$	$\boxed{}$	$\boxed{}$
Decimal	$\boxed{}$	$\boxed{}$	$\boxed{}$	0.75	1.00
Percent	$\boxed{}$	$\boxed{}$	52%	$\boxed{}$	$\boxed{}$

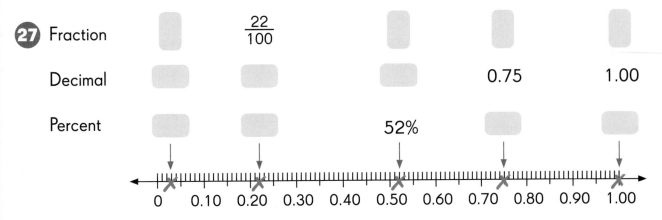

Let's Practice

Express as a fraction with a denominator of 100 and then as a percent.

1 11 out of 100

2 73 out of 100

3 8 out of 100

4 9 out of 10

Express the shaded part of each whole as a percent.

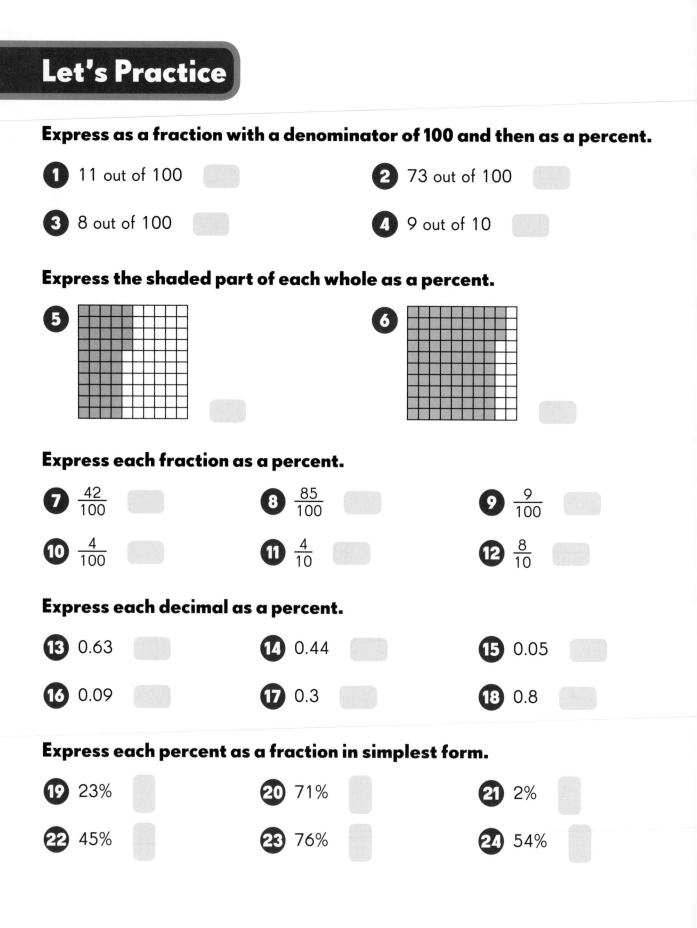

5

6

Express each fraction as a percent.

7 $\frac{42}{100}$

8 $\frac{85}{100}$

9 $\frac{9}{100}$

10 $\frac{4}{100}$

11 $\frac{4}{10}$

12 $\frac{8}{10}$

Express each decimal as a percent.

13 0.63

14 0.44

15 0.05

16 0.09

17 0.3

18 0.8

Express each percent as a fraction in simplest form.

19 23%

20 71%

21 2%

22 45%

23 76%

24 54%

Express each percent as a decimal.

25 24% [ ]

26 3% [ ]

27 17% [ ]

28 70% [ ]

29 69% [ ]

30 33% [ ]

Solve.

31 Of the 100 people who visited a museum last Wednesday, 63 were tourists.

  a What percent of the people who visited the museum were tourists?

  b What percent of the people who visited the museum were not tourists?

32 Out of 100 pieces of fruit that Harry picked in an orchard, 34 were oranges. The rest were apples.

  a What percent of the fruits were oranges?

  b What percent of the fruits were apples?

Copy the number line. Mark ✗ to show where each percent is located.

33 28%   **34** 49%   **35** 4%   **36** 77%

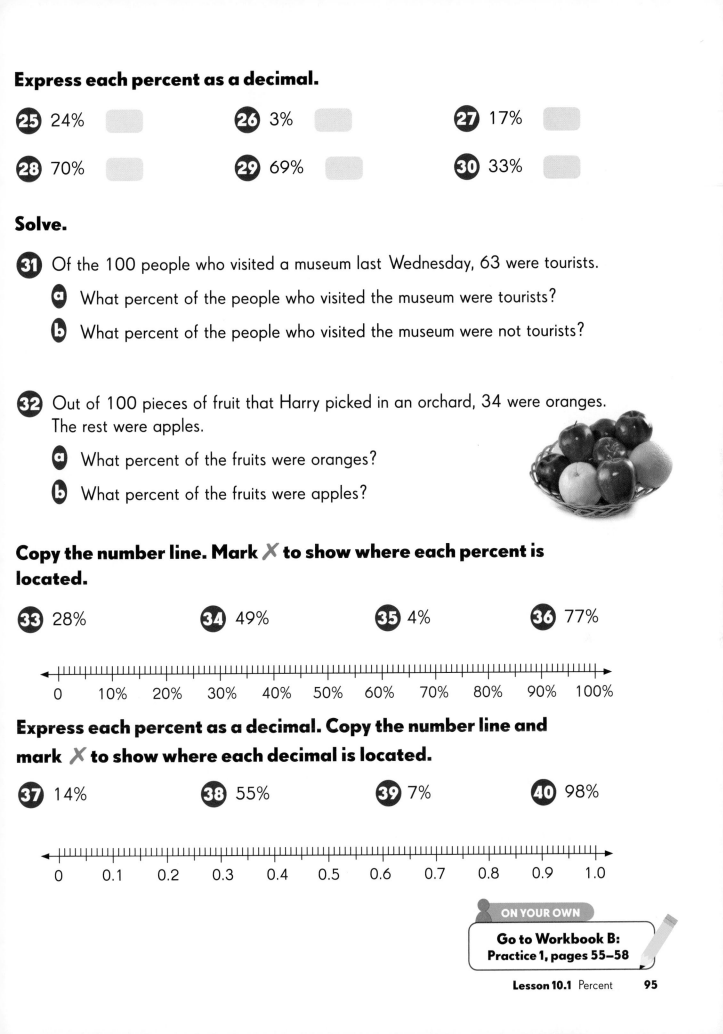

0 10% 20% 30% 40% 50% 60% 70% 80% 90% 100%

Express each percent as a decimal. Copy the number line and mark ✗ to show where each decimal is located.

37 14%   **38** 55%   **39** 7%   **40** 98%

0 0.1 0.2 0.3 0.4 0.5 0.6 0.7 0.8 0.9 1.0

ON YOUR OWN

**Go to Workbook B:
Practice 1, pages 55–58**

10.2 Expressing Fractions as Percents

Lesson Objective

• Express fractions as percents.

Learn **Express fractions as percents.**

Jessica spent $\frac{1}{4}$ of her money on a pair of shoes. What percent of her money did she spend on the shoes?

Method 1

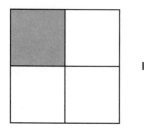 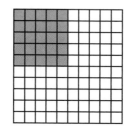

To express $\frac{1}{4}$ as a fraction with a denominator of 100, multiply both the numerator and denominator by 25.

$$\frac{1}{4} = \frac{1 \times 25}{4 \times 25} = \frac{25}{100} = 25\%$$

Method 2

Whole Amount	Spent
$1 = \frac{4}{4}$	$\frac{1}{4}$
100%	?%

A whole is $\frac{4}{4}$ or 100%.

1 whole $\longrightarrow$ 100%

4 parts $\longrightarrow$ 100%

1 part $\longrightarrow$ 100% ÷ 4 = 25%

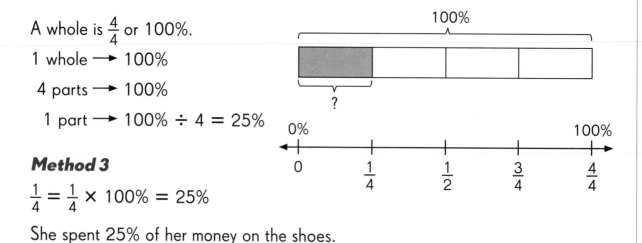

Method 3

$$\frac{1}{4} = \frac{1}{4} \times 100\% = 25\%$$

She spent 25% of her money on the shoes.

Guided Practice

Express each fraction as a percent. Use models and number lines to help you.

1 $\frac{3}{4}$

4 parts ⟶ 100%

1 part ⟶ ☐ % ÷ ☐ = ☐ %

3 parts ⟶ 3 × ☐ % = ☐ %

So, $\frac{3}{4}$ = ☐ %

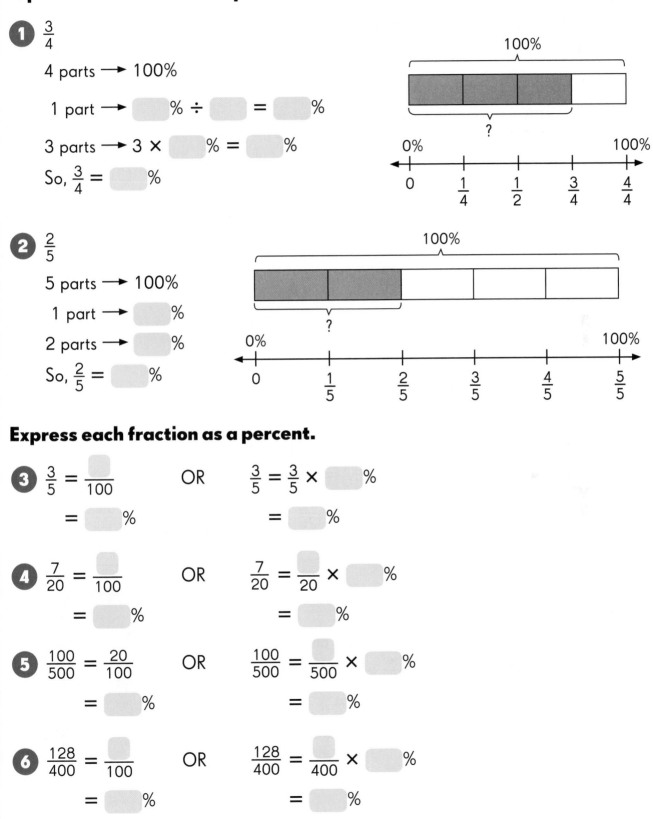

2 $\frac{2}{5}$

5 parts ⟶ 100%

1 part ⟶ ☐ %

2 parts ⟶ ☐ %

So, $\frac{2}{5}$ = ☐ %

Express each fraction as a percent.

3 $\frac{3}{5} = \frac{\square}{100}$ OR $\frac{3}{5} = \frac{3}{5} \times$ ☐ %

  = ☐ %   = ☐ %

4 $\frac{7}{20} = \frac{\square}{100}$ OR $\frac{7}{20} = \frac{\square}{20} \times$ ☐ %

  = ☐ %   = ☐ %

5 $\frac{100}{500} = \frac{20}{100}$ OR $\frac{100}{500} = \frac{\square}{500} \times$ ☐ %

  = ☐ %   = ☐ %

6 $\frac{128}{400} = \frac{\square}{100}$ OR $\frac{128}{400} = \frac{\square}{400} \times$ ☐ %

  = ☐ %   = ☐ %

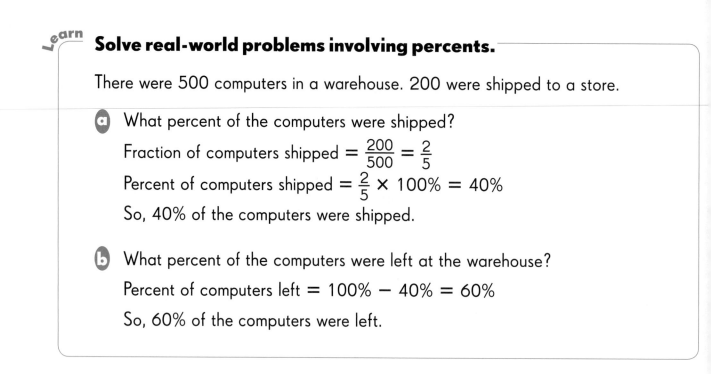

Solve real-world problems involving percents.

There were 500 computers in a warehouse. 200 were shipped to a store.

ⓐ What percent of the computers were shipped?

Fraction of computers shipped $= \dfrac{200}{500} = \dfrac{2}{5}$

Percent of computers shipped $= \dfrac{2}{5} \times 100\% = 40\%$

So, 40% of the computers were shipped.

ⓑ What percent of the computers were left at the warehouse?

Percent of computers left $= 100\% - 40\% = 60\%$

So, 60% of the computers were left.

Guided Practice

Solve. Use models to help you.

7 A bakery had 250 pounds of flour. On Monday, 120 pounds of the flour was used to make bread. The rest was used on Tuesday.

ⓐ What percent of the flour was used on Monday?

Fraction of flour used on Monday $= \dfrac{120}{250} = \dfrac{12}{25}$

Percent of flour used on Monday $= \dfrac{12}{25} \times 100\%$

$\qquad\qquad\qquad\qquad\qquad\qquad = \boxed{}\%$

> 120 pounds is about half or 50% of the weight of 250 pounds.

$\boxed{}$% of the flour was used on Monday.

ⓑ What percent of the flour was used on Tuesday?

Percent of flour used on Tuesday $= \boxed{}\% - \boxed{}\%$

$\qquad\qquad\qquad\qquad\qquad\qquad = \boxed{}\%$

$\boxed{}$% of the flour was used on Tuesday.

Hands-On Activity

WORK IN PAIRS

Set A   4   10   20   25   50

Set B   2   5   11   12   28   49

STEP 1 Form a proper fraction. Choose the denominator from Set A and the numerator from Set B.

STEP 2 Draw a model to show the fraction as a percent.

Let's Practice

Express each fraction as a percent.

1 $\frac{3}{20}$

2 $\frac{24}{25}$

3 $\frac{9}{50}$

4 $\frac{4}{5}$

5 $\frac{21}{50}$

6 $\frac{17}{25}$

Express each fraction as a percent.

7 $\frac{78}{200}$

8 $\frac{260}{400}$

9 $\frac{237}{300}$

Solve. Show your work.

10 A bakery sold $\frac{2}{5}$ of its loaves of whole-wheat bread before noon. What percent of the loaves of bread were sold?

11 Chef Lee bought 20 kilograms of rice. He cooked 7 kilograms of it. What percent of the rice did Chef Lee cook?

12 There are 900 students in a school. 540 of them are boys. What percent of the students in the school are boys?

13 Shawn painted $\frac{13}{25}$ of a wall.

a What percent of the wall was painted?

b What percent of the wall was not painted?

14 Of the total school population, $\frac{11}{25}$ travel to school by bus, $\frac{7}{25}$ get a ride in a car, and the rest walk.

a What percent of the students ride in a bus or car?

b What percent of the students walk?

15 In a certain school, $\frac{3}{20}$ of the students wear glasses.

a What percent of the students wear glasses?

b What percent of the students do not wear glasses?

16 Norma earns $800 a month. She saves $240 of her earnings and uses the rest to pay for her expenses.

a What percent of her money does she save?

b What percent of her money is used to pay expenses?

17 Of the 250 cartons of milk sold, 225 of them are chocolate-flavored. The rest are strawberry-flavored. $\frac{24}{25}$ of the chocolate-flavored cartons of milk are sold to students.

a What percent of the cartons of milk are strawberry-flavored?

b What percent of the chocolate-flavored cartons of milk are sold to students?

18 Of the 30,000 visitors to a theme park in one week, 18,000 were adults. Of the adults at the theme park, $\frac{9}{20}$ were men.

a What percent of the visitors were children?

b What percent of the adults were men?

ON YOUR OWN

Go to Workbook B: Practice 2, pages 59–62

10.3 Percent of a Number

Lesson Objective

•   Use different ways to find the number represented by a percent.

Find the number represented by the percent.

Of the 400 seats on an airplane, 80% of the seats are in the economy-class cabin. How many seats are in the economy-class cabin?

Method 1

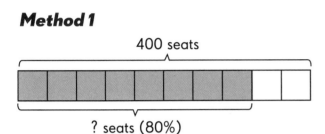

400 seats

? seats (80%)

100% → 400 seats

  1% → 400 ÷ 100 = 4 seats

80% → 80 × 4 = 320 seats

There are 320 seats in the economy-class cabin.

100% of the seats is the total number of seats.

Method 2

80% of seats = 80% of 400

$= \frac{80}{100} \times 400$

= 320

There are 320 seats in the economy-class cabin.

Guided Practice

Solve. Use models to help you.

1 Lily had $800. She spent 20% of her money. How much money did she spend?

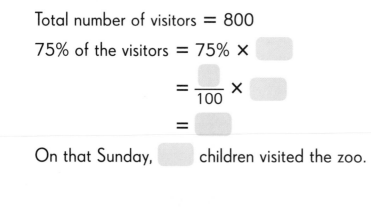

$ [ ]

$? ([ ] %)

100% ⟶ $ [ ]

1% ⟶ $ [ ] ÷ [ ] = $ [ ]

20% ⟶ [ ] × $ [ ] = $ [ ]

Lily spent $ [ ] .

2 One Sunday, 800 people visited a zoo, and 75% of the visitors were children. How many children visited the zoo on that Sunday?

Total number of visitors = 800

75% of the visitors = 75% × [ ]

$$= \frac{[\quad]}{100} \times [\quad]$$

$$= [\quad]$$

On that Sunday, [ ] children visited the zoo.

Find the percent and number represented by the percent.

Mr. Sanjay earns a monthly salary of $4,400. He spends 25% of the salary on rent and 30% of the salary on food.

ⓐ What percent of his salary is left?

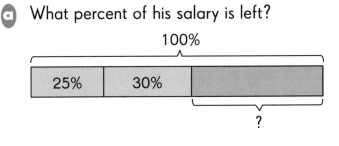

100% − 25% − 30% = 45%

45% of his salary is left.

ⓑ How much of his salary is left?

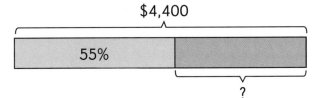

Method 1

100% ⟶ $4,400

1% ⟶ $4,400 ÷ 100 = $44

45% ⟶ 45 × $44 = $1,980

Mr. Sanjay has $1,980 left.

Method 2

45% of $4,400 = 45% × $4,400

$$= \frac{45}{100} \times \$4,400$$

$$= \$1,980$$

Mr. Sanjay has $1,980 left.

Guided Practice

Solve. Use models to help you.

 Of the 1,200 goats, chickens and ducks on Maria's farm, 20% are goats and 45% are chickens.

ⓐ What percent of the animals are ducks?

100% − ⬜% − ⬜% = ⬜%

⬜% of the animals are ducks.

ⓑ How many ducks are there on the farm?

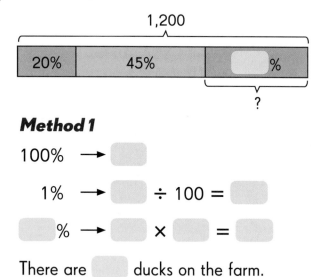

Method 1

100% ⟶ ⬜

1% ⟶ ⬜ ÷ 100 = ⬜

⬜% ⟶ ⬜ × ⬜ = ⬜

There are ⬜ ducks on the farm.

Method 2

⬜% of 1,200 = ⬜% × 1,200

$$= \frac{⬜}{100} × 1{,}200$$

$$= ⬜$$

There are ⬜ ducks on the farm.

Hands-On Activity

WORK IN PAIRS

STEP 1 Draw a model to show each situation.

1 Marianne has 440 milliliters of milk. She uses 75% of it to make biscuits.

2 Felix earns $720 monthly. He saves 25% of the money and spends the rest.

STEP 2 Write word problems that can be solved using your model.

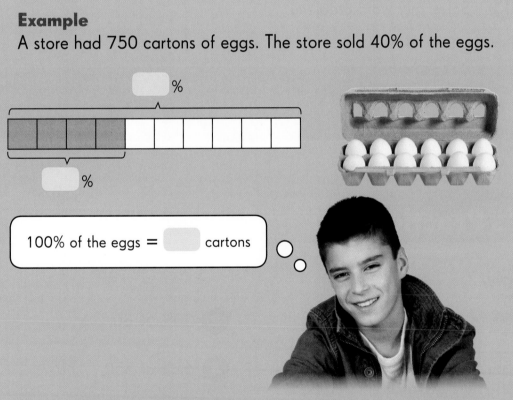

Example
A store had 750 cartons of eggs. The store sold 40% of the eggs.

◻ %

◻ %

100% of the eggs = ◻ cartons

You may use the model to help you solve these word problems.
- How many cartons of eggs did the store sell?
- How many cartons of eggs were not sold?
- What percent of the eggs were not sold?

Math Journal

STEP 1 Write a word problem that can be solved using these sentences.

$$40\% \times 825 = 330 \qquad 825 - 330 = 495$$

STEP 2 Copy and complete the model to solve the problem.

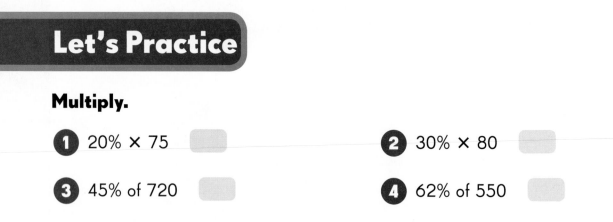

STEP 3 Solve your word problem.

Let's Practice

Multiply.

1 20% × 75

2 30% × 80

3 45% of 720

4 62% of 550

Solve. Use models to help you.

5 A can of tomatoes had a mass of 560 grams. Sylvia used 70% of the can to make soup. How many grams of tomatoes did she use in her soup?

6 Sarah earns $20 a day working after school. She spent 30% of her daily earnings on Monday.

  a How much money did she spend on Monday?

  b How much money was left on Monday?

7 450 children attended the school play. Of the total attendance, 40% were boys. How many girls attended the school play?

8 Of the 200 students at Central School, 75% live more than a mile from the school. How many students live less than a mile from the school?

9 Raymond had $900. He spent 20% of his money on a wireless phone, 45% on a television set, and the rest on a camera.

  a What percent of his money was spent on the camera?

  b How much money was spent on the camera?

10 Of the 30 pounds of fish served for lunch at a restaurant, 15% was swordfish, 60% was salmon, and the rest was haddock.

  a What percent of the fish was haddock?

  b How many pounds of haddock were served?

11 Of the 2,500 apartments in a new development, 15% have one bedroom, 25% have two bedrooms, and the rest have three bedrooms.

  a What percent of the apartments have three bedrooms?

  b How many three-bedroom apartments are there?

12 In a 250-gram package of dried fruit, 22% are cherries, 28% are pineapples, and 44% are apples. The rest are apricots.

  a What percent of the package are apricots?

  b What is the mass of the apricots?

ON YOUR OWN

Go to Workbook B:
Practice 3, pages 63–66

Lesson 10.4 Real-World Problems: Percent

Lesson Objective

- Solve real-world problems involving percents.

Learn **Solve word problems involving sales tax.**

A television set costs $1,500. There is a 7% sales tax on the television set.

(a) How much is the sales tax?

Method 1

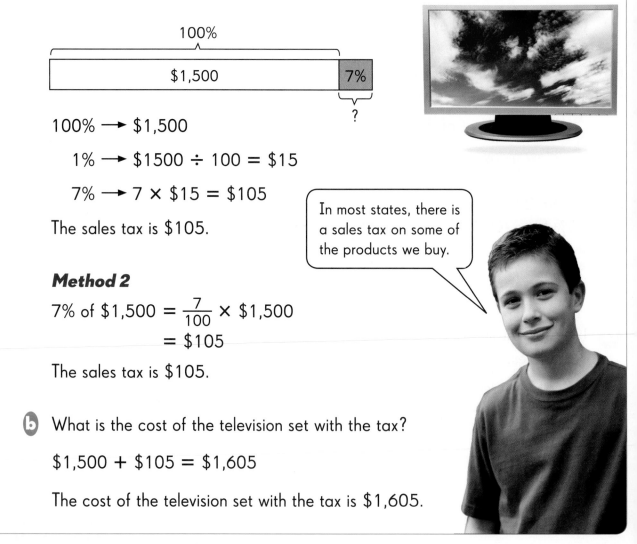

100% → $1,500

1% → $1500 ÷ 100 = $15

7% → 7 × $15 = $105

The sales tax is $105.

> In most states, there is a sales tax on some of the products we buy.

Method 2

$7\% \text{ of } \$1,500 = \frac{7}{100} \times \$1,500$

$= \$105$

The sales tax is $105.

(b) What is the cost of the television set with the tax?

$1,500 + $105 = $1,605

The cost of the television set with the tax is $1,605.

Guided Practice

Solve.

1 The Carlson family went out to dinner. The cost of the food they ordered was $82. In addition, they paid a 7% **meals tax**.

a How much was the meals tax?

Method 1

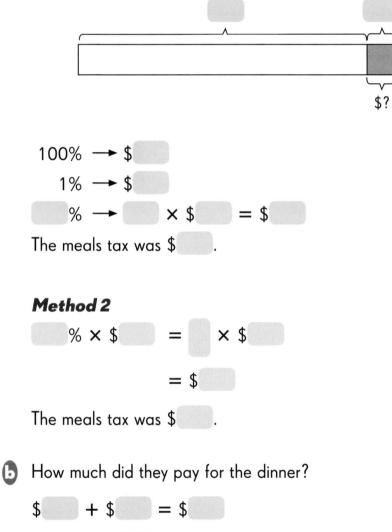

100% ⟶ $[   ]

1% ⟶ $[   ]

[   ]% ⟶ [   ] × $[   ] = $[   ]

The meals tax was $[   ].

Method 2

[   ]% × $[   ] = [   ] × $[   ]

= $[   ]

The meals tax was $[   ].

b How much did they pay for the dinner?

$[   ] + $[   ] = $[   ]

They paid $[   ] for the dinner.

The regular price of a sofa was $2,000. During a sale, Mrs. Wong bought the sofa at a discount of 15%.

ⓐ What was the dollar amount of the discount?

Method 1

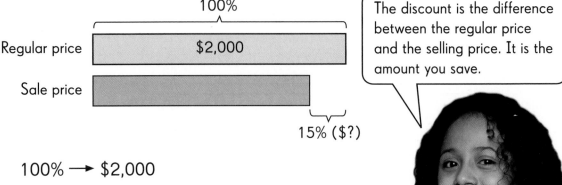

100% → $2,000

1% → $2,000 ÷ 100 = $20

15% → 15 × $20 = $300

The dollar amount of the discount was $300.

Method 2

Discount = 15% of regular price

$$= \frac{15}{100} \times \$2,000$$

$$= \$300$$

The dollar amount of the discount was $300.

ⓑ How much did she pay for the sofa?

$2,000 − $300 = $1,700

She paid $1,700 for the sofa.

> Subtract the dollar amount of the discount from the regular price.

Guided Practice

Solve.

2 The regular price of a pair of inline skates was $150. At a sale, Joanne bought the pair of skates at a discount of 20%.

ⓐ What was the dollar amount of the discount?

Method 1

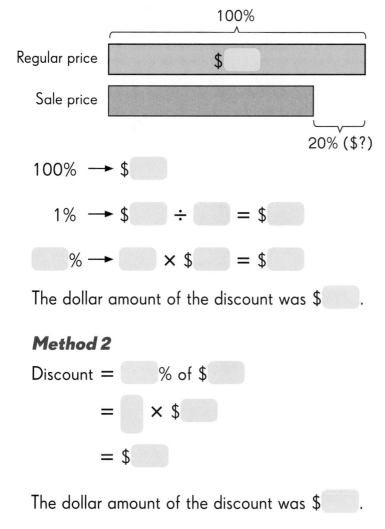

100% ⟶ $ ⬚

1% ⟶ $ ⬚ ÷ ⬚ = $ ⬚

⬚% ⟶ ⬚ × $ ⬚ = $ ⬚

The dollar amount of the discount was $ ⬚ .

Method 2

Discount = ⬚% of $ ⬚

= ⬚ × $ ⬚

= $ ⬚

The dollar amount of the discount was $ ⬚ .

ⓑ How much did she pay for the skates?

$ ⬚ − $ ⬚ = $ ⬚

Joanne paid $ ⬚ for the skates.

^earn Solve word problems involving **interest**.

The Historical Society has $15,000 in an account that pays an interest of 4% per year. How much money will it have in the account at the end of 1 year?

Interest = 4% of $15,000

$$= \frac{4}{100} \times \$15,000$$

$$= \$600$$

> Add the interest to the amount in the account. Interest is the amount that a bank pays you for depositing your money with them.

Amount of money in the account at the end of 1 year
= $15,000 + $600

= $15,600

The Historical Society will have $15,600 in the account at the end of 1 year.

Guided Practice

Solve.

3 A company has $200,000 in an investment fund. The interest is 6% per year. How much money will the company have in the fund at the end of 1 year?

Interest = ____ % of $ ____

= ____ × $ ____

= $ ____

> $200,000 + Interest

Amount of money in the fund at the end of 1 year
= $ ____ + $ ____

= $ ____

The company will have $ ____ in the fund at the end of 1 year.

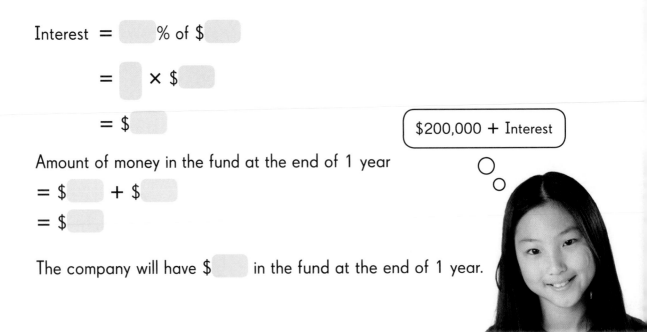

 **Hands-On Activity**

Take turns to draw a model to show each situation. Help your partner label each model with the appropriate numbers.

1 Linda bought a shelf that cost $149. She paid 7% sales tax on $149. Draw a model to show the price of the shelf before and after the sales tax was included.

2 The original price of a chair is $50. The shop owner increases the price by 30%. Draw a model to show the original price and new price of the chair.

3 The regular price of a book was $16. The shop gave a discount of 10% off the regular price. Draw a model to show the regular price and sale price of the book.

Mysteries ?

4 Mr. Whitman has $4,500 in an account that pays 3% interest per year. Draw a model to show the amount of money in the account now and at the end of 1 year.

Math Journal

The regular price of a jacket was $78. Gretchen bought the jacket at a 5% discount. How much did she pay for the jacket?

Bob, Marcos and Selena drew models to represent this word problem. Whose model is correct? Explain why.

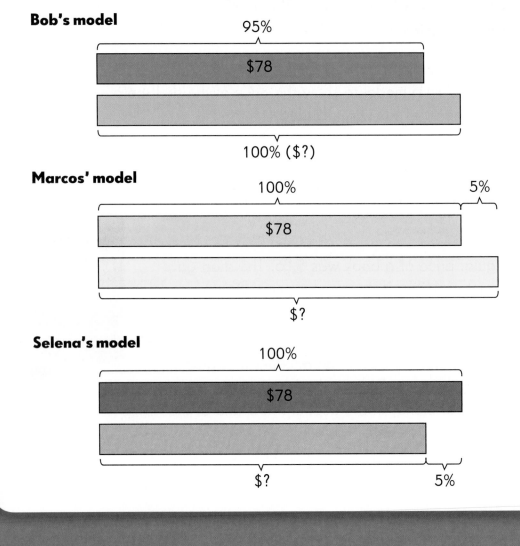

Bob's model

95%
$78
100% ($?)

Marcos' model

100%   5%
$78
$?

Selena's model

100%
$78
$?   5%

Let's Practice

Solve. Show your work.

1 David bought a digital camera that cost $320. He paid 5% sales tax on the price of the camera. How much sales tax did David pay?

2 A restaurant meal cost $90 and there was a 6% meals tax on the price of the meal.

   a How much was the meals tax?

   b What was the total price of the meal with meals tax?

3 Jack bought an airline ticket which cost $520. In addition, he paid 7% sales tax on the ticket. How much did he pay for the ticket?

4 Desmond went to dinner with a group of friends. The dinner cost $240. They left the waiter a 20% tip. How much did they pay for the dinner with the tip?

5 The regular price of a notebook computer was $650. Kwan bought the notebook computer at a discount of 5%. How much did Kwan pay for the notebook computer?

6 For a field trip, 35 students went to the zoo. How much did they pay for the tickets in all?

> **Zoo Admission Ticket**
> $15 each
> 20% discount for students

7 Company ABC invests $185,000 in a fund which pays 6% interest per year. How much money will the company have in the fund at the end of 1 year?

ON YOUR OWN

**Go to Workbook B:
Practice 4, pages 67–70**

CRITICAL THINKING SKILLS
Put On Your Thinking Cap!

PROBLEM SOLVING

Use a model to solve the problem.
In a school fund-raising project, 40% of the total funds collected were from the teachers. Parents and students contributed the remaining amount. The parents contributed twice as much as the students. What percent of the total funds collected was contributed by the students?

ON YOUR OWN

**Go to Workbook B:
Put on Your Thinking Cap!
pages 71– 72**

Chapter Wrap Up

Study Guide

You have learned...

Percent

Percent, Fraction, and Decimal

- Percent means 'out of 100'. 75% means 75 out of 100.

- Express a fraction as a percent.

$$\frac{24}{100} = 24\%$$

$$\frac{9}{10} = \frac{90}{100} = 90\%$$

$$\frac{1}{5} = \frac{20}{100} = 20\%$$

$$\frac{21}{300} = \frac{7}{100} = 7\%$$

- Express a percent as a fraction.

$$15\% = \frac{15}{100} = \frac{3}{20}$$

- Express a decimal as a percent.

$$0.2 = \frac{2}{10} = \frac{20}{100} = 20\%$$

- Express a percent as a decimal.

$$5\% = \frac{5}{100} = 0.05$$

Percent of a Number

Find 25% of 400.

Method 1

$$100\% \longrightarrow 400$$

$$1\% \longrightarrow 400 \div 100 = 4$$

$$25\% \longrightarrow 25 \times 4 = 100$$

Method 2

$$\frac{25}{100} \times 400 = 100$$

Real-World Problems

Solve real-world problems involving
- fractions
- percents
- sales tax
- meals tax
- discount
- interest

Chapter Review/Test

Vocabulary

Choose the correct word.

 1 ▢ means 'out of 100'.

2 When a ▢ is given on an item, its selling price is lower than its regular price.

3 A bank pays you ▢ when you deposit money in the bank.

> percent
> sales tax
> meals tax
> discount
> interest

Concepts and Skills

Complete.

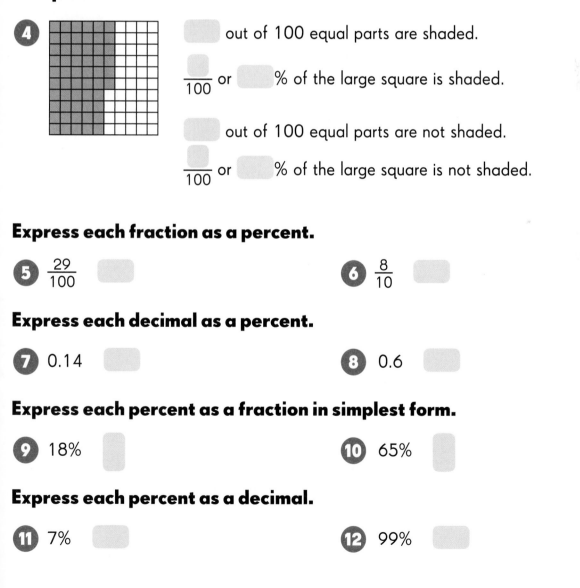

4 ▢ out of 100 equal parts are shaded.

$\frac{▢}{100}$ or ▢ % of the large square is shaded.

▢ out of 100 equal parts are not shaded.

$\frac{▢}{100}$ or ▢ % of the large square is not shaded.

Express each fraction as a percent.

5 $\frac{29}{100}$ ▢

6 $\frac{8}{10}$ ▢

Express each decimal as a percent.

7 0.14 ▢

8 0.6 ▢

Express each percent as a fraction in simplest form.

9 18% ▢

10 65% ▢

Express each percent as a decimal.

11 7% ▢

12 99% ▢

Express each fraction as a percent.

13 $\frac{1}{2}$

14 $\frac{3}{4}$

15 $\frac{9}{20}$

16 $\frac{4}{5}$

17 $\frac{15}{300}$

18 $\frac{84}{400}$

Multiply.

19 25% × 160

20 30% × 300

21 52% × 350

22 78% × 650

23 5% × 270

24 60% × 480

Problem Solving

Solve. Show your work.

25 A baker has 50 pounds of flour. She uses 12 pounds of flour to make bread. What percent of the flour does she use?

26 Karen earns $1,800 a month. She spends 40% of it and saves the rest. How much does she save each month?

27 Tony buys a pair of running shoes for $80. He pays 9% sales tax. How much does the pair of running shoes cost in total?

28 The regular price of a book is $36. The book is sold at a discount of 10%. What is the price of the book after the discount?

29 A company has $54,000 in a bank account that pays an interest of 2% per year. How much money can it withdraw at the end of 1 year?

11 Graphs and Probability

I tossed a number cube 30 times. Look at my results in the table.

Number on Cube	Number of Tosses	
1	‖‖‖ ‖	7
2	‖‖‖	5
3	‖‖‖	5
4	‖‖	3
5	‖‖‖	4
6	‖‖‖ ‖	6

Do you know the experimental probability of getting a 6? What is the theoretical probability of getting a 6 with one toss of the number cube?

Lessons

BIG IDEAS

▶ Displaying data in a graph highlights some features of the data.
▶ Probability measures the likelihood of an event occurring.

Recall Prior Knowledge

Making and interpreting a bar graph

You can make a bar graph to compare data.
The data may be in a table, a tally chart, or another form.

Type of Fruit	Number of Pieces of Fruit Bought
apple	8
orange	10
grapefruit	16
pear	12

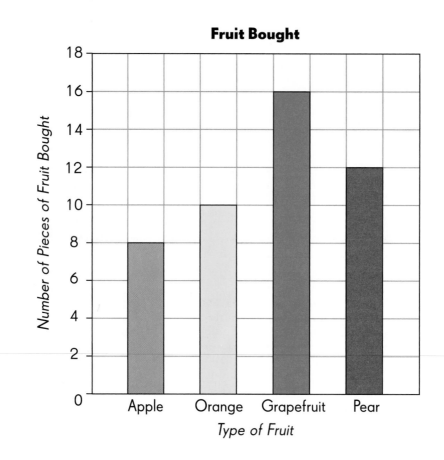

Fruit Bought

10 oranges were bought.
Twice as many grapefruit as apples were bought.
46 pieces of fruit were bought.

Finding the average or mean

At a game, James scores 5 points, Betty scores 3 points, Cynthia scores 7 points.

Average or mean number of points $= \dfrac{\text{Total number of points}}{\text{Numbers of players}}$

$$= \dfrac{5 + 3 + 7}{3}$$

$$= 5$$

Writing probability as a fraction

A favorable outcome is a result you are looking for. The probability of getting a favorable outcome can be written as a fraction.

Probability of a favorable outcome $= \dfrac{\text{Number of favorable outcomes}}{\text{Total number of possible outcomes}}$

You can represent probability on a number line. The closer a probability of an outcome is to 1, the more likely the outcome is to occur.

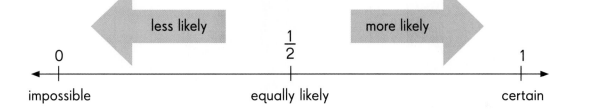

This spinner is divided into 6 equal parts.

Probability of landing on an even number $= \dfrac{3}{6} = \dfrac{1}{2}$

Probability of landing on 1 or 2 $= \dfrac{4}{6} = \dfrac{2}{3}$

Probability of landing on 3 or 4 $= \dfrac{2}{6} = \dfrac{1}{3}$

Probability of landing on 1, 2, 3, or 4 $= \dfrac{6}{6} = 1$

Probability of landing on 5 $= 0$

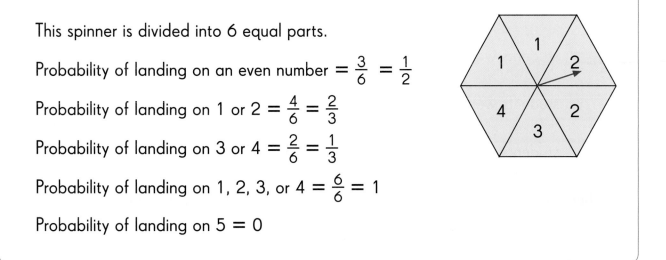

✔ Quick Check

Complete. Use the data in the graph.

The bar graph shows the number of students absent from school from Monday to Friday.

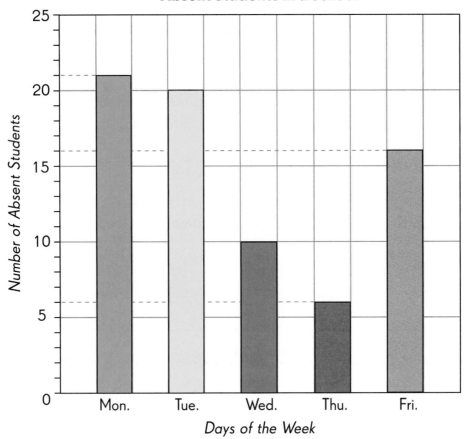

Absent Students in a School

Number of Absent Students

Days of the Week

1 [   ] students were absent on Monday.

2 [   ] students were absent on Tuesday.

3 [   ] students were absent on Thursday and Friday.

4 There were [   ] more students absent on Tuesday than on Wednesday.

5 The least number of students were absent on [   ].

Solve.

6 The masses of 3 boys are 45 kilograms, 62 kilograms, and 58 kilograms. Find the average mass of the boys.

Complete with more likely, less likely, equally likely, certain, and impossible.

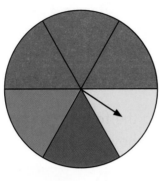

7 It is ____ that the spinner will land on yellow.

8 It is ____ that the spinner will land on black.

9 It is ____ that the spinner will land on red.

Look at the above spinner. Express each probability as a fraction.

10 The probability that the spinner will land on blue is ____.

11 The probability that the spinner will land on red is ____.

12 The probability that the spinner will land on red, green, yellow or blue is ____.

13 The probability that the spinner will land on purple is ____.

11.1 Making and Interpreting Double Bar Graphs

Lesson Objective

- Make and interpret a double bar graph.

Vocabulary
double bar graph

key

Learn **Make a double bar graph from two sets of similar data.**

Susan conducts a survey to find the favorite yogurt flavor of students in Class 5A and Class 5B. She shows the results of her survey in a table.

Class	Favorite Yogurt Flavor			
	Vanilla	**Blueberry**	**Peach**	**Strawberry**
A	9	16	2	9
B	7	12	4	10

Next, Susan presents the two sets of data in two bar graphs.

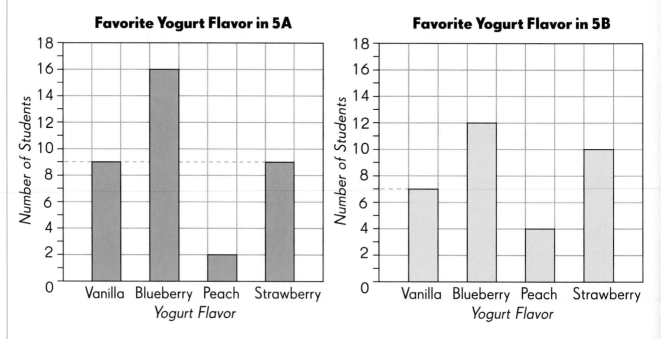

Susan combines the two graphs to compare the two sets of data.
This type of graph is a **double bar graph**.

In a double bar graph, each item on the horizontal axis is represented by two bars, one for each data set.

Susan makes her double bar graph by following these steps.

Step 1
Draw and label the vertical axis. Choose a suitable scale and mark equal intervals.

Step 2
Draw and label the horizontal axis. List the items to be displayed on this axis.

Step 3
Draw one bar for each data set that relates to the item.
Use a different color for each data set.
Give a **key** to show what data set each color represents.

Step 4
Give the graph a title.

Susan uses a scale from 0 to 18 and equal intervals of 2.
She uses green for the bar that represents Class 5A data, and yellow for Class 5B data.

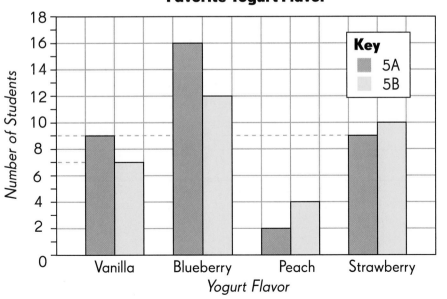

^{earn} **Interpret a double bar graph.**

Use the double graph on page 125.

1 To find the most popular flavor in each class, look for the tallest bar for each class. The two bars representing blueberry are the tallest for each class.
Blueberry is the most popular flavor in each class.

2 To find how many more students in 5A than in 5B prefer vanilla, read the values from the two bars that represent this flavor.
Then subtract the number of students that each bar represents.

$9 - 7 = 2$

There are 2 more students in 5A than in 5B who prefer vanilla.

3 To find the flavor showing the least difference between the two classes, look for the pair of bars with the least difference in height.
Then subtract the values for the number of students.

$10 - 9 = 1$

The strawberry flavor shows the least difference between the two classes.

A double bar graph presents two data sets for comparison.

Guided Practice

The table shows the amount of money collected at counters A and B during a fair.
A double bar graph of the data is started below.

Period (Time)	Counter A	Counter B
first hour	$250	$150
second hour	$450	$250
third hour	$300	$400
fourth hour	$500	$450
fifth hour	$750	$800

Describe what is missing for each numbered box in the graph.

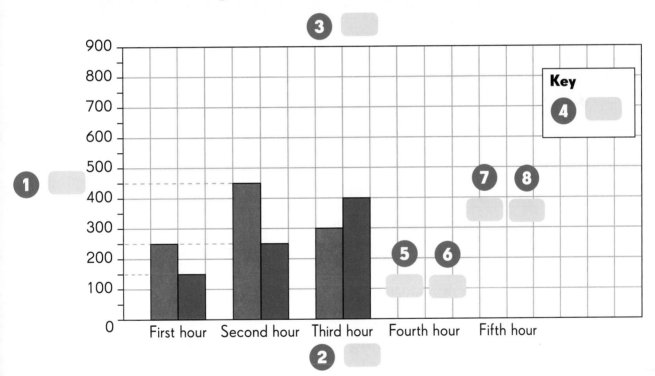

Complete. Use the data in the graph.

9 A total of $ ____ was collected at both counters in the third hour.

10 In the ____ hour, the least amount of money was collected at both counters.
Explain your answer.

11 In the ____ hour, the most amount of money was collected at both counters.
Explain your answer.

12 The average amount of money collected per hour at counter B was ____ .

 **Hands-On Activity**

Materials:
• a paper bag
• one paper slip of each color: red, blue, green, yellow
• 3 pink paper slips

WORK IN PAIRS

STEP
1 Draw a paper slip from a bag containing red, blue, green, yellow, and pink paper slips.

STEP
2 Record the color of the paper slip drawn in the table. Then, return the paper slip to the bag.

Color	Student A		Student B	
	Tally	Number of Times	Tally	Number of Times
red				
blue				
green				
yellow				
pink				

STEP
3 Take turns to repeat STEP **1** and STEP **2** to make up 50 draws.

STEP
4 Use the data in the table to draw a double bar graph.

Answer these questions using the data in the graph.

a What is the total number of paper slips drawn?

b Which color was drawn the most often by each of you?

c Which color was drawn the least often by each of you?

d How many more or fewer pink paper slips were drawn by you than your partner?

e What do you notice when you compare the difference between the number of times each color is drawn?

Let's Practice

The double bar graph shows the number of pieces of fruit Gina and Kim bought at a supermarket.

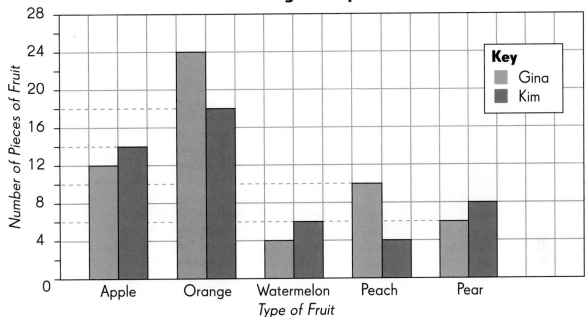

Copy and complete the table. Use the data in the graph.

1

Type of Fruit	⬜	⬜
apple		
orange		
watermelon		
peach		
pear		

Complete. Use the data in the table and the graph.

2 Which fruit did each girl buy the most?

Gina ⬜   Kim ⬜

3 Which fruit did each girl buy the least?

Gina ⬜   Kim ⬜

Complete. Use the data in the table and the graph on page 129.

4 Gina buys more [ ] and [ ] than Kim.

5 Gina bought [ ] pieces of fruit.

6 Kim bought [ ] pieces of fruit.

7 Kim must buy [ ] more pieces of fruit so that both girls have the same number of pieces.

The table shows the number of hours Sarah and Henry spent on each activity in a week.

Activity	Number of Hours Spent on the Activity by Sarah	Number of Hours Spent on the Activity by Henry
swimming	10	7
playing piano	6	1
playing tennis	2	6
reading	12	6
playing basketball	14	18

Use the data in the table to draw a double bar graph. Then use your graph to answer each question.

8 How many more hours does Sarah swim than Henry? [ ]

9 How many fewer hours does Henry spend on playing piano compared to Sarah? [ ]

10 Find the total number of hours Sarah and Henry spent on playing tennis. [ ]

11 Who do you think prefers to read? Why? [ ]

12 On which activity do both students spend the most number of hours? [ ]

ON YOUR OWN

Go to Workbook B:
Practice 1, pages 83–84

Lesson 11.2 Graphing an Equation

Lesson Objectives

- Read points on a coordinate grid.
- Plot points on a coordinate grid.
- Graph an equation.

Vocabulary

coordinate grid	ordered pair
x-axis	x-coordinate
y-axis	y-coordinate
coordinate plane	origin
coordinates	straight line graph
	equation

ˡᵉᵃʳⁿ Read and plot points on a coordinate grid.

You can use a **coordinate grid** to locate points in a plane. A coordinate grid has a horizontal number line and a vertical number line.

> The horizontal number line is called the **x-axis** and the vertical number line is called the **y-axis**.

These axes are number lines, so they are marked with numbers.
You can name or locate any point on this **coordinate plane** with two numbers, called **coordinates**.

This coordinate grid is marked with two points, A (2, 5) and B (4, 3).

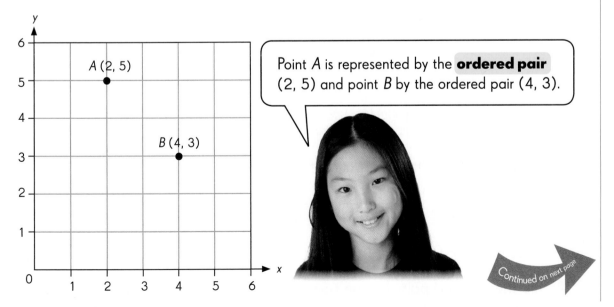

Point A is represented by the **ordered pair** (2, 5) and point B by the ordered pair (4, 3).

Continued on next page

The first coordinate (**x-coordinate**) is a number located on the *x*-axis.
The second coordinate (**y-coordinate**) is a number located on the *y*-axis.

> A pair of coordinates is always named in order, the *x*-coordinate
> first, the *y*-coordinate second, and so, it is called an ordered pair.

In the coordinate grid, to plot point *A* (2, 5), locate 2 units to the right of
the *y*-axis and 5 units above the *x*-axis. Then mark the point with a dot.

To plot point *B* (4, 3), locate 4 units to the right of the *y*-axis and 3 units
above the *x*-axis. Then mark the point with a dot.

> A point *A* (*x*, *y*) means the point *A* is located *x* units
> from the *y*-axis and *y* units above the *x*-axis.

The *x*-axis and *y*-axis intersect at right angles at a point called the **origin**.
The coordinates of the origin are (0, 0).

Guided Practice

Copy the coordinate grid and complete.

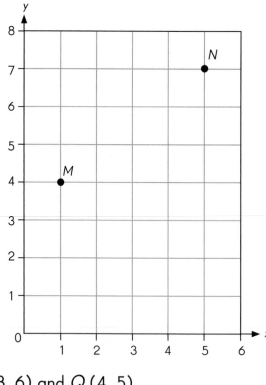

1 Plot the points *P* (3, 6) and *Q* (4, 5).

2 Name the ordered pairs for the points *M* and *N*.

Learn Graph an equation.

Alice buys some granola bars from a supermarket. Each granola bar costs $2. The table shows the total cost of the granola bars.

Number of Granola Bars	1	2	3	4	5
Total Cost ($)	2	4	6	8	10

Alice uses the data in the table to plot the ordered pairs
(1, 2), (2, 4), (3, 6), (4, 8), and (5, 10) in a coordinate grid.
The *x*-axis shows the number of granola bars.
The *y*-axis shows the total cost of the granola bars.

Alice joins the points in the coordinate grid using a straight line. This line is called a **straight line graph**. From the graph, you can find the *x*-coordinate if the *y*-coordinate is known and vice versa.
There is an **equation** connecting *x* and *y*. The equation is $y = 2x$.

An equation is a statement that joins two equal expressions by an '='.

In the equation $y = 2x$, the expression $2x$ is joined to the expression *y*.
So, the equation shows the relationship between *x* and *y*.

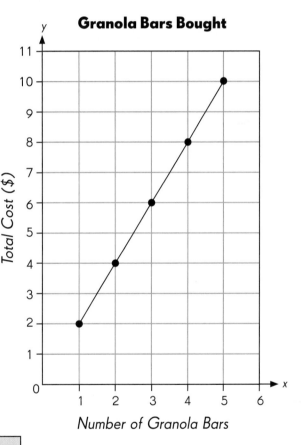

Granola Bars Bought

x	1	2	3	4	5
y = 2x	2	4	6	8	10

The straight line passing through the ordered pairs
in the table is called the graph of the equation $y = 2x$.

Continued on next page

The dimensions of a building are shown.

length = 18 yards   width = 15 yards   height = 24 yards

Mr. Gonzales wants to build an apartment house with the same dimensions labeled in feet. He uses a graph to help him find the measurements.

Mr. Gonzales knows that 1 yard equals 3 feet. So, he uses the equation $y = 3x$ to draw a straight line graph for values of x from 0 to 24. Each point on the graph shows the measurement in yards and the corresponding measurement in feet.

x (yards)	0	3	6	9	12	15	18	21	24
y = 3x (feet)	0	9	18	27	36	45	54	63	72

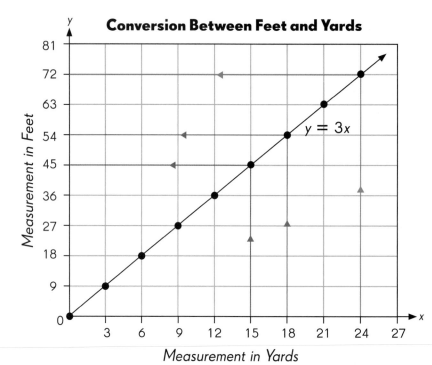

Conversion Between Feet and Yards

From the graph, 18 yards on the x-axis corresponds to 54 feet on the y-axis. Also, 15 yards corresponds to 45 feet and 24 yards corresponds to 72 feet.

The dimensions of Mr. Gonzales' apartment house are 54 feet by 45 feet by 72 feet. A door 9 feet high will have a height of 3 yards. A nearby warehouse 27 yards high will have a height of 81 feet.

Guided Practice

Use the data in the graph to answer the questions.

The graph $y = 8x$ shows the cost of fabric measured in yards.

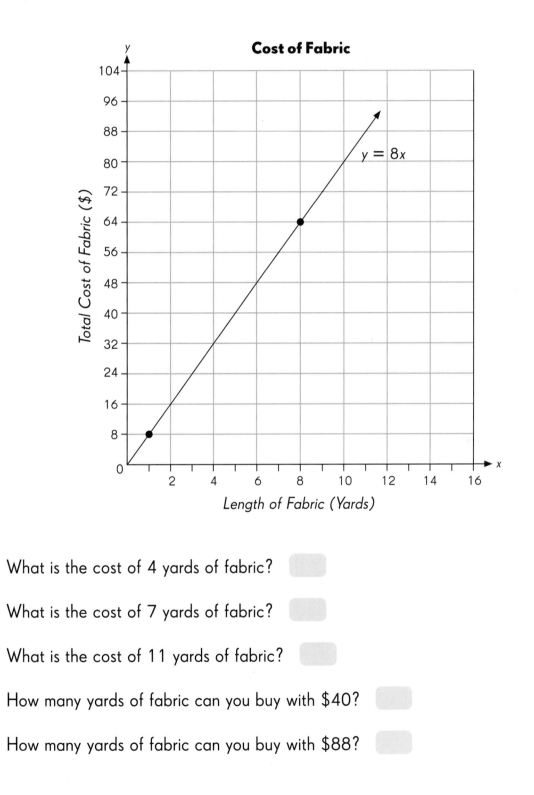

Cost of Fabric

$y = 8x$

Total Cost of Fabric ($)

Length of Fabric (Yards)

3 What is the cost of 4 yards of fabric?

4 What is the cost of 7 yards of fabric?

5 What is the cost of 11 yards of fabric?

6 How many yards of fabric can you buy with $40?

7 How many yards of fabric can you buy with $88?

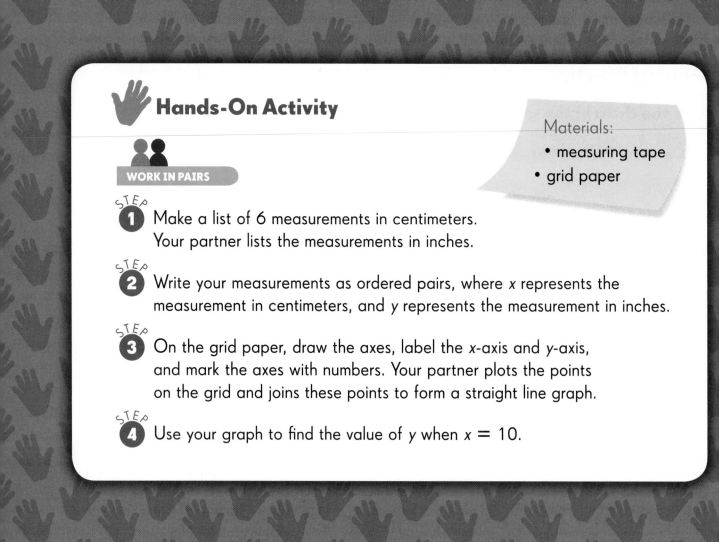

Hands-On Activity

Materials:
• measuring tape
• grid paper

WORK IN PAIRS

STEP 1 Make a list of 6 measurements in centimeters. Your partner lists the measurements in inches.

STEP 2 Write your measurements as ordered pairs, where x represents the measurement in centimeters, and y represents the measurement in inches.

STEP 3 On the grid paper, draw the axes, label the x-axis and y-axis, and mark the axes with numbers. Your partner plots the points on the grid and joins these points to form a straight line graph.

STEP 4 Use your graph to find the value of y when $x = 10$.

Let's Practice

Copy the coordinate grid and plot the points on the grid.

1 Plot the points A (2, 3), B (4, 5), C (0, 7), and D (3, 8) on a coordinate grid.

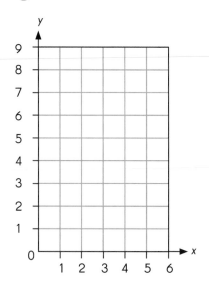

Use the coordinate grid to find the ordered pair that describes each location.

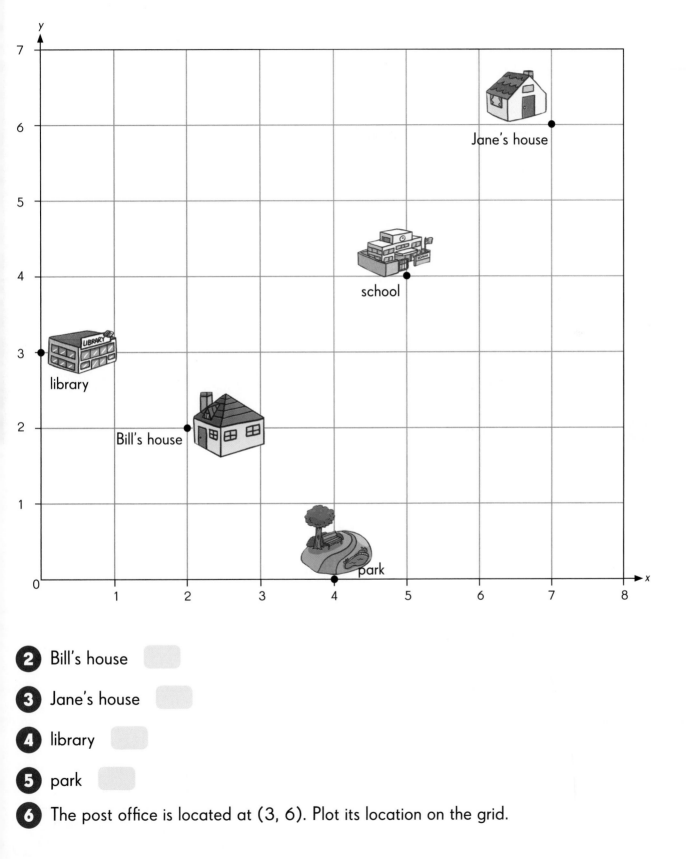

2 Bill's house [ ]

3 Jane's house [ ]

4 library [ ]

5 park [ ]

6 The post office is located at (3, 6). Plot its location on the grid.

Use the data in the graph to answer the questions.

The graph shows the cost of ribbons measured in yards.

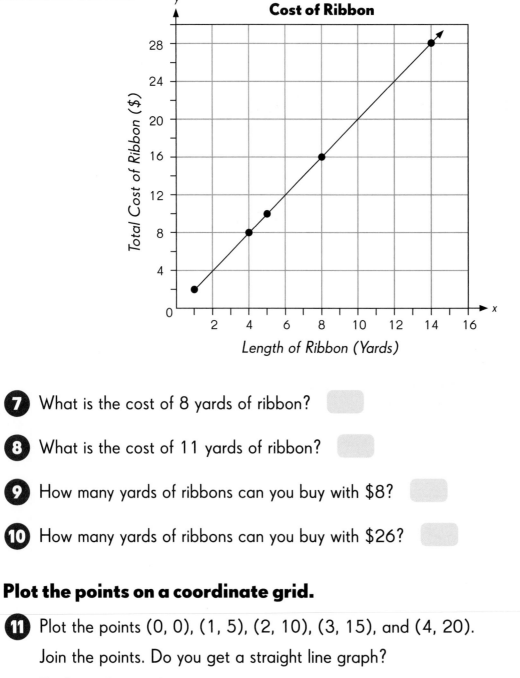

7 What is the cost of 8 yards of ribbon?

8 What is the cost of 11 yards of ribbon?

9 How many yards of ribbons can you buy with $8?

10 How many yards of ribbons can you buy with $26?

Plot the points on a coordinate grid.

11 Plot the points (0, 0), (1, 5), (2, 10), (3, 15), and (4, 20).

Join the points. Do you get a straight line graph?

Explain why or why not.

ON YOUR OWN

Go to Workbook B:
Practice 2, pages 85–88

Lesson 11.3 Combinations

Lesson Objectives

- List and count all possible combinations.
- Draw a tree diagram to show all possible combinations.
- Use multiplication to find the number of combinations.

Vocabulary
combinations
organized list
tree diagram

Learn Find the number of combinations.

Marion has to paint a rectangle and a triangle. She can paint each shape red or blue. There are different ways or **combinations** to paint the shapes.

> The number of combinations means the number of ways of selecting or grouping items, where the order is not important.

You can make an **organized list** to show the combinations. Then find the number of combinations.

> An organized list helps you to record combinations in a systematic order.

red rectangle, red triangle
red rectangle, blue triangle
blue rectangle, red triangle
blue rectangle, blue triangle

> An organized list helps me count the combinations.

There are 4 combinations for painting the two shapes.

Guided Practice

Make an organized list to find the number of combinations.

Keith wants to order a sandwich and a drink. The sandwiches are tuna, chicken, and ham. The drinks are lemonade and orange juice.

 Make an organized list of the combinations.

There are ⬚ combinations.

 If a roast beef sandwich is also available, then Keith can choose from ⬚ combinations.

Learn **Draw a tree diagram.**

A **tree diagram** is another way to show combinations.

You can use the example on page 139 to draw a tree diagram. Then compare it with the organized list.

The tree diagram shows the possible combinations for painting Marion's rectangle and triangle in red or blue. Each stem on the tree diagram can be traced from left to right and represents a combination.

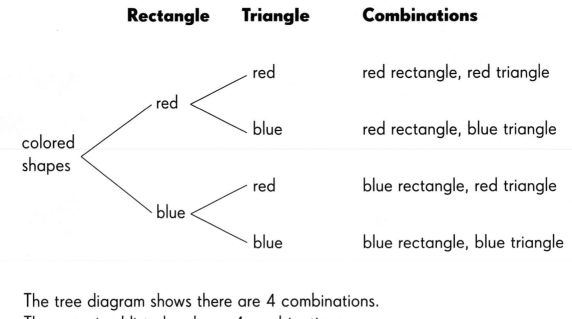

Rectangle	Triangle	Combinations
red	red	red rectangle, red triangle
red	blue	red rectangle, blue triangle
blue	red	blue rectangle, red triangle
blue	blue	blue rectangle, blue triangle

The tree diagram shows there are 4 combinations.
The organized list also shows 4 combinations.

Guided Practice

Draw a tree diagram to find the number of combinations.

3 Ms. Davis has 2 pairs of shoes and 4 dresses. The colors of her shoes are red and black. The colors of her dresses are white, black, maroon, and beige. If Ms. Davis wants to match a pair of shoes to a dress, how many combinations does she have?

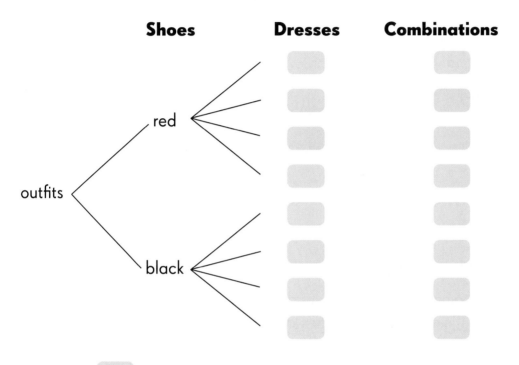

There are [ ] combinations.

Use multiplication to find the number of combinations.

Look at the example on page 139.
Marion has 2 colors for painting each rectangle and 2 colors for painting each triangle.
Multiply to find the number of combinations.

Color choices   ×   Color choices   =   Number of
for rectangle   for triangle   combinations
       ↓   ↓
       2   ×   2   =   4

There are 4 combinations.

Guided Practice

Multiply to find the number of combinations.

4 Mr. Atkins has 5 shirts and 3 pairs of pants.
Find the number of combinations of matching a shirt and a pair of pants.

Number of combinations =  × ☐

=

🖐 Hands-On Activity

👥
WORK IN PAIRS

A café sells 4 choices of sandwiches and
5 choices of fruit juice. The sandwiches are ham,
tuna, egg, and cheese. The juices are apple,
orange, pineapple, peach, and cranberry.
Find the number of combinations
of a sandwich and juice.

Materials:
• paper
• colored markers
• straightedge

STEP 1 Use markers and a straightedge to draw a tree diagram
to find the combinations.

STEP 2 Count the number of combinations.

STEP 3 Use multiplication to check if the number of combinations
shown on the tree diagram is correct.

Math Journal

Write a word problem about combining groups of 2 and 5 items. Draw a tree diagram to show the number of combinations based on your word problem.

Let's Practice

Solve. Show your work.

1 Jack has 4 pairs of socks in different colors. He has 2 pairs of shoes, one of which does not have shoelaces.

a Make an organized list to find the number of combinations of shoes and socks.

b Draw a tree diagram to find the number of combinations.

2 A teacher has 6 different chapter books and 3 different mathematics books. She wants to give one chapter book, and one mathematics book to one student.

a Use a tree diagram to show the number of combinations the teacher can choose.

b Use multiplication to check that the number of combinations is correct.

3 A pizza shop has 4 kinds of meat toppings, and 3 kinds of vegetable toppings. Find the number of combinations of 1 meat and 1 vegetable topping the shop can offer.

a Make an organized list to find the number of combinations.

b Use multiplication to check that the number of combinations is correct.

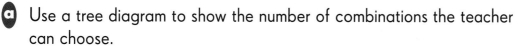

ON YOUR OWN

Go to Workbook B: Practice 3, pages 89–92

Lesson 11.4 Theoretical Probability and Experimental Probability

Lesson Objectives

- Find the experimental probability of an outcome.
- Compare the results of an experiment with the theoretical probability.

Vocabulary
favorable outcome
theoretical probability
experimental probability

Learn Understand theoretical probability.

There are 6 possible color outcomes when spinning the spinner shown. The probability of getting any 1 of the 6 outcomes is $\frac{1}{6}$. Because the sections are of equal size, each outcome is equally likely.

A coin has both a head or a tail. When you toss it, it lands as a head or a tail. There are 2 possible outcomes. If you are hoping the coin will land as a head, then the **favorable outcome** is a head.

head   tail

> The possible outcomes of tossing a coin are a head or a tail.

So, the probability of getting heads is 1 out of 2 or $\frac{1}{2}$.

The probability of getting tails is also $\frac{1}{2}$.

This is **theoretical probability**. You know that the coin lands either as a head or a tail. You predict the outcomes are equally likely.

> If each outcome is equally likely, the theoretical probability of an event is
>
> $$\frac{\text{Number of favorable outcomes}}{\text{Total number of possible outcomes}}.$$

If the coin is tossed only a few times, you may get more heads than tails. If the coin is tossed many times, theoretically, the probability of getting a head or tail is $\frac{1}{2}$.

Similarly, the theoretical probability of spinning any 1 of the 6 colors on the spinner with 6 equal sections is $\frac{1}{6}$.

Guided Practice

Complete.

A bag has 3 yellow beads and 5 green beads.

1 The number of yellow beads is ____ .

2 The number of green beads is ____ .

3 The total number of beads is ____ .

4 What is the theoretical probability of

a drawing a yellow bead?

$$\frac{\text{Number of yellow beads}}{\text{Total number of beads}} = \boxed{}$$

b drawing a green bead?

$$\frac{\text{Number of green beads}}{\text{Total number of beads}} = \boxed{}$$

Solve.

Brad rolls a cube numbered 1 to 6 on its faces. Then he tosses a nickel.

5 Draw a tree diagram to show all the combinations of outcomes.

6 What is the theoretical probability of getting a head and an odd number?

7 What is the theoretical probability of getting a tail and a zero?

8 What is the theoretical probability of getting a head or a number less than 5?

9 What is the theoretical probability of getting a tail and a number more than 1 and less than 6?

Hands-On Activity

WORK IN PAIRS

Materials:
- a paper bag
- 2 red connecting cubes
- 3 green connecting cubes
- 5 blue connecting cubes

STEP 1 Draw a connecting cube from a
bag containing 2 red, 3 green, and 5 blue cubes.
Return each cube to the bag before drawing another.

STEP 2 Record the color of the cube drawn in the table.

Outcome	Number of Favorable Outcomes	Probability
blue cube		
green cube		
red cube		

STEP 3 Take turns to repeat **STEP 1** and **STEP 2** to make up 20 draws.
Complete the table.

Answer these questions using the data in the table.

a What is the experimental probability of drawing a cube of each color?

Blue ____   Green ____   Red ____

b What is the theoretical probability of drawing a cube of each color?

Blue ____   Green ____   Red ____

c Compare the experimental probability and theoretical probability
in each case. Are the probabilities close?

Let's Explore!

Work in groups of 4.

STEP 1 Each member tosses a coin 50 times and records the results.

STEP 2 Combine your results with members of your group. Record the results of 200 tosses.

STEP 3 Combine your group results with those of other groups. Get the results of at least 1,000 tosses.

What is the experimental probability of getting a tail in each case? Compare the probabilities. What do you observe? Explain your answer.

Let's Practice

Solve. Show your work.

1 A cube is numbered 1 to 6 on its faces.

a What is the theoretical probability of getting a 5?

b What is the theoretical probability of getting a 0?

Marcus tossed a number cube with 1 to 6 on its faces 20 times.
The table shows the results.

Number Tossed	1	2	3	4	5	6
Number of Times	5	2	3	1	6	3

 What is the experimental probability of getting a 6?

b What is the theoretical probability of getting a 6?

 A coin has both a head and a tail.
A spinner has 4 equal sections numbered 1 to 4.

 Draw a tree diagram to show the possible combinations of outcomes
when the coin is tossed and the spinner is spun.

b What is the total number of possible outcomes?

c What is the theoretical probability of getting

i a head and a 4?

ii a tail and a 0?

iii a tail and an even number?

iv a head and a prime number?

 Ms. Jackson wants to prepare a menu with one meat dish, and
one vegetable dish. She can prepare fish, chicken, turkey, or beef.
For a vegetable, she can prepare carrots, peas, or squash.

 Draw a tree diagram to show all the combinations of dishes.

 If she chooses randomly, what is the theoretical probability of preparing fish,
and any of the vegetable dishes?

c If she chooses randomly, what is the theoretical probability of preparing carrots,
and any meat dish?

5 There are 4 yellow cubes and 6 brown cubes in a bag.
In an experiment, Leslie and Mandy take turns to draw a cube from
the bag 50 times. Each time they return the cube to the bag.
The outcomes are recorded in the table.

a Copy and complete the table.

Student	Number of Yellow Cubes Drawn	Number of Brown Cubes Drawn	Probability a Yellow Cube is Drawn	Probability a Brown Cube is Drawn
Leslie	16	34		
Mandy	22	28		

b What is the difference between the theoretical probability and the
experimental probability of drawing a yellow cube in both cases?

6 Tony has a bag of 10 pens in different colors. He takes a pen from
the bag, records its color in a tally chart and, returns it to the bag.
He does this 25 times and records the results in a table.

Outcome	Tally	Number
purple	~~HHH~~ ~~HHH~~	10
blue	//	2
red	~~HHH~~ ///	8
yellow	~~HHH~~	5

a For each color, what is the experimental probability of picking a pen in that
color?

b Which color has the highest probability of being picked?

c What is the probability of picking a purple, blue, red or yellow pen?

d How many pens of each color do you think are
in the bag? Explain your answers.

ON YOUR OWN

**Go to Workbook B:
Practice 4, pages 93–96**

Math Journal

A spinner is divided into 5 sections, of which 4 are equal in size. The sections are numbered from 1 to 5, with 5 on the larger section. Joe spins the spinner 25 times and records the outcomes in a table.

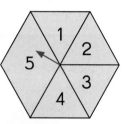

Number on Section	Number of Times Spinner Lands on Each Number	Probability
1	5	$\frac{1}{5}$
2	2	$\frac{2}{25}$
3	5	$\frac{1}{5}$
4	3	$\frac{3}{25}$
5	10	$\frac{2}{5}$

1 Are the probabilities in the third column of the table correct? Explain.

2 The theoretical probability of landing on each number is $\frac{1}{5}$. Is this true? Explain.

PROBLEM SOLVING

1 Dakota tosses two number cubes, each numbered 1 to 6 on its faces. She notes the two numbers tossed each time. Then she records the difference between the two numbers on a line plot.

```
        X
        X
        X    X
        X    X
   X    X    X
   X    X    X    X
   X    X    X    X    X
   X    X    X    X    X
   X    X    X    X    X    X
   X    X    X    X    X    X
 ◄─┼────┼────┼────┼────┼────┼────┼─►
   0    1    2    3    4    5    6
          Difference in Number
```

a Find the experimental probability of each possible outcome.

b The line plot shows that the probability of getting a difference of 1 is the highest. Explain.

c What is the theoretical probability of getting a difference of 1?

d What is the theoretical probability of getting a difference of 6?

ON YOUR OWN

**Go to Workbook B:
Put on Your Thinking Cap!
pages 97 – 100**

Chapter Wrap Up

Study Guide

You have learned...

BIG IDEAS

▶ Displaying data in a graph highlights some features of the data.
▶ Probability measures the likelihood of an event occurring.

Data

Double Bar Graphs

- Present data in a double bar graph.
- Interpret and compare two data sets.
- Draw double bar graphs.

Graphing an Equation

- Read points on a coordinate grid.
- Plot points on a coordinate grid.
- Join the points on a coordinate grid to draw a straight line graph.
- Graph an equation.

Probability

Combinations

To find the number of possible combinations,

- make an organized list.
- draw a tree diagram.
- use multiplication.

Theoretical and Experimental Probabilities

- If each outcome is equally likely, the theoretical probability that an event occurs

$$= \frac{\text{Number of favorable outcomes}}{\text{Total number of possible outcomes}}$$

- The probability of an event that is based on the actual results of trials is an experimental probability. Experimental probability

$$= \frac{\text{Number of favorable outcomes in an actual experiment}}{\text{Total number of trials}}$$

- Theoretical probability predicts the results of an experiment. Experimental probability describes the actual results of an experiment.

Chapter Review/Test

Vocabulary
Choose the correct word.

1 $y = 6x$ is an example of an ____ .

2 The number of ways of selecting items, where the order is not important, is known as the number of ____ .

3 From the results of an experiment repeated a large number of times, the ____ of an outcome can be calculated.

4 A ____ can be used to compare two sets of data.

5 An ____ shows the combinations in a systematic order.

6 In a graph, (5, 8) and (2, 3) are the ____ of two points.

> double bar graph
> key
> coordinates
> x-axis
> y-axis
> origin
> equation
> organized list
> combinations
> tree diagram
> favorable outcomes
> experimental probability
> theoretical probability

Concepts and Skills
Use the data in the graph to answer the questions.

The double bar graph shows the number of students who represent their college in tennis and basketball.

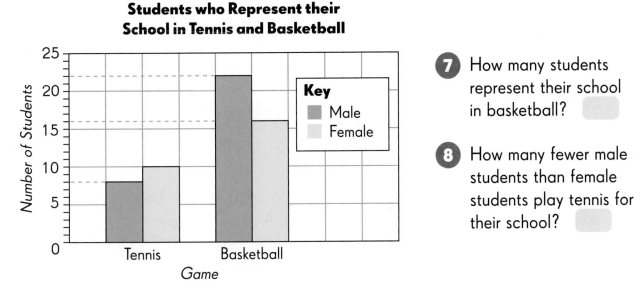

Students who Represent their School in Tennis and Basketball

7 How many students represent their school in basketball? ____

8 How many fewer male students than female students play tennis for their school? ____

Complete.

The graph shows the weight of bags of flour.

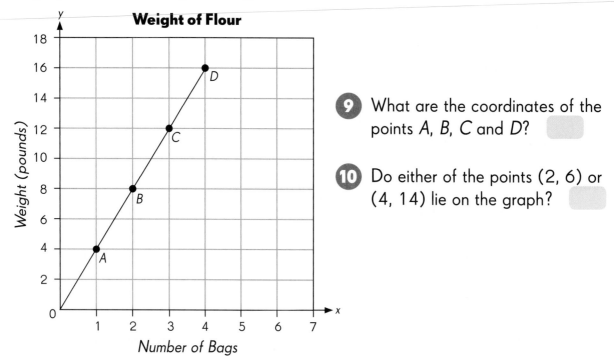

9 What are the coordinates of the points *A, B, C* and *D*?

10 Do either of the points (2, 6) or (4, 14) lie on the graph?

Use a tree diagram to find the number of combinations.

There are 4 handbags and 3 belts that Lena likes.
She wants to buy a handbag and a belt.

11 Draw a tree diagram to show the possible combinations of a handbag and a belt Lena can buy.

There are ____ combinations.

Problem Solving
Solve. Show your work.

12 Each letter of the word WORK is written on separate cards. One card is picked and returned to the stack. Then another card is picked. How many combinations of two letters can be picked?

13 A bag contains 5 pieces of paper numbered 1 to 5. Another bag contains 3 pieces of paper numbered 6 to 8. A piece of paper is drawn from each bag. The sum of the numbers is then noted. Find the number of combinations with a sum that is 10 or greater.

12 Angles

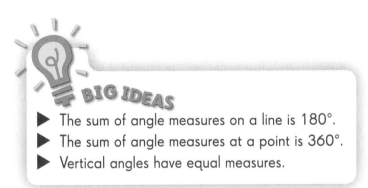

BIG IDEAS

► The sum of angle measures on a line is 180°.
► The sum of angle measures at a point is 360°.
► Vertical angles have equal measures.

Recall Prior Knowledge

Identifying point, line, line segment, and ray

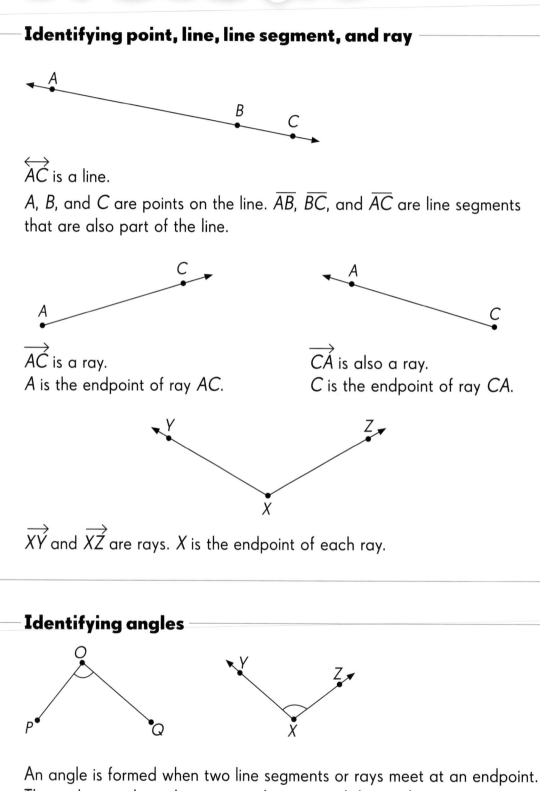

$\overleftrightarrow{AC}$ is a line.

A, B, and C are points on the line. $\overline{AB}$, $\overline{BC}$, and $\overline{AC}$ are line segments that are also part of the line.

$\overrightarrow{AC}$ is a ray.
A is the endpoint of ray AC.

$\overrightarrow{CA}$ is also a ray.
C is the endpoint of ray CA.

$\overrightarrow{XY}$ and $\overrightarrow{XZ}$ are rays. X is the endpoint of each ray.

Identifying angles

An angle is formed when two line segments or rays meet at an endpoint. The endpoint where they meet is the vertex of the angle.

Naming angles

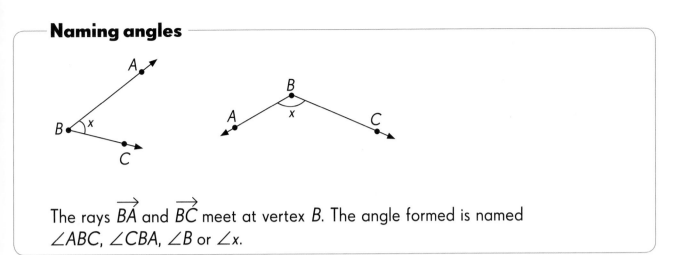

The rays $\overrightarrow{BA}$ and $\overrightarrow{BC}$ meet at vertex B. The angle formed is named
$\angle ABC$, $\angle CBA$, $\angle B$ or $\angle x$.

Measuring angles with a protractor

The measure of an angle is given in degrees.

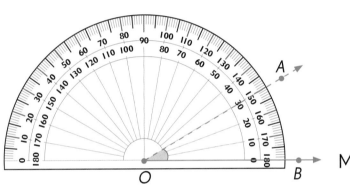

Measure of $\angle BOA = 30°$

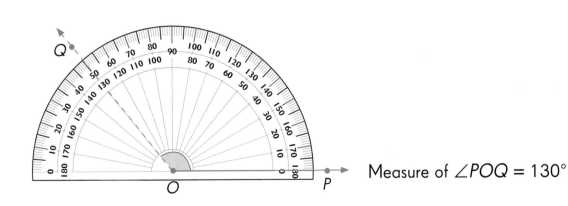

Measure of $\angle POQ = 130°$

Identifying right angles and perpendicular lines

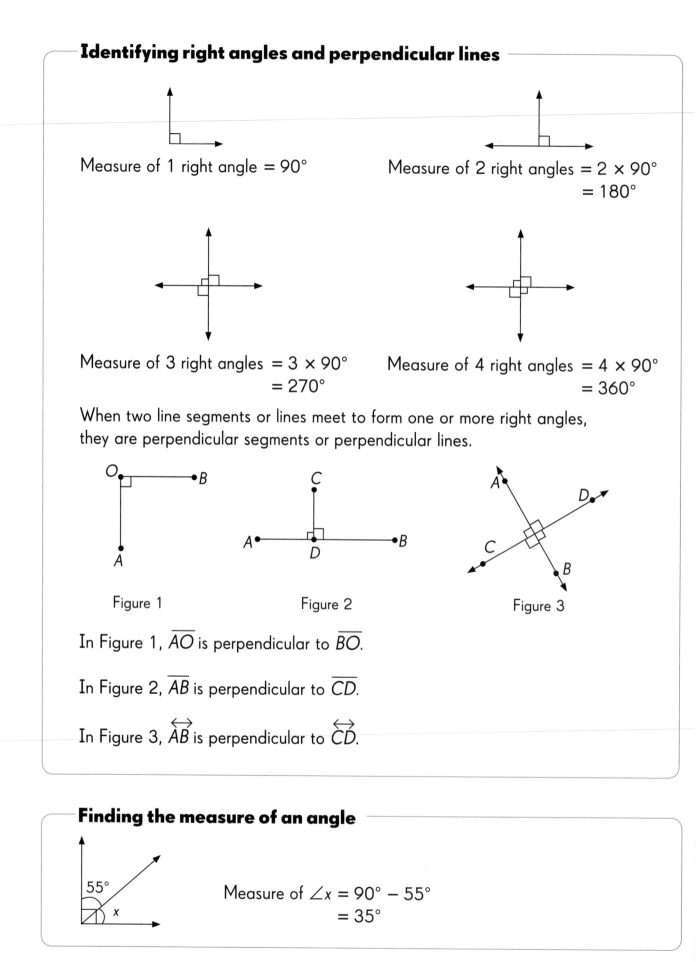

Measure of 1 right angle = 90°

Measure of 2 right angles = 2 × 90°
= 180°

Measure of 3 right angles = 3 × 90°
= 270°

Measure of 4 right angles = 4 × 90°
= 360°

When two line segments or lines meet to form one or more right angles, they are perpendicular segments or perpendicular lines.

Figure 1

Figure 2

Figure 3

In Figure 1, $\overline{AO}$ is perpendicular to $\overline{BO}$.

In Figure 2, $\overline{AB}$ is perpendicular to $\overline{CD}$.

In Figure 3, $\overleftrightarrow{AB}$ is perpendicular to $\overleftrightarrow{CD}$.

Finding the measure of an angle

55°

x

Measure of $\angle x = 90° - 55°$
= 35°

✔ Quick Check

Complete.

1

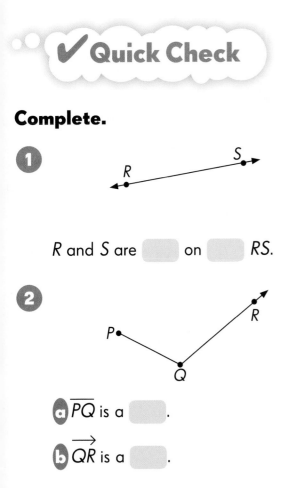

R and S are ⬚ on ⬚ RS.

2

a PQ̄ is a ⬚.

b QR⃗ is a ⬚.

Mark the angles.

3 Copy and mark three angles in the figure.

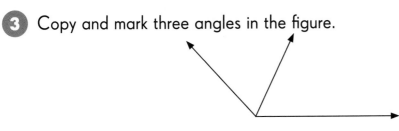

Name these marked angles.

4

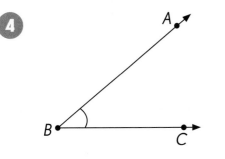

⬚

5

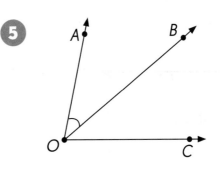

⬚

Use a protractor to measure the marked angles.

6

B

A ◄——————► O

Angle measure = ▢

7

A

O   B

Angle measure = ▢

Complete.

8 **a** The pairs of perpendicular line segments in the figure are ▢.

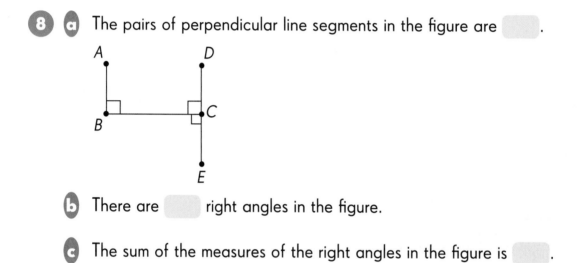

A   D

B   C

E

b There are ▢ right angles in the figure.

c The sum of the measures of the right angles in the figure is ▢.

Find the unknown angle measures.

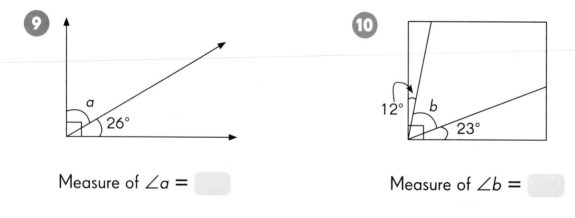

9

a

26°

Measure of ∠a = ▢

10

12°   b

23°

Measure of ∠b = ▢

Lesson 12.1 Angles on a Line

Lesson Objective

- Understand and apply the property that the sum of angle measures on a line is 180°.

Vocabulary
angles on a line

Learn **Use a protractor to show the sum of the angle measures on a line is 180°.**

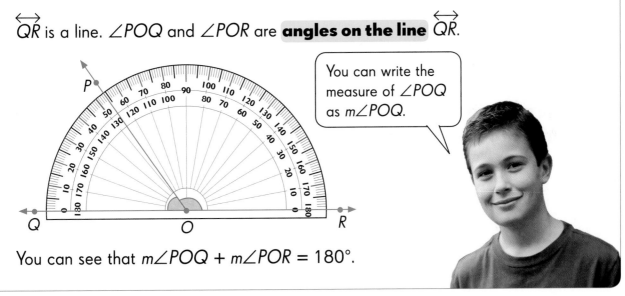

$\overleftrightarrow{QR}$ is a line. $\angle POQ$ and $\angle POR$ are **angles on the line** $\overleftrightarrow{QR}$.

You can write the measure of $\angle POQ$ as $m\angle POQ$.

You can see that $m\angle POQ + m\angle POR = 180°$.

Learn **Use reasoning to show the sum of the angle measures on a line is 180°.**

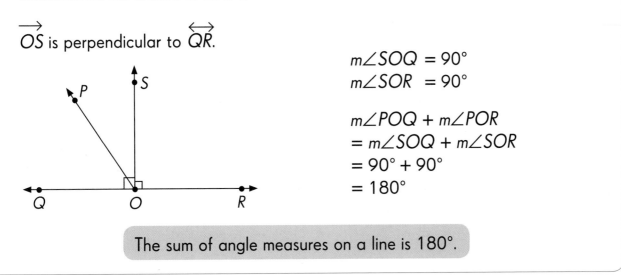

$\overrightarrow{OS}$ is perpendicular to $\overleftrightarrow{QR}$.

$m\angle SOQ = 90°$
$m\angle SOR = 90°$

$m\angle POQ + m\angle POR$
$= m\angle SOQ + m\angle SOR$
$= 90° + 90°$
$= 180°$

The sum of angle measures on a line is 180°.

Guided Practice

Use a protractor to find the measures of the angles.

1

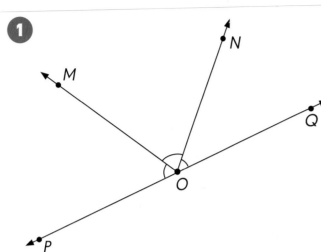

$m\angle POM$ = ☐

$m\angle MON$ = ☐

$m\angle NOQ$ = ☐

$m\angle POM + m\angle MON + m\angle NOQ$ = ☐

Are these angles on a line? ☐

Name the marked angles on the line $\overleftrightarrow{XY}$.
State the sum of the measures of the angles.

2

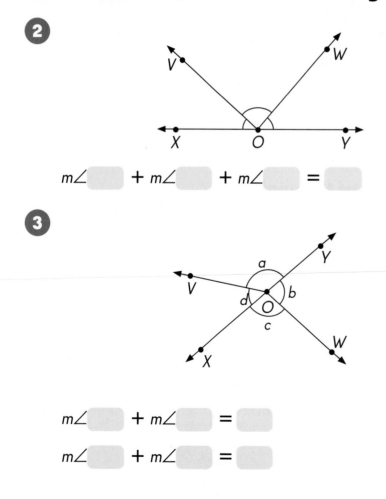

$m\angle$ ☐ $+ \, m\angle$ ☐ $+ \, m\angle$ ☐ = ☐

3

$m\angle$ ☐ $+ \, m\angle$ ☐ = ☐

$m\angle$ ☐ $+ \, m\angle$ ☐ = ☐

Find the unknown measures of angles on a line.

$\overleftrightarrow{AC}$ is a line. Find the measure of $\angle x$.

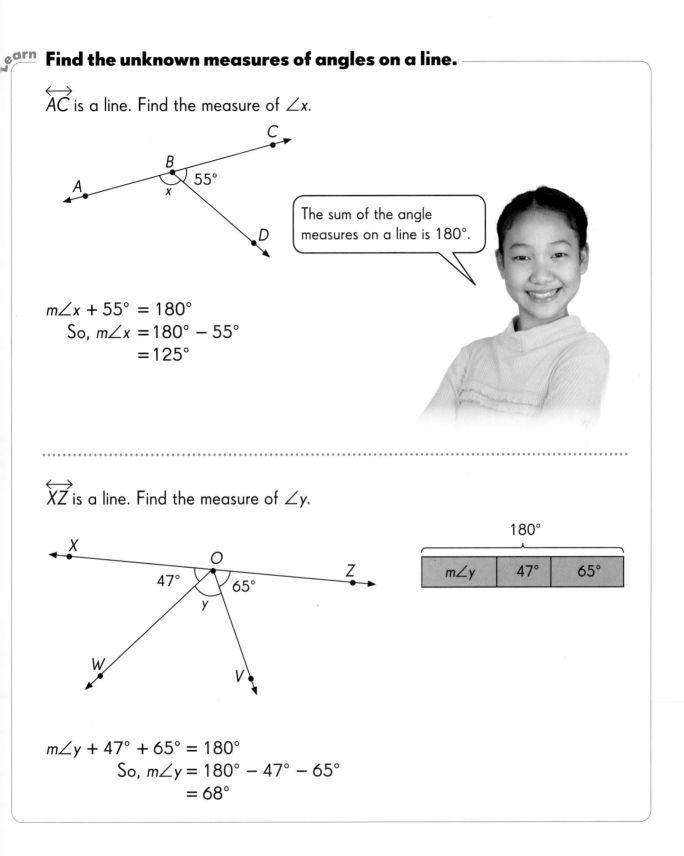

The sum of the angle measures on a line is 180°.

$m\angle x + 55° = 180°$

So, $m\angle x = 180° - 55°$

$= 125°$

$\overleftrightarrow{XZ}$ is a line. Find the measure of $\angle y$.

180°		
$m\angle y$	47°	65°

$m\angle y + 47° + 65° = 180°$

So, $m\angle y = 180° - 47° - 65°$

$= 68°$

Guided Practice

Complete.

4 $\overleftrightarrow{XZ}$ is a line. Find the measure of $\angle y$.

$m\angle y = $ ▢ $-$ ▢

$\quad\quad = $ ▢

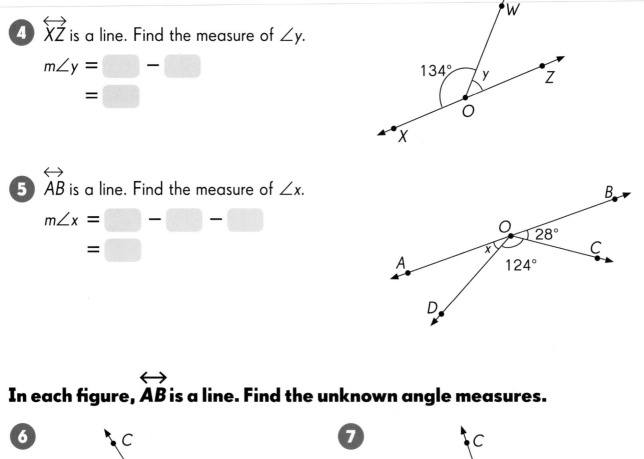

5 $\overleftrightarrow{AB}$ is a line. Find the measure of $\angle x$.

$m\angle x = $ ▢ $-$ ▢ $-$ ▢

$\quad\quad = $ ▢

In each figure, $\overleftrightarrow{AB}$ is a line. Find the unknown angle measures.

6

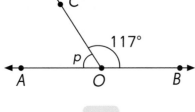

▢

7

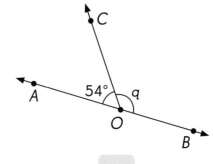

▢

8

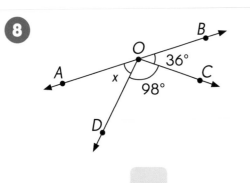

▢

9

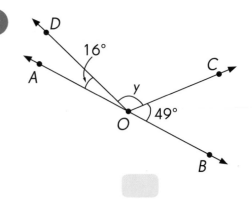

▢

Hands-On Activity

WORK IN PAIRS

1 Choose the sets of angles that can form angles on a line.

a $m\angle a = 98°$, $m\angle b = 82°$

b $m\angle p = 78°$, $m\angle q = 35°$, $m\angle r = 77°$

c $m\angle w = 34°$, $m\angle x = 29°$, $m\angle y = 16°$, $m\angle z = 101°$

2 Write a set of three angle measures that have

a a sum of 180°,

b a sum greater or less than 180°.

Ask your partner to draw the set of three angles that can form angles on a line.

READING AND WRITING MATH
Math Journal

In this figure, $\overleftrightarrow{AB}$ is a line and $\overrightarrow{OD}$ is perpendicular to $\overleftrightarrow{AB}$.
Explain why the sum of measures of $\angle x$, $\angle y$, and $\angle z$ is 180°.

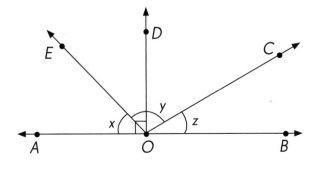

Let's Practice

Identify angles on a line.

1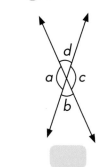

2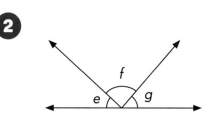

Answer the questions.

3 What is the sum of the measures of angles on a line?

4 Can angles of 70°, 45° and 65° form angles on a line?
Explain your answer   .

5 Can angles of 10°, 90°, 45° and 45° form angles on a line?
Explain your answer.

Find the unknown angle measures.

6 $\overleftrightarrow{AB}$ is a line.

Find the measure of ∠x.

7 $\overleftrightarrow{MN}$ is a line.
$\overrightarrow{XQ}$ is perpendicular to $\overleftrightarrow{MN}$.
Find the measures of ∠c and ∠d.

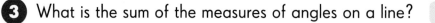

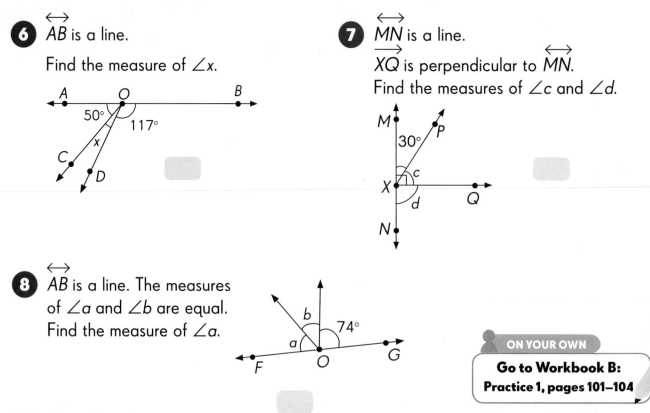

8 $\overleftrightarrow{AB}$ is a line. The measures
of ∠a and ∠b are equal.
Find the measure of ∠a.

ON YOUR OWN

Go to Workbook B:
Practice 1, pages 101–104

12.2 Angles at a Point

Lesson Objective

• Understand and apply the property that the sum of angle measures at a point is 360°.

Learn **Use reasoning to show the sum of the angle measures at a point is 360°.**

$\overrightarrow{OA}$, $\overrightarrow{OB}$ and $\overrightarrow{OC}$ are rays that meet at the point O.
$\angle x$, $\angle y$ and $\angle z$ are known as **angles at a point**.

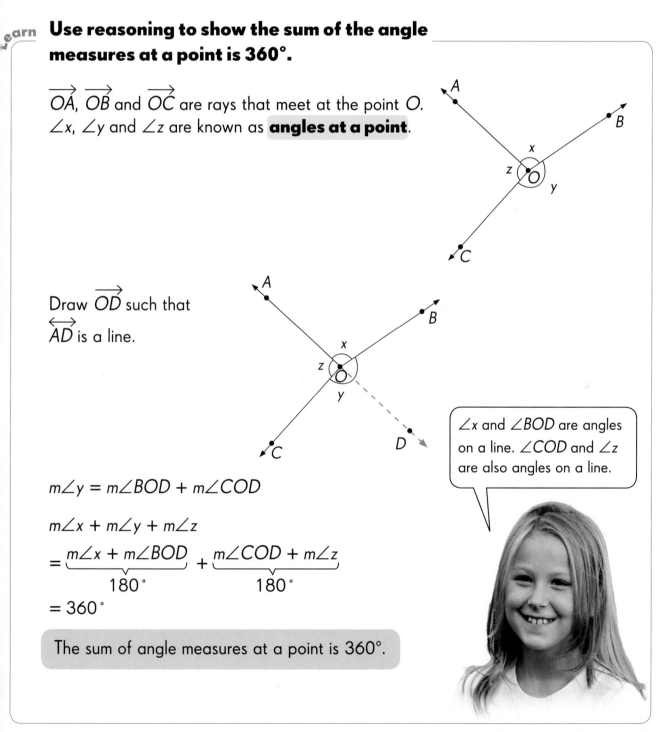

Draw $\overrightarrow{OD}$ such that
$\overleftrightarrow{AD}$ is a line.

$\angle x$ and $\angle BOD$ are angles on a line. $\angle COD$ and $\angle z$ are also angles on a line.

$m\angle y = m\angle BOD + m\angle COD$

$m\angle x + m\angle y + m\angle z$

$= \underbrace{m\angle x + m\angle BOD}_{180°} + \underbrace{m\angle COD + m\angle z}_{180°}$

$= 360°$

The sum of angle measures at a point is 360°.

Guided Practice

Use a protractor to find the measures of the angles.

1

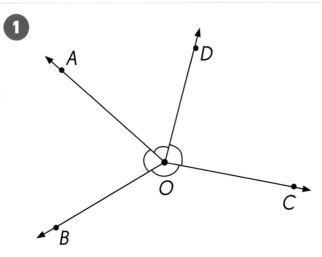

$m\angle AOD =$ ▢

$m\angle DOC =$ ▢

$m\angle BOC =$ ▢

$m\angle AOB =$ ▢

$m\angle AOD + m\angle DOC + m\angle BOC + m\angle AOB =$ ▢ $+$ ▢ $+$ ▢ $+$ ▢

$=$ ▢

Are these angles at a point? ▢

Name the marked angles at point O. State the sum of the measures of the angles.

2

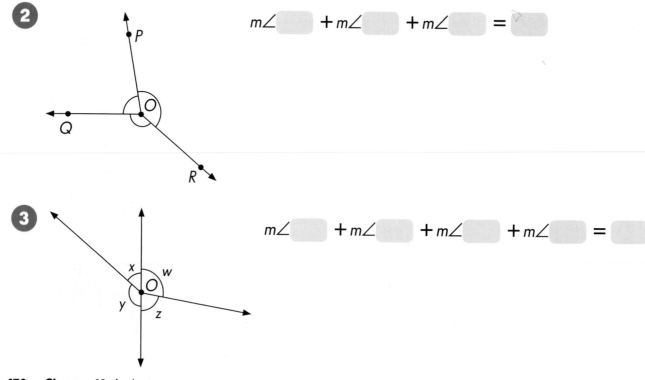

$m\angle$ ▢ $+ m\angle$ ▢ $+ m\angle$ ▢ $=$ ▢

3

$m\angle$ ▢ $+ m\angle$ ▢ $+ m\angle$ ▢ $+ m\angle$ ▢ $=$ ▢

Find the unknown measures of angles at a point.

Find the measure of $\angle a$.

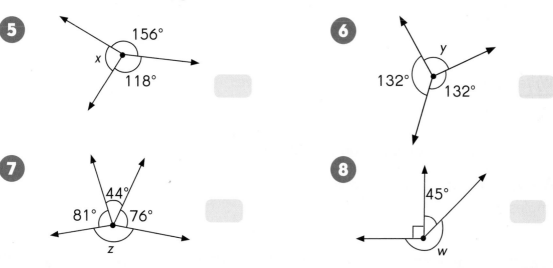

The sum of angle measures at a point is $360°$.

$360°$

| 152° | 97° | $m\angle a$ |

$m\angle a + 152° + 97° = 360°$

So, $m\angle a = 360° - 152° - 97°$

$= 111°$

Guided Practice

Complete.

4 Find the measure of $\angle t$.

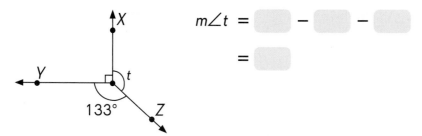

$m\angle t = \boxed{} - \boxed{} - \boxed{}$

$= \boxed{}$

Find the unknown angle measures.

5

156°

x

118°

$\boxed{}$

6

y

132°   132°

$\boxed{}$

7

44°

81°   76°

z

$\boxed{}$

8

45°

w

$\boxed{}$

Hands-On Activity

Material:
• protractor

WORK IN PAIRS

1 Choose the sets of angles that can form angles at a point.

a $m\angle a = 87°$, $m\angle b = 98°$, $m\angle c = 175°$

b $m\angle p = 36°$, $m\angle q = 69°$, $m\angle r = 107°$, $m\angle s = 58°$

c $m\angle w = 95°$, $m\angle x = 48°$, $m\angle y = 48°$, $m\angle z = 169°$

2 Take turns to measure and write down the measures of angles in each set. Which set of angles can form angles at a point?
Explain your answer.

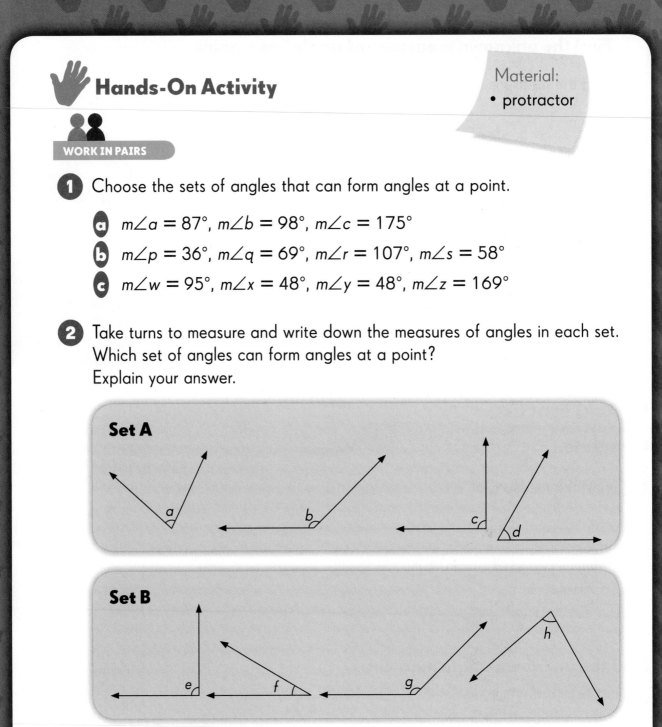

Set A

Set B

3 Write a set of four angle measures that have

a a sum of 360°,

b a sum greater or less than 360°.

Ask your partner to draw the set of four angles that can form angles at a point.

Identify angles at a point.

1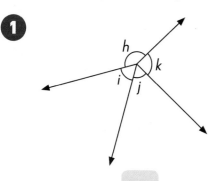

2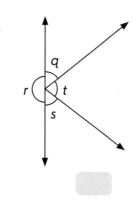

Answer the questions.

3 What is the sum of the measures of angles at a point?

4 Can angles of 25°, 85°, 138° and 112° form angles at a point? Explain your answer.

Find the unknown angle measures.

5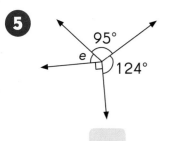
95°
e
124°

6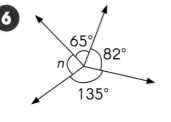
65°
82°
n
135°

7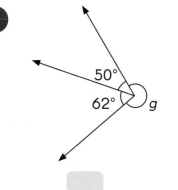
50°
62°
g

8 $\overleftrightarrow{AB}$ is a line.

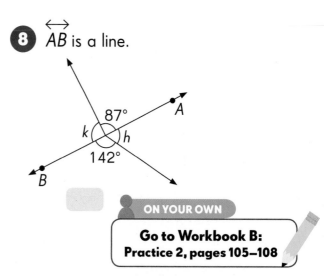
87°
k   h
142°
A
B

ON YOUR OWN

Go to Workbook B:
Practice 2, pages 105–108

12.3 Vertical Angles

Lesson Objective

- Understand and apply the property that vertical angles have equal measures.

Vocabulary
intersecting lines
vertical angles

Learn **Vertical angles formed by intersecting lines have equal measures.**

$\overleftrightarrow{EF}$ and $\overleftrightarrow{GH}$ are two lines that intersect each other forming the four angles, $\angle a$, $\angle b$, $\angle c$, and $\angle d$. The pair of angles $\angle a$ and $\angle c$ are called **vertical angles**.
Similarly, the pair of angles $\angle b$ and $\angle d$ are called vertical angles.

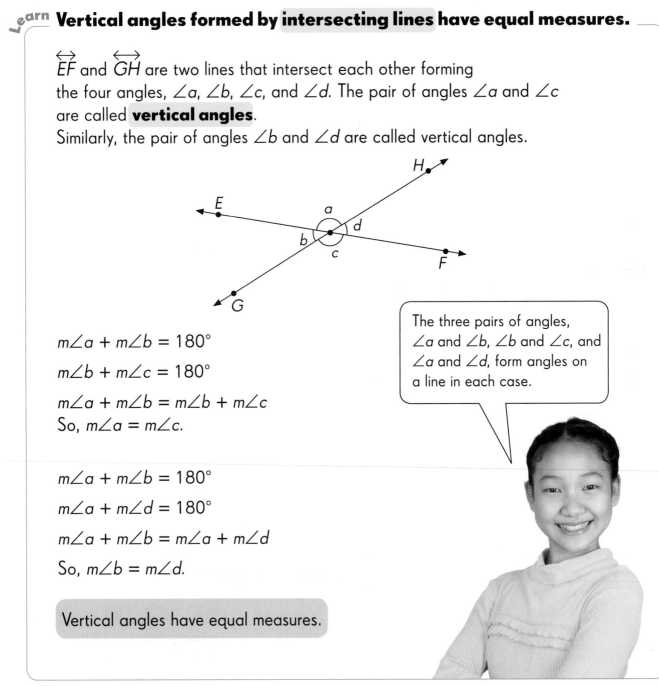

$m\angle a + m\angle b = 180°$

$m\angle b + m\angle c = 180°$

$m\angle a + m\angle b = m\angle b + m\angle c$
So, $m\angle a = m\angle c$.

> The three pairs of angles, $\angle a$ and $\angle b$, $\angle b$ and $\angle c$, and $\angle a$ and $\angle d$, form angles on a line in each case.

$m\angle a + m\angle b = 180°$

$m\angle a + m\angle d = 180°$

$m\angle a + m\angle b = m\angle a + m\angle d$

So, $m\angle b = m\angle d$.

Vertical angles have equal measures.

Hands-On Activity

WORK IN PAIRS

Materials:
- tracing paper
- ruler

STEP 1 Copy $\overleftrightarrow{AB}$ and $\overleftrightarrow{CD}$ on a piece of tracing paper.
Your partner folds the paper along the red dotted line.

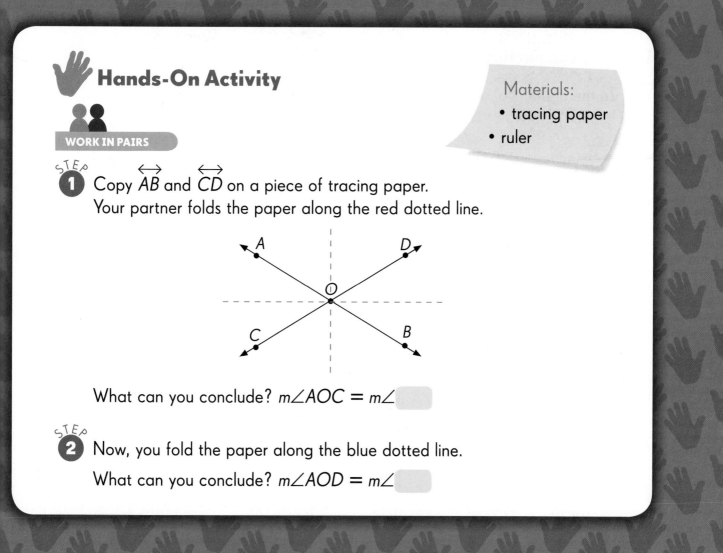

What can you conclude? $m\angle AOC = m\angle \boxed{}$

STEP 2 Now, you fold the paper along the blue dotted line.

What can you conclude? $m\angle AOD = m\angle \boxed{}$

Guided Practice

Use a protractor to find the measures of the angles.

1 The figure shows the four angles formed when two lines intersect.

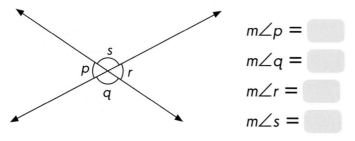

$m\angle p = \boxed{}$

$m\angle q = \boxed{}$

$m\angle r = \boxed{}$

$m\angle s = \boxed{}$

Which are the two pairs of vertical angles? $\boxed{}$

Identify the vertical angles.

2 In the figure, $\overleftrightarrow{PQ}$ and $\overleftrightarrow{RS}$ are lines.
Name the pairs of vertical angles.

$\angle POR$ and $\angle$ ⬚ are vertical angles.

Also, $\angle$ ⬚ and $\angle$ ⬚ are vertical angles.

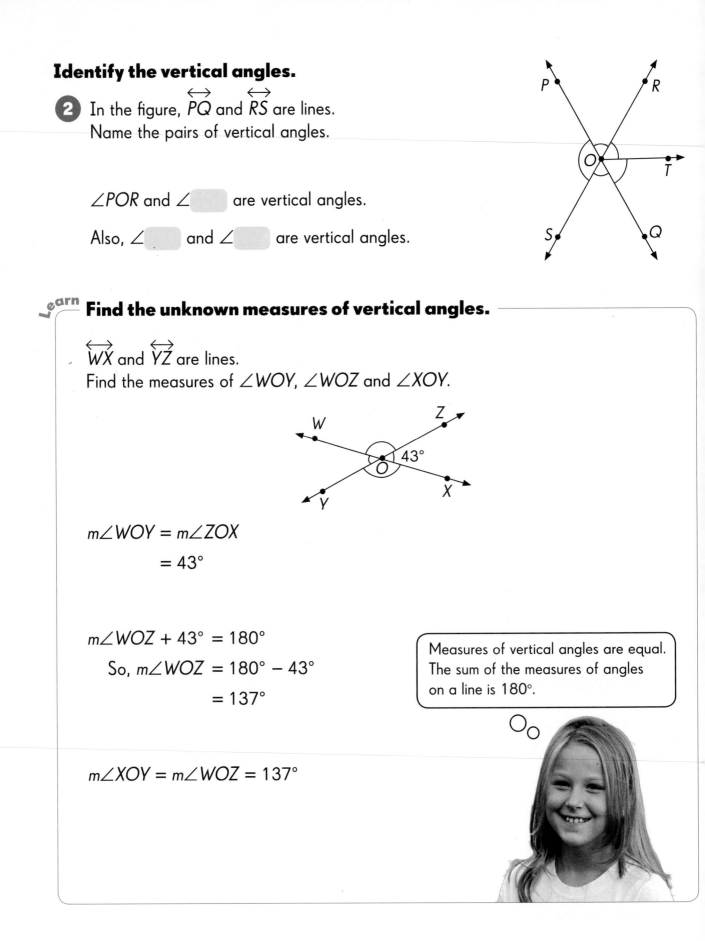

Find the unknown measures of vertical angles.

$\overleftrightarrow{WX}$ and $\overleftrightarrow{YZ}$ are lines.
Find the measures of $\angle WOY$, $\angle WOZ$ and $\angle XOY$.

$$m\angle WOY = m\angle ZOX$$
$$= 43°$$

$$m\angle WOZ + 43° = 180°$$
$$\text{So, } m\angle WOZ = 180° - 43°$$
$$= 137°$$

Measures of vertical angles are equal.
The sum of the measures of angles
on a line is 180°.

$$m\angle XOY = m\angle WOZ = 137°$$

Guided Practice

Complete.

3 $\overleftrightarrow{PQ}$ and $\overleftrightarrow{RS}$ are lines.

$\overrightarrow{OT}$ is perpendicular to $\overleftrightarrow{PQ}$. Find the measure of $\angle x$.

$\angle POR$ and $\angle SOQ$ are vertical angles.

$m\angle x +$ ☐ $=$ ☐

$m\angle x =$ ☐ $-$ ☐

$=$ ☐

Find the unknown angle measures.

$\overleftrightarrow{AB}$ and $\overleftrightarrow{CD}$ are lines in each figure.

4
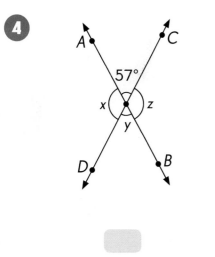

☐

5
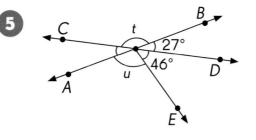

☐

Let's Practice

Identify each pair of vertical angles.

1

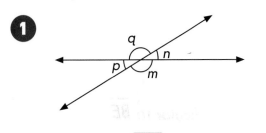

2

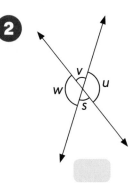

Answer the questions. Explain your answer.

3 Can angles of 50°, 50°, 130° and 130° form

   a angles at a point?

   b vertical angles?

4 $\overleftrightarrow{AB}$ and $\overleftrightarrow{CD}$ are lines.
Find the measures of $\angle j$ and $\angle k$.

5 $\overleftrightarrow{MN}$, $\overleftrightarrow{PQ}$ and $\overleftrightarrow{RS}$ are lines.
Find the sum of the measures of
$\angle b$, $\angle d$ and $\angle f$.

6 $\overleftrightarrow{PQ}$, $\overleftrightarrow{MN}$ and $\overleftrightarrow{XY}$ are lines
and $m\angle a = m\angle c = m\angle e$.
Find the measure of $\angle b$.

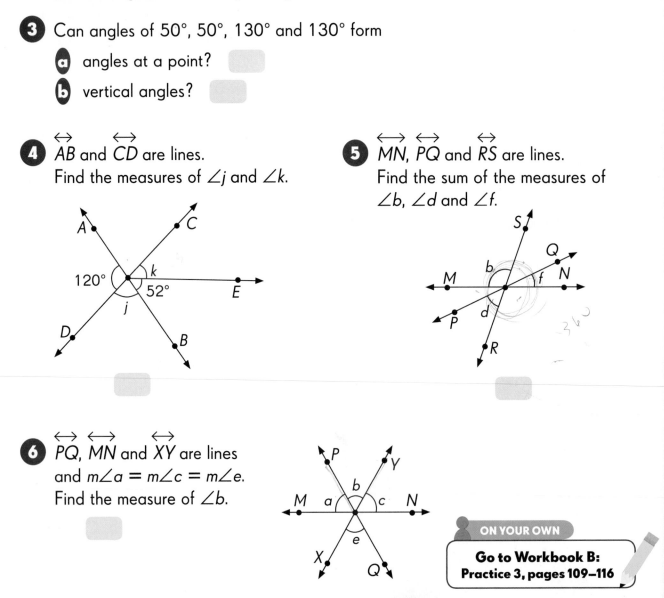

ON YOUR OWN

**Go to Workbook B:
Practice 3, pages 109–116**

Put On Your Thinking Cap!

PROBLEM SOLVING

Solve.

1 In the figure, $\overrightarrow{BA}$ is perpendicular to $\overrightarrow{BD}$, $\overrightarrow{BC}$ is perpendicular to $\overrightarrow{BE}$ and $\angle ABC = 2°$.

Is *DE* a line?
Explain your answer.

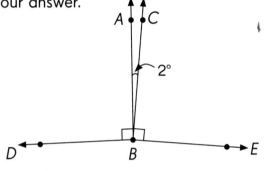

2 $\overleftrightarrow{KL}$ and $\overleftrightarrow{PN}$ are lines.

a The figure shows that $\angle MON$ and $\angle QOL$ are right angles.
Name another right angle.

b Name the angle equal to $\angle KOM$.
Explain your answer.

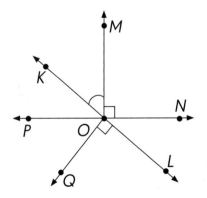

ON YOUR OWN

Go to Workbook B:
Put on Your Thinking Cap!
pages 117–120

Chapter Wrap Up

Study Guide

You have learned...

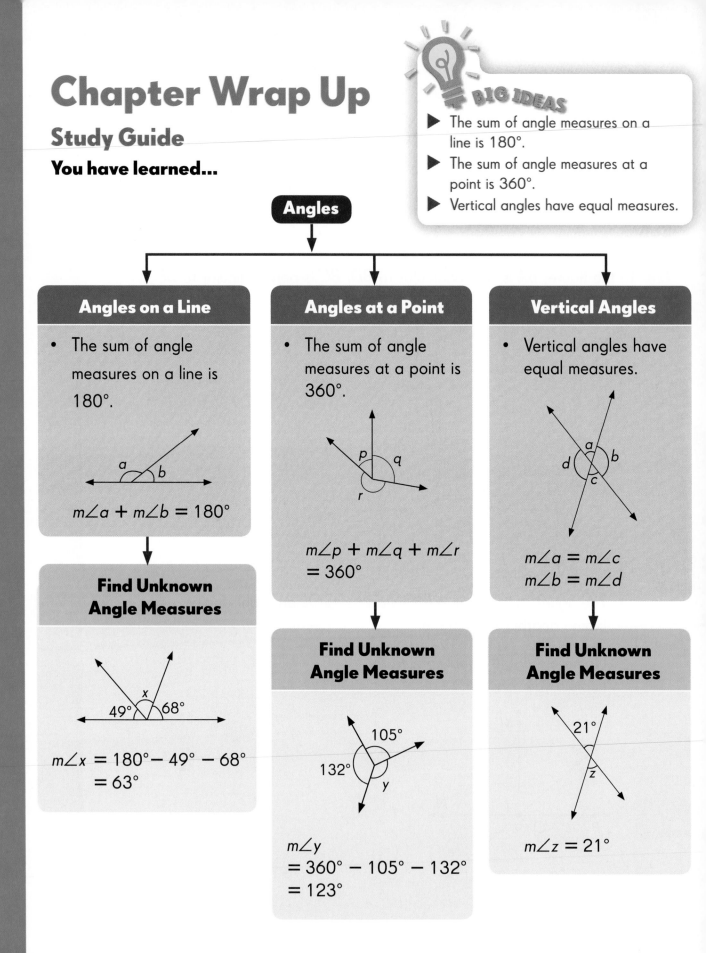

Angles

Angles on a Line

- The sum of angle measures on a line is 180°.

$$m\angle a + m\angle b = 180°$$

Find Unknown Angle Measures

$$m\angle x = 180° - 49° - 68°$$
$$= 63°$$

Angles at a Point

- The sum of angle measures at a point is 360°.

$$m\angle p + m\angle q + m\angle r = 360°$$

Find Unknown Angle Measures

$$m\angle y$$
$$= 360° - 105° - 132°$$
$$= 123°$$

Vertical Angles

- Vertical angles have equal measures.

$$m\angle a = m\angle c$$
$$m\angle b = m\angle d$$

Find Unknown Angle Measures

$$m\angle z = 21°$$

Chapter Review/Test

cabulary

omplete.

The following box appears at the right:

> angles on a line
> angles at a point
> intersecting lines
> vertical angles

1 The sum of ▢ is 180°.

2 The sum of ▢ is 360°.

3 The measures of ▢ are equal.

Concepts and Skills

Find the unknown angle measures.

4 $\overleftrightarrow{AB}$ and $\overleftrightarrow{CD}$ are lines.

5 $\overleftrightarrow{AB}$ is a line.

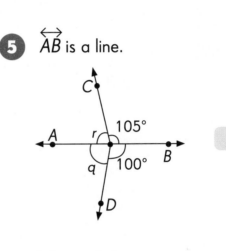

6 $\overleftrightarrow{AB}$ is a line.

7 $\overleftrightarrow{AB}$ and $\overleftrightarrow{CD}$ are lines.

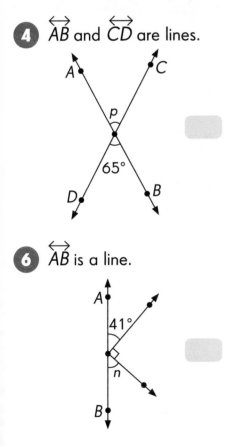

Solve.

8 $\overleftrightarrow{ST}$, $\overleftrightarrow{UV}$ and $\overleftrightarrow{KL}$ are lines.
$\angle a$, $\angle c$, and $\angle e$ have equal measures.
What is the sum of the measures of $\angle b$,
$\angle d$, and $\angle f$? ▢

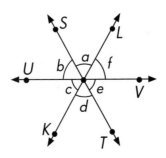

13 Properties of Triangles and Four-sided Figures

A tangram is a puzzle that is formed by cutting a square into seven pieces as shown.

You can create other geometric figures using the pieces of the tangram. Try making these!

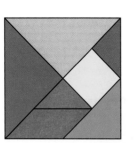

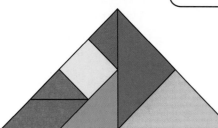
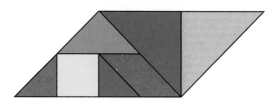

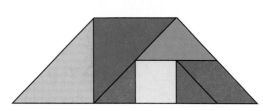
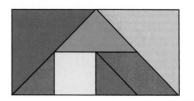

Lessons

BIG IDEAS

▶ Properties of geometric figures state relationships among angles or sides of the figures.

▶ Triangles and four-sided figures have their own special properties.

Recall Prior Knowledge

Classifying polygons

Name of Polygon	Definition of Polygon
Triangle	A triangle has three sides and three angles.
Parallelogram	A parallelogram is a four-sided figure in which the opposite sides are parallel.
Rectangle	A rectangle is a parallelogram with four right angles.
Rhombus	A rhombus is a parallelogram with all sides of equal length.
Square	A square is a rectangle with all sides of equal length.
Trapezoid	A trapezoid is a four-sided figure in which only one pair of opposite sides are parallel.

Finding measures of angles on a line

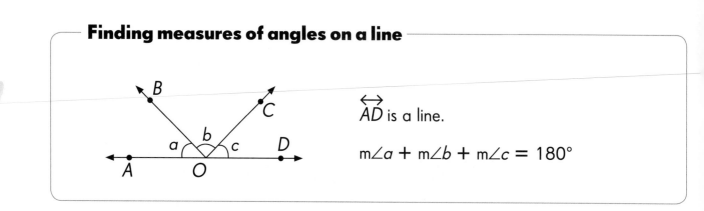

$\overleftrightarrow{AD}$ is a line.

$m\angle a + m\angle b + m\angle c = 180°$

Comparing expressions

When expressions are not equal, they form an inequality.
< means *less than* and > means *greater than*.

If $x = 10$, then $x + 15 < 35$.
If $x = 25$, then $x + 15 > 35$.
If $x = 20$, then $x + 15 = 35$.

✔ Quick Check

Name the sides and angles of triangle *PQR*.

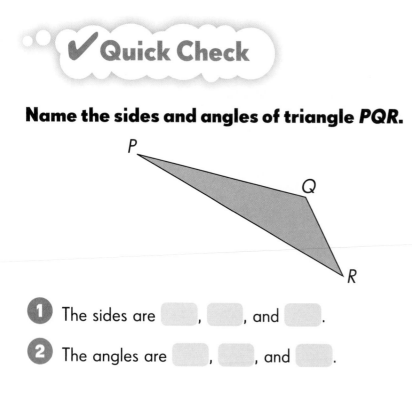

1 The sides are [ ] , [ ] , and [ ] .

2 The angles are [ ] , [ ] , and [ ] .

Complete.

3 The opposite [ ] of a parallelogram are parallel.

4 A rectangle has [ ] sides of equal length.

5 The measure of each angle of a rectangle is [ ].

6 A parallelogram with four right angles is a [ ].

7 The four sides of a square are of [ ] length.

8 Each angle of a square is a [ ] angle.

9 A rectangle with four sides of equal length is a [ ].

10 The four sides of a rhombus are of [ ] length.

11 A trapezoid has only one pair of opposite sides that is [ ].

Complete.

$\overleftrightarrow{AB}$ is a line.

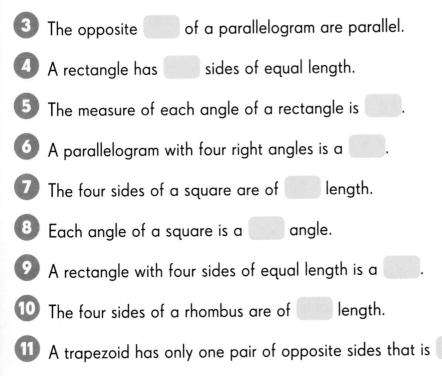

12 m∠ [ ] + m∠ [ ] = 180°

13 m∠ [ ] + m∠ [ ] = 180°

Complete. Use >, <, or =.

14 If $x = 5$, then $x - 2$ ◯ 10.

15 If $x = 20$, then $x + 5$ ◯ 15.

16 If $x = 30$, then $x + 10$ ◯ 40.

13.1 Classifying Triangles

Lesson Objective

- Classify triangles by the lengths of their sides, and angle measures.

Learn **Identify equilateral, isosceles, and scalene triangles.**

You can classify triangles by the lengths of their sides.

In triangle ABC, all the sides are of equal length.
It is an **equilateral triangle**.

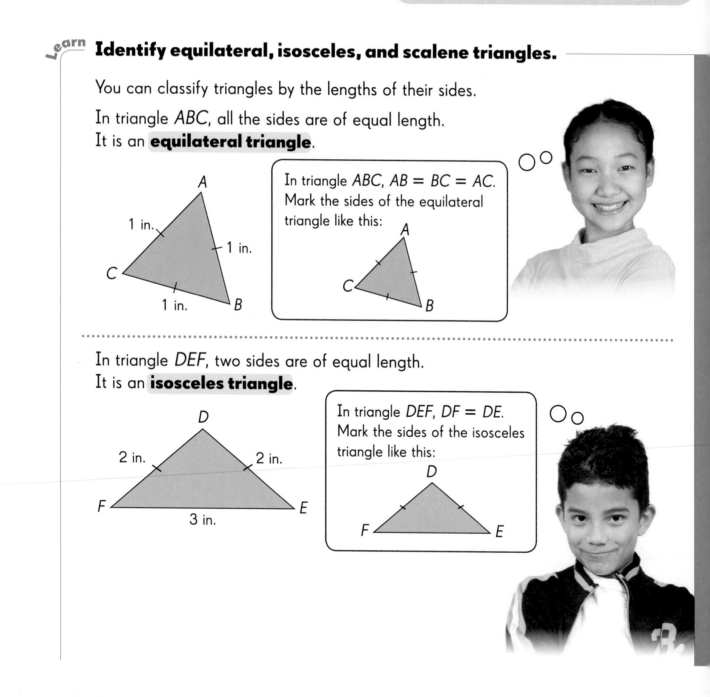

In triangle ABC, $AB = BC = AC$.
Mark the sides of the equilateral triangle like this:

In triangle DEF, two sides are of equal length.
It is an **isosceles triangle**.

In triangle DEF, $DF = DE$.
Mark the sides of the isosceles triangle like this:

In triangle *GHI*, the three sides have different lengths.
It is a **scalene triangle**.

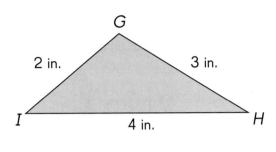

G

2 in.   3 in.

I   4 in.   H

Guided Practice

Which of these triangles is equilateral, isosceles, or scalene?
Use a centimeter ruler to find out.

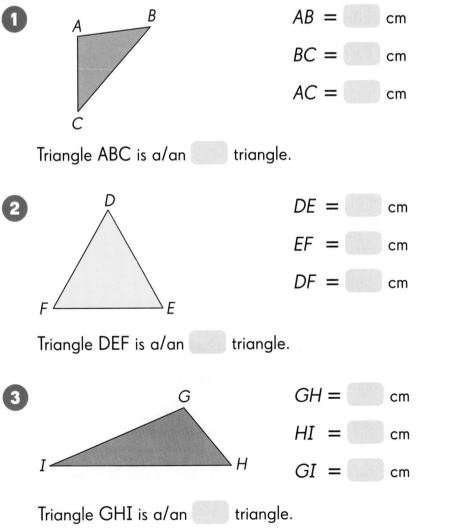

1

A   B

C

$AB = $ ⬚ cm

$BC = $ ⬚ cm

$AC = $ ⬚ cm

Triangle ABC is a/an ⬚ triangle.

2

D

F   E

$DE = $ ⬚ cm

$EF = $ ⬚ cm

$DF = $ ⬚ cm

Triangle DEF is a/an ⬚ triangle.

3

G

I   H

$GH = $ ⬚ cm

$HI = $ ⬚ cm

$GI = $ ⬚ cm

Triangle GHI is a/an ⬚ triangle.

Identify right, obtuse, and acute triangles.

You can classify triangles by the measures of their angles.

In triangle *PQR*, ∠*R* is a right angle.
Triangle *PQR* is a **right triangle**.
A right triangle has one right angle.

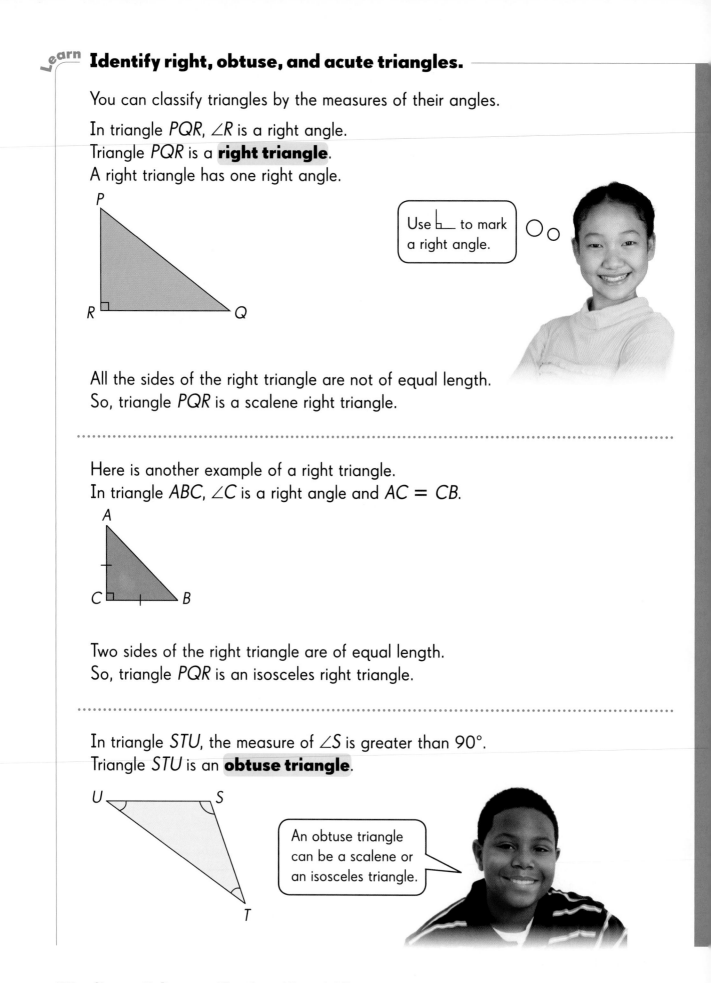

Use ⌐ to mark a right angle.

All the sides of the right triangle are not of equal length.
So, triangle *PQR* is a scalene right triangle.

- -

Here is another example of a right triangle.
In triangle *ABC*, ∠*C* is a right angle and *AC* = *CB*.

Two sides of the right triangle are of equal length.
So, triangle *PQR* is an isosceles right triangle.

- -

In triangle *STU*, the measure of ∠*S* is greater than 90°.
Triangle *STU* is an **obtuse triangle**.

An obtuse triangle can be a scalene or an isosceles triangle.

In triangle *XYZ*, the measures of all the angles are acute or less than 90°. It is an **acute triangle**.

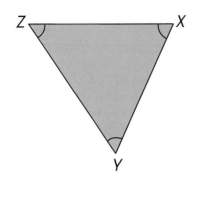

Z   X

Y

An acute triangle can be an equilateral, isosceles or a scalene triangle.

Guided Practice

Which of these triangles is right, obtuse, or acute?
Use a protractor to find out.

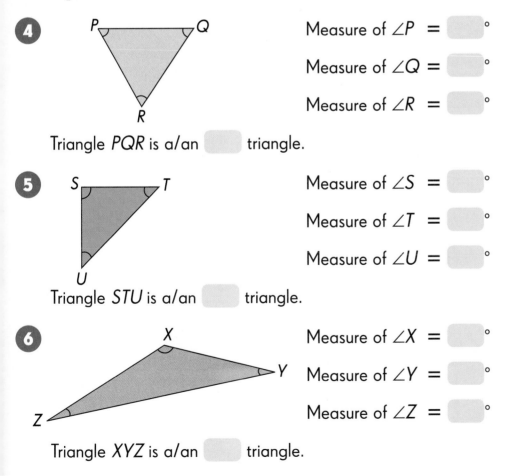

4

P   Q

R

Measure of ∠P = ☐°

Measure of ∠Q = ☐°

Measure of ∠R = ☐°

Triangle *PQR* is a/an ☐ triangle.

5

S   T

U

Measure of ∠S = ☐°

Measure of ∠T = ☐°

Measure of ∠U = ☐°

Triangle *STU* is a/an ☐ triangle.

6

X

Y

Z

Measure of ∠X = ☐°

Measure of ∠Y = ☐°

Measure of ∠Z = ☐°

Triangle *XYZ* is a/an ☐ triangle.

Classify each triangle as equilateral, isosceles, or scalene.
Also classify it as right, obtuse, or acute.
Use a centimeter ruler and a protractor to help you.

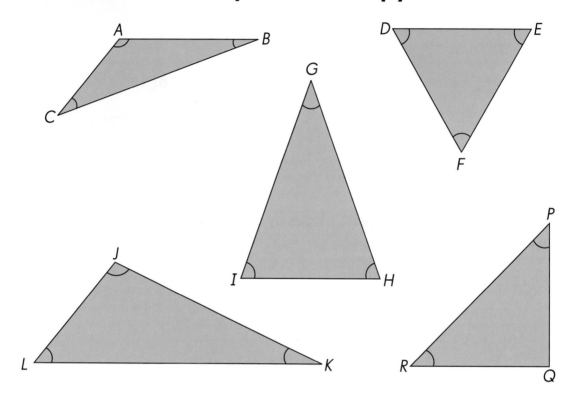

Name of Triangle	Triangles
equilateral triangle	
isosceles triangle	
scalene triangle	
right triangle	
obtuse triangle	
acute triangle	

ON YOUR OWN

**Go to Workbook B:
Practice 1, pages 121–122**

Lesson 13.2 Measures of Angles of a Triangle

Lesson Objective

- Understand and apply the property that the sum of the angle measures of a triangle is 180°.

Show that the sum of all angle measures in a triangle is 180°.

Trace each triangle and cut it out. Then cut out the angles and arrange them on a line as shown.

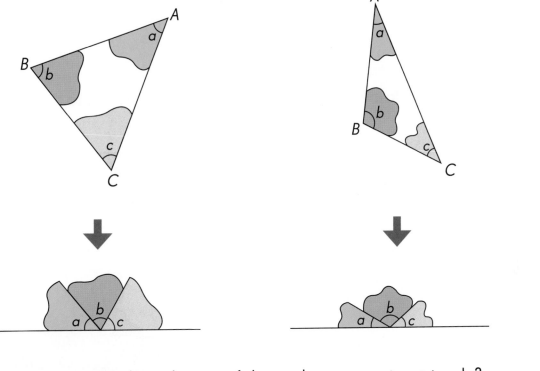

What can you say about the sum of the angle measures in a triangle?

$m\angle a + m\angle b + m\angle c = 180°$

The sum of the three angle measures in any triangle is 180°.

^{Learn} Find unknown angle measures in a triangle.

In triangle *ABC*, find the measure of ∠*B*.

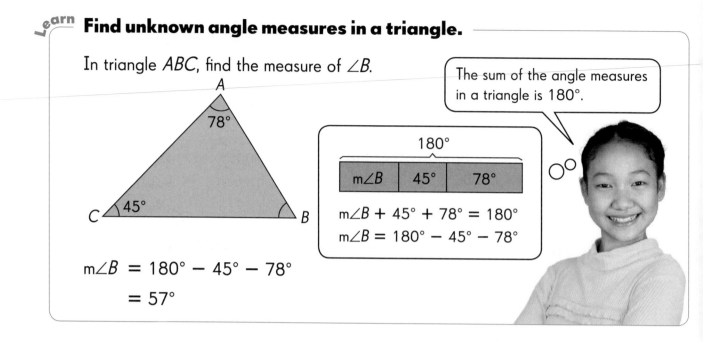

The sum of the angle measures in a triangle is 180°.

180°		
m∠B	45°	78°

m∠B + 45° + 78° = 180°

m∠B = 180° − 45° − 78°

m∠B = 180° − 45° − 78°

= 57°

Guided Practice

Complete. Find the unknown angle measure in each triangle.

1

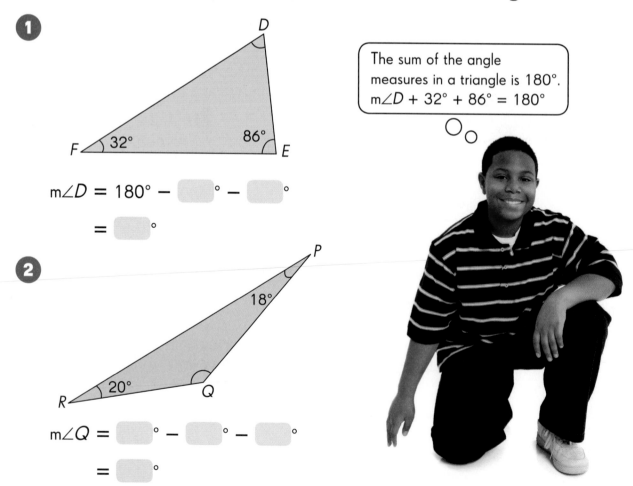

The sum of the angle measures in a triangle is 180°.

m∠D + 32° + 86° = 180°

m∠D = 180° − ⬜° − ⬜°

= ⬜°

2

m∠Q = ⬜° − ⬜° − ⬜°

= ⬜°

1 In triangle *ABC*, m∠*A* = 50°. Three possible examples of triangle *ABC* are shown.

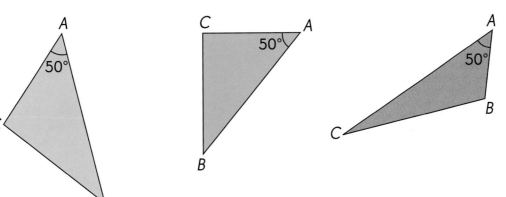

a What is the sum of the measures of ∠*B* and ∠*C*?

b State five possible sets of values for the measures of ∠*B* and ∠*C*.

c Can the measure of ∠*B* be 120°? Explain your answer.

d Can the measure of ∠*B* be 130°? Explain your answer.

2 Suppose that ∠*X*, ∠*Y*, and ∠*Z* are the three angles of triangle *XYZ*.

a If ∠*X* is an obtuse angle, can ∠*Y* also be an obtuse angle? Explain your answer.

b If the measure of ∠*X* is greater than 90°, what can you say about the sum of the measures of ∠*Y* and ∠*Z*?

Let's Practice

These triangles are not drawn to scale. Find the unknown angle measure in each triangle.

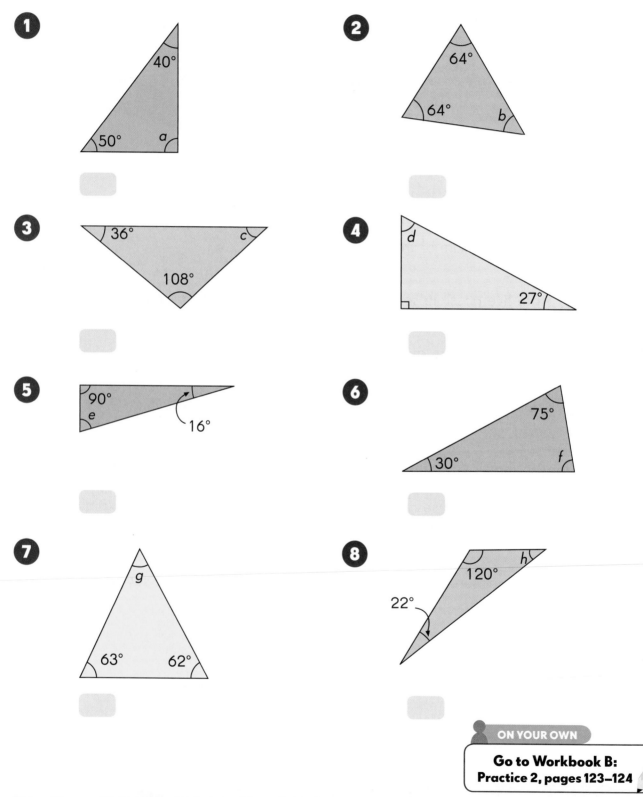

1 40° 50° a

2 64° 64° b

3 36° c 108°

4 d 27°

5 90° e 16°

6 75° 30° f

7 g 63° 62°

8 120° 22° h

ON YOUR OWN

Go to Workbook B:
Practice 2, pages 123–124

13.3 Right, Isosceles, and Equilateral Triangles

Lesson

Lesson Objective

- Understand and apply the properties of right, isosceles, and equilateral triangles.

Learn

Show that the sum of the measures of the two acute angles in a right triangle is 90°.

Triangle ABC is a right triangle. $\angle B$ is a right angle.

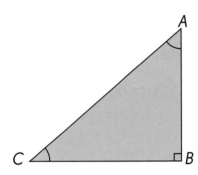

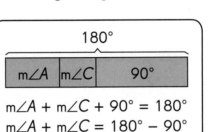

$m\angle A + m\angle C + 90° = 180°$
$m\angle A + m\angle C = 180° - 90°$

$m\angle B = 90°$

$m\angle A + m\angle C + m\angle B = 180°$

$m\angle A + m\angle C + 90° = 180°$

$\qquad m\angle A + m\angle C = 180° - 90°$

$\qquad\qquad\qquad = 90°$

> In a right triangle, the sum of the measures of the two acute angles is 90°.

✋ Hands-On Activity

Use a computer drawing tool to draw three right triangles. Print them out. For each triangle, use a protractor to measure the acute angles. Is the sum of the measures of the acute angles 90°?

Learn Find unknown angle measures in a right triangle.

In triangle ABC, $\angle A$ is a right angle and the measure of $\angle B = 60°$. Find the measure of $\angle C$.

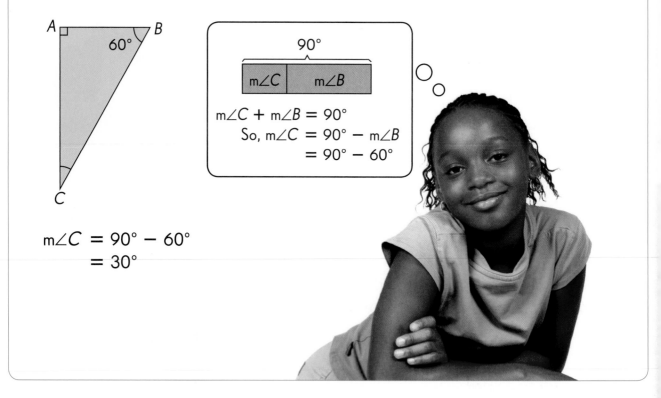

$$90°$$

| $m\angle C$ | $m\angle B$ |

$m\angle C + m\angle B = 90°$
So, $m\angle C = 90° - m\angle B$
$= 90° - 60°$

$m\angle C = 90° - 60°$
$= 30°$

Guided Practice

These triangles are not drawn to scale. Find the unknown angle measures.

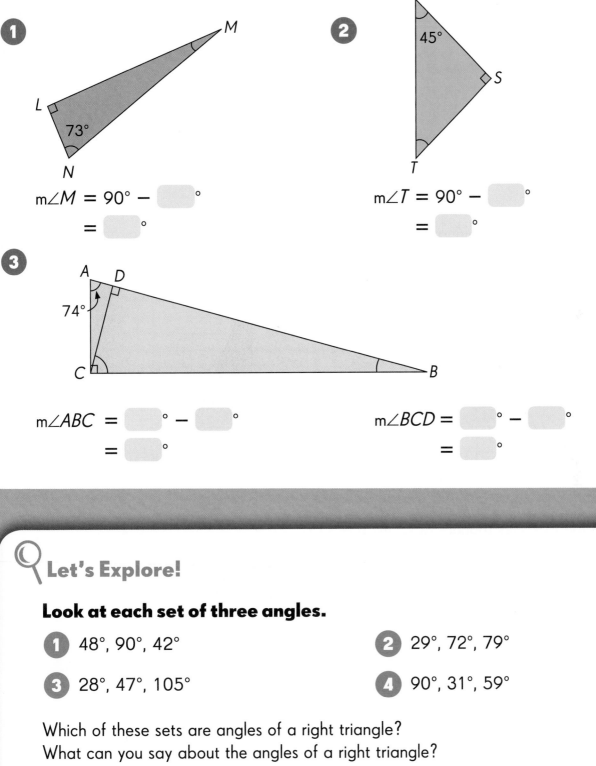

1

$m\angle M = 90° - \boxed{}°$

$\quad\quad = \boxed{}°$

2

$m\angle T = 90° - \boxed{}°$

$\quad\quad = \boxed{}°$

3

$m\angle ABC = \boxed{}° - \boxed{}°$

$\quad\quad\quad = \boxed{}°$

$m\angle BCD = \boxed{}° - \boxed{}°$

$\quad\quad\quad = \boxed{}°$

Let's Explore!

Look at each set of three angles.

1 48°, 90°, 42°

2 29°, 72°, 79°

3 28°, 47°, 105°

4 90°, 31°, 59°

Which of these sets are angles of a right triangle?
What can you say about the angles of a right triangle?

Show that in an isosceles triangle, the measures of the angles opposite the equal sides are equal.

Make a copy of the isosceles triangle *ABC* and cut it out.

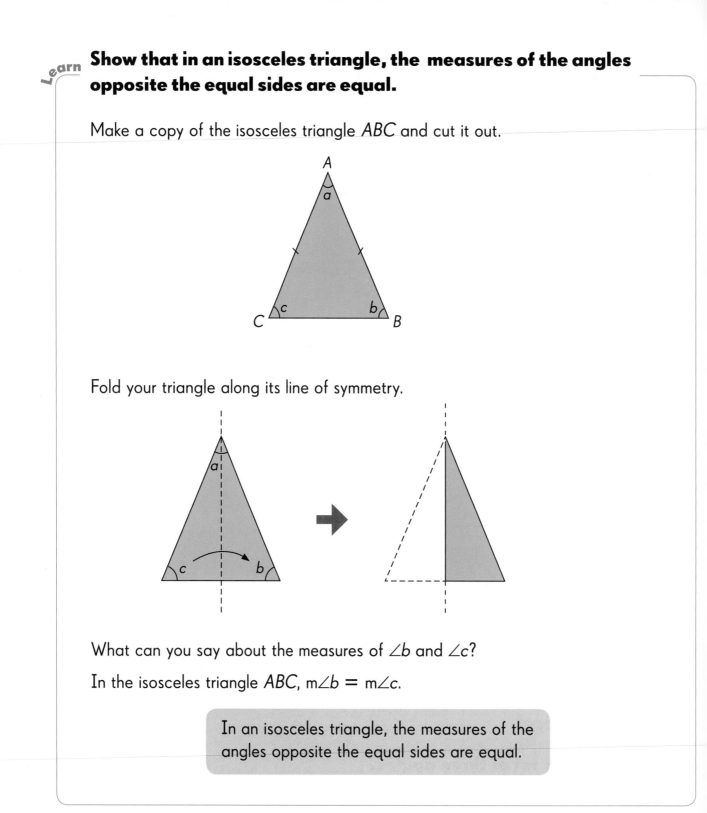

Fold your triangle along its line of symmetry.

What can you say about the measures of ∠*b* and ∠*c*?

In the isosceles triangle *ABC*, m∠*b* = m∠*c*.

> In an isosceles triangle, the measures of the angles opposite the equal sides are equal.

Find unknown angle measures in an isosceles triangle.

In triangle ABC, $AC = BC$ and the measure of $\angle B = 62°$.
Find the measures of $\angle A$ and $\angle C$.

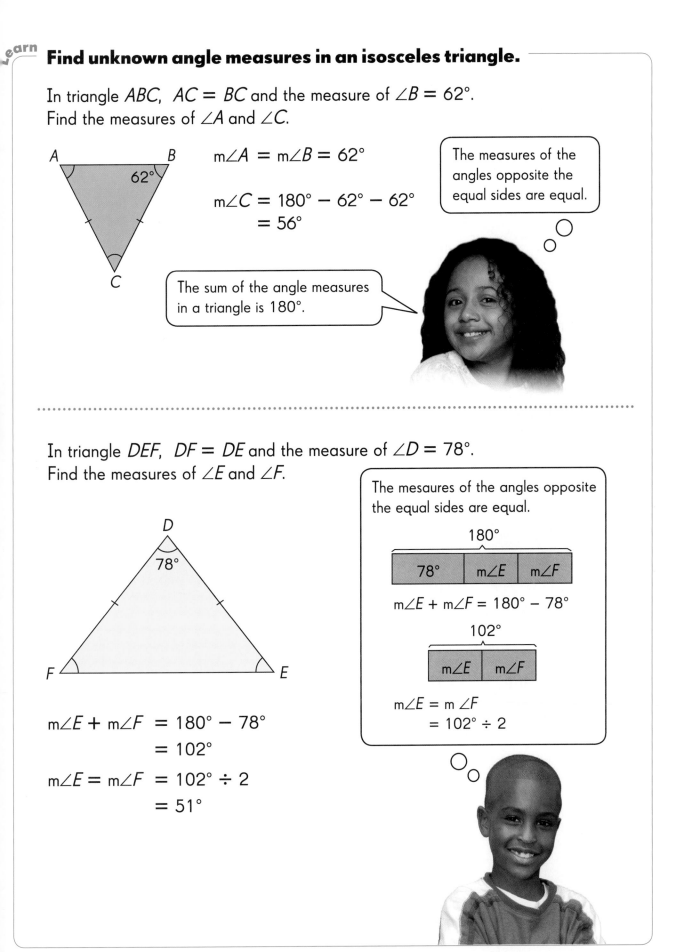

$m\angle A = m\angle B = 62°$

$m\angle C = 180° - 62° - 62°$
$\quad\quad = 56°$

The measures of the angles opposite the equal sides are equal.

The sum of the angle measures in a triangle is 180°.

In triangle DEF, $DF = DE$ and the measure of $\angle D = 78°$.
Find the measures of $\angle E$ and $\angle F$.

The mesaures of the angles opposite the equal sides are equal.

180°

78°	m∠E	m∠F

$m\angle E + m\angle F = 180° - 78°$

102°

m∠E	m∠F

$m\angle E = m\angle F$
$\quad\quad = 102° \div 2$

$m\angle E + m\angle F = 180° - 78°$
$\quad\quad\quad\quad\quad = 102°$

$m\angle E = m\angle F = 102° \div 2$
$\quad\quad\quad\quad\quad = 51°$

Guided Practice

These triangles are not drawn to scale. Find the unknown angle measures.

4 In triangle ABC, $AB = AC$ and the measure of $\angle C = 39°$.
Find the measure of $\angle A$.

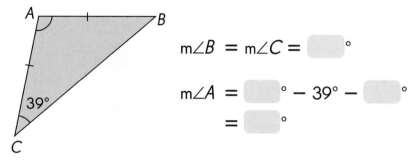

$$m\angle B = m\angle C = \boxed{}°$$

$$m\angle A = \boxed{}° - 39° - \boxed{}°$$

$$= \boxed{}°$$

5 In triangle DEF, $DE = FE$ and the measure of $\angle E = 74°$.
Find the measures of $\angle D$ and $\angle F$.

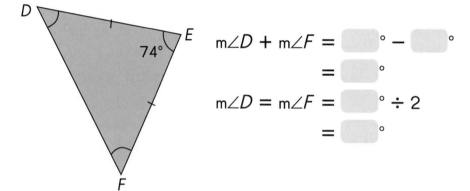

$$m\angle D + m\angle F = \boxed{}° - \boxed{}°$$

$$= \boxed{}°$$

$$m\angle D = m\angle F = \boxed{}° \div 2$$

$$= \boxed{}°$$

6 In triangle ABC, $AC = BC$.
Find the measure of $\angle BCD$.

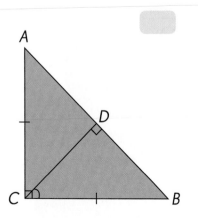

7 In triangle ABC, $m\angle BAC = 42°$,
$\angle ABC = 90°$, and $BC = BD$.
Find the measure of $\angle CBD$.

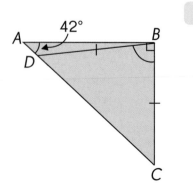

Show that the measures of all the angles of an equilateral triangle are equal and each angle measures 60°.

XYZ is an equilateral triangle.

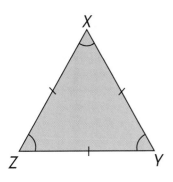

I can also think of an equilateral triangle as an isosceles triangle.

In triangle *XYZ*, *XZ = XY*, *ZY = ZX*, *YX = YZ*.
So, m∠Z = m∠Y, m∠Y = m∠X, m∠X = m∠Z.
So, m∠X = m∠Y = m∠Z.

The measures of all the angles of an equilateral triangle are equal.

m∠X + m∠Y + m∠Z = 180°
m∠X = m∠Y = m∠Z = 180° ÷ 3
= 60°

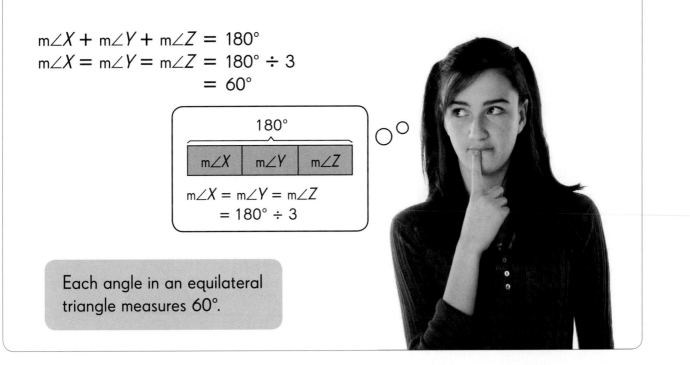

180°

m∠X	m∠Y	m∠Z

m∠X = m∠Y = m∠Z
= 180° ÷ 3

Each angle in an equilateral triangle measures 60°.

Guided Practice

Which of these are equilateral triangles?

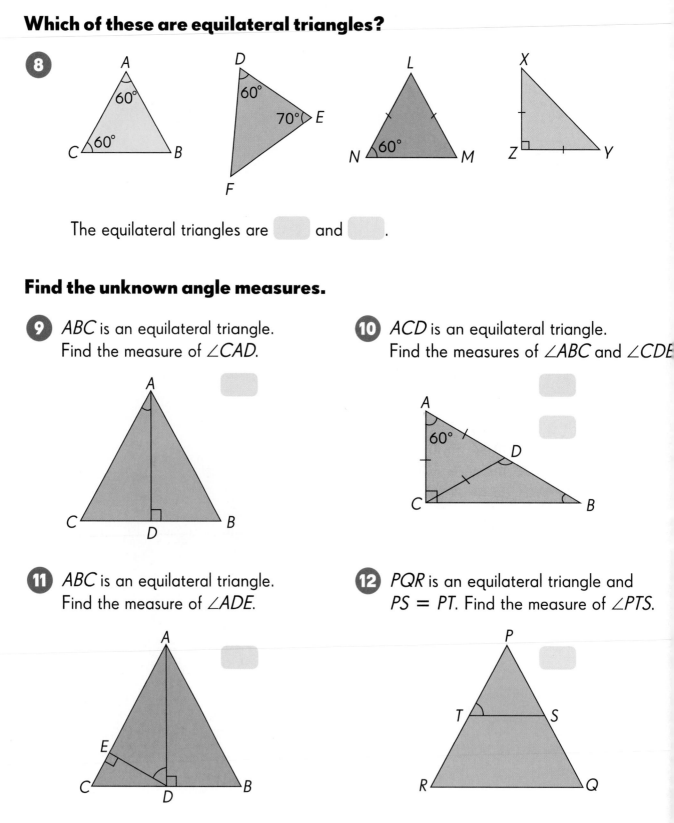

The equilateral triangles are [   ] and [   ].

Find the unknown angle measures.

9 *ABC* is an equilateral triangle.
Find the measure of ∠*CAD*.

10 *ACD* is an equilateral triangle.
Find the measures of ∠*ABC* and ∠*CDE*

11 *ABC* is an equilateral triangle.
Find the measure of ∠*ADE*.

12 *PQR* is an equilateral triangle and
PS = *PT*. Find the measure of ∠*PTS*.

Let's Explore!

Draw these triangles on grid paper. Which triangles cannot be drawn? Classify the triangles that can be drawn.

① A triangle with two sides of equal length and one angle greater than 90°.

② A triangle with three equal angle measures.

③ A right triangle with three sides of equal length.

④ A right triangle with two sides of equal length.

⑤ A triangle with two sides of equal length and all three angles measuring less than 90°.

⑥ A triangle with all three sides of different lengths and two equal angle measures.

⑦ A right triangle with all three sides of different lengths.

Math Journal

① In triangle *PQR, PR = PQ.* and the measure of ∠*P* = 30°. Write what you know about triangle *PQR.*

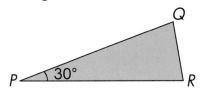

② In triangle *XYZ,* ∠*XZY* = 43° and ∠*XYZ* = 47°. Write what you know about triangle *XYZ.*

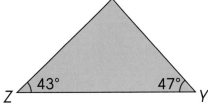

Let's Practice

These triangles are not drawn to scale. Find the unknown angle measures. Then classify each triangle in two ways.

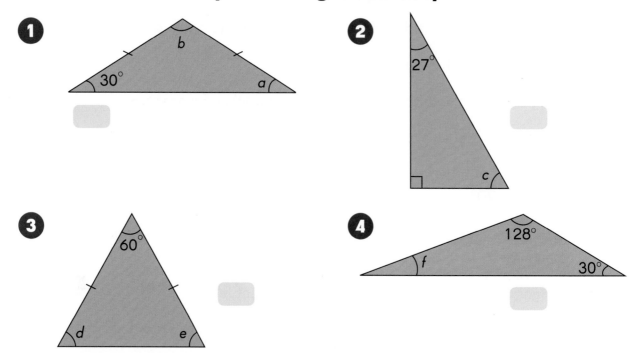

1 b, 30°, a

2 27°, c

3 60°, d, e

4 128°, f, 30°

These triangles are not drawn to scale. Find the unknown angle measures.

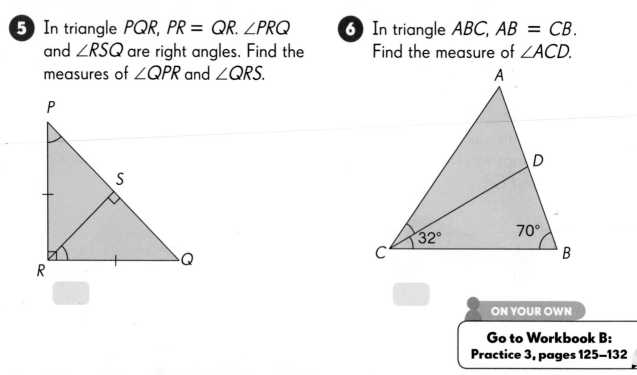

5 In triangle *PQR*, *PR* = *QR*. ∠*PRQ* and ∠*RSQ* are right angles. Find the measures of ∠*QPR* and ∠*QRS*.

P, S, R, Q

6 In triangle *ABC*, *AB* = *CB*. Find the measure of ∠*ACD*.

A, D, 70°, 32°, C, B

ON YOUR OWN

**Go to Workbook B:
Practice 3, pages 125–132**

13.4 Triangle Inequalities

Lesson Objective

- Understand that the sum of the length of any two sides of a triangle is greater than the length of the third side.

Learn **Show that the sum of the lengths of two sides of a triangle is greater than the length of the third side.**

In triangle ABC, $AB = 7$ cm, $BC = 5$ cm, and $AC = 4$ cm

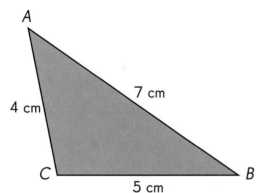

Compare		
$AC + BC$ to AB	$AC + AB$ to BC	$AB + BC$ to AC
$AC + BC = 4$ cm $+ 5$ cm $= 9$ cm $AB = 7$ cm $9 > 7$ So, $AC + BC > AB$	$AC + AB = 4$ cm $+ 7$ cm $= 11$ cm $BC = 5$ cm $11 > 5$ So, $AC + AB > BC$	$AB + BC = 7$ cm $+ 5$ cm $= 12$ cm $AC = 4$ cm $12 > 4$ So, $AB + BC > AC$

$9 > 7$, $11 > 5$, and $12 > 4$ are examples of inequalities.

> The sum of the lengths of any two sides of a triangle is greater than the length of the third side.

Hands-On Activity

Materials:
• centimeter ruler
• inch ruler

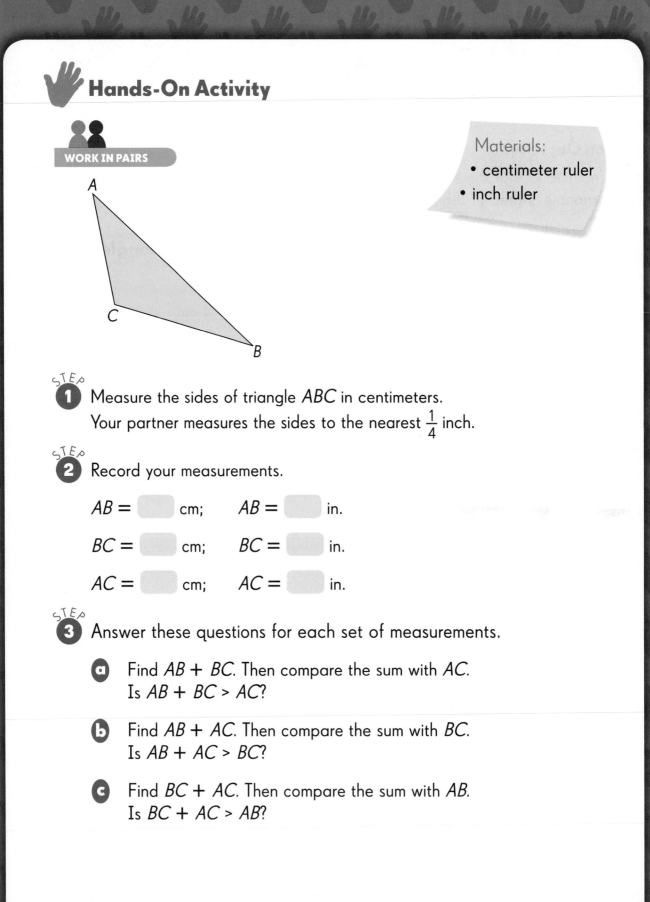

STEP 1 Measure the sides of triangle *ABC* in centimeters.
Your partner measures the sides to the nearest $\frac{1}{4}$ inch.

STEP 2 Record your measurements.

$AB =$ ⬜ cm; $AB =$ ⬜ in.

$BC =$ ⬜ cm; $BC =$ ⬜ in.

$AC =$ ⬜ cm; $AC =$ ⬜ in.

STEP 3 Answer these questions for each set of measurements.

ⓐ Find $AB + BC$. Then compare the sum with AC.
Is $AB + BC > AC$?

ⓑ Find $AB + AC$. Then compare the sum with BC.
Is $AB + AC > BC$?

ⓒ Find $BC + AC$. Then compare the sum with AB.
Is $BC + AC > AB$?

Guided Practice

PQR is a triangle in which $PQ = 8$ centimeters, $QR = 10$ centimeters and $PR = 6$ centimeters.

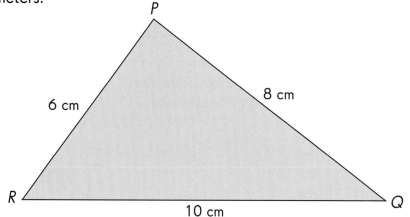

Complete. Use >, <, or = to compare.

1 Find $PQ + QR$. Then compare the sum with PR.

$PQ + QR = \boxed{}$ cm $+ \boxed{}$ cm

$ = \boxed{}$ cm

$PQ + QR \enspace \boxed{} \enspace PR$

2 Find $QR + PR$. Then compare the sum with PQ.

$QR + PR = \boxed{}$ cm $+ \boxed{}$ cm

$ = \boxed{}$ cm

$QR + PR \enspace \boxed{} \enspace PQ$

3 Find $PQ + PR$. Then compare the sum with QR.

$PQ + PR = \boxed{}$ cm $+ \boxed{}$ cm

$ = \boxed{}$ cm

$PQ + PR \enspace \boxed{} \enspace QR$

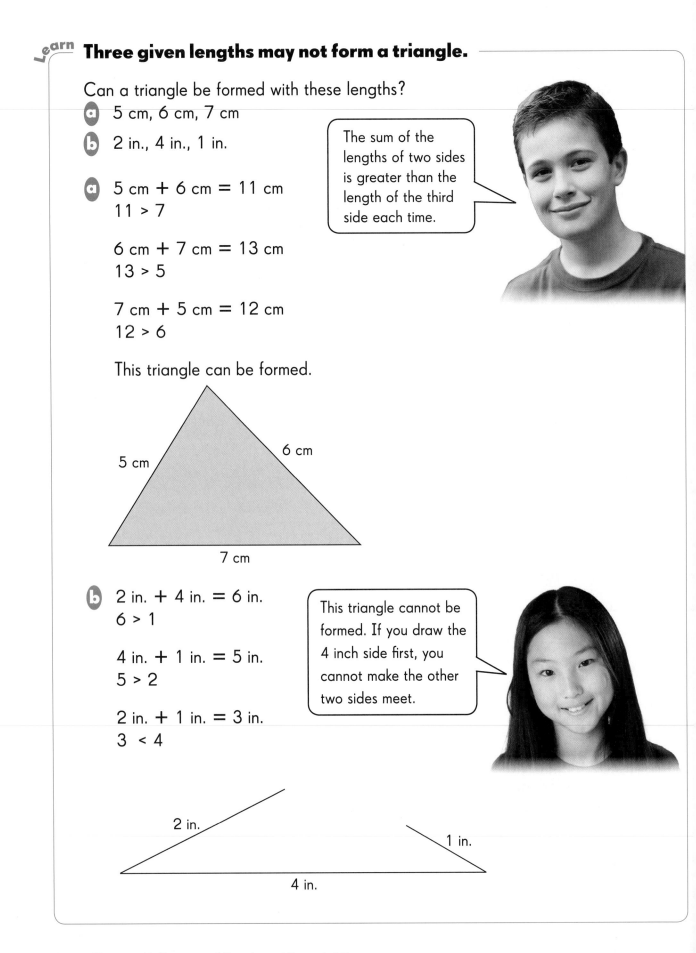

Learn Three given lengths may not form a triangle.

Can a triangle be formed with these lengths?

ⓐ 5 cm, 6 cm, 7 cm

ⓑ 2 in., 4 in., 1 in.

> The sum of the lengths of two sides is greater than the length of the third side each time.

ⓐ 5 cm + 6 cm = 11 cm
11 > 7

6 cm + 7 cm = 13 cm
13 > 5

7 cm + 5 cm = 12 cm
12 > 6

This triangle can be formed.

5 cm   6 cm
7 cm

ⓑ 2 in. + 4 in. = 6 in.
6 > 1

4 in. + 1 in. = 5 in.
5 > 2

2 in. + 1 in. = 3 in.
3 < 4

> This triangle cannot be formed. If you draw the 4 inch side first, you cannot make the other two sides meet.

2 in.   1 in.
4 in.

Guided Practice

Can a triangle be formed with these lengths?
Complete. Use >, <, or = to compare.

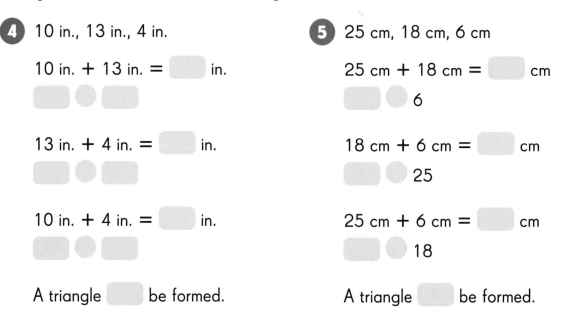

4 10 in., 13 in., 4 in.

10 in. + 13 in. = ⬜ in.

⬜ ⬤ ⬜

13 in. + 4 in. = ⬜ in.

⬜ ⬤ ⬜

10 in. + 4 in. = ⬜ in.

⬜ ⬤ ⬜

A triangle ⬜ be formed.

5 25 cm, 18 cm, 6 cm

25 cm + 18 cm = ⬜ cm

⬜ ⬤ 6

18 cm + 6 cm = ⬜ cm

⬜ ⬤ 25

25 cm + 6 cm = ⬜ cm

⬜ ⬤ 18

A triangle ⬜ be formed.

Learn **Find the possible lengths of a side of a triangle given the lengths of the other two sides.**

The sides of triangle ABC are in whole centimeters.
$AB = 11$ centimeters, $BC = 14$ centimeters and $AC > 20$ centimeters.
Find the possible lengths of $\overline{AC}$ in whole centimeters.

$AB + BC = 11$ cm $+ 14$ cm
$\qquad\quad = 25$ cm

$AB + BC > AC$
$\quad 25$ cm $> AC$

So AC is greater than 20 centimeters and less than 25 centimeters.
The possible lengths of $\overline{AC}$ are 21 centimeters, 22 centimeters,
23 centimeters, and 24 centimeters.

Guided Practice

Complete. Use >, <, or = to compare.

6 XYZ is a triangle in which $XY = 11$ inches and $XZ = 19$ inches.
The length of $\overline{YZ}$ is in whole inches and is greater than 26 inches.
Find the possible lengths of $\overline{YZ}$.

$XY + XZ = \boxed{}$ in. + $\boxed{}$ in.

$ = \boxed{}$ in.

$XY + XZ \enspace \bigcirc \enspace YZ$

$\boxed{}$ in. $\bigcirc \boxed{}$

So YZ is greater than $\boxed{}$ inches and less than $\boxed{}$ inches.

The possible lengths of $\overline{YZ}$ are $\boxed{}$ inches, $\boxed{}$ inches, and $\boxed{}$ inches.

Let's Practice

Which of these lengths can form a triangle? Answer yes or no.

1 9 cm, 17 cm, 20 cm $\boxed{}$

2 5 cm, 25 cm, 29 cm $\boxed{}$

3 14 cm, 16 cm, 31 cm $\boxed{}$

4 8 in., 15 in., 16 in. $\boxed{}$

5 4 in., 18 in., 24 in. $\boxed{}$

6 10 in., 12 in., 21 in. $\boxed{}$

Solve.

7 PQR is a triangle in which $PQ = 18$ centimeters and $QR = 19$ centimeters.
The length of $\overline{PR}$ is in whole centimeters and is greater than 32 centimeters.
What are the possible lengths of $\overline{PR}$? Explain.

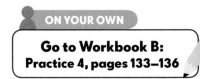

ON YOUR OWN

Go to Workbook B:
Practice 4, pages 133–136

Parallelogram, Rhombus, and Trapezoid

Lesson Objective

• Understand and apply the properties of parallelogram, rhombus, and trapezoid.

Identify parallelograms.

Besides squares and rectangles, there are other four-sided figures that have their own special properties. In the figure $ABCD$, $\overline{AB}$ is parallel to $\overline{DC}$ and $\overline{AD}$ is parallel to $\overline{BC}$.

> I can write $\overline{AB}$ is parallel to $\overline{DC}$ as $\overline{AB} \parallel \overline{DC}$ and $\overline{BC}$ is parallel to $\overline{AD}$ as $\overline{AD} \parallel \overline{BC}$.

Figure $ABCD$ is a **parallelogram**.

Here are three other examples of parallelograms.

A parallelogram is a four-sided figure in which opposite sides are parallel.

Guided Practice

Use a ruler and a drawing triangle to find out which of these figures are not parallelograms.

1

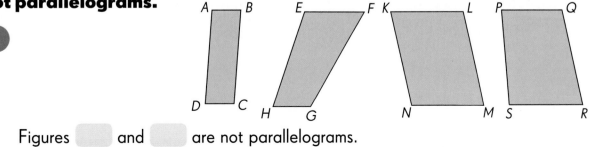

Figures ☐ and ☐ are not parallelograms.

👋 Hands-On Activity

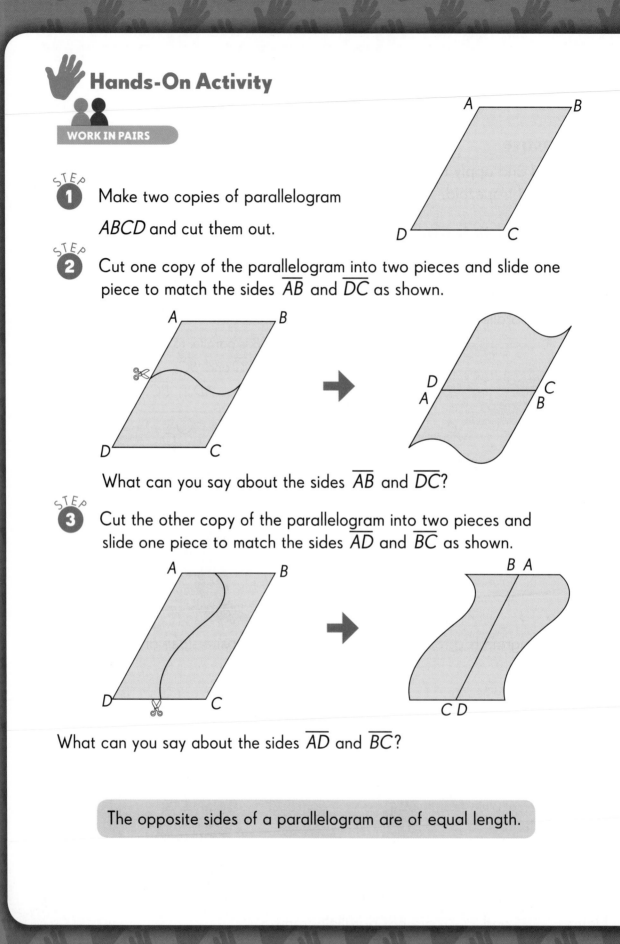

STEP 1 Make two copies of parallelogram *ABCD* and cut them out.

STEP 2 Cut one copy of the parallelogram into two pieces and slide one piece to match the sides $\overline{AB}$ and $\overline{DC}$ as shown.

What can you say about the sides $\overline{AB}$ and $\overline{DC}$?

STEP 3 Cut the other copy of the parallelogram into two pieces and slide one piece to match the sides $\overline{AD}$ and $\overline{BC}$ as shown.

What can you say about the sides $\overline{AD}$ and $\overline{BC}$?

> The opposite sides of a parallelogram are of equal length.

Hands-On Activity

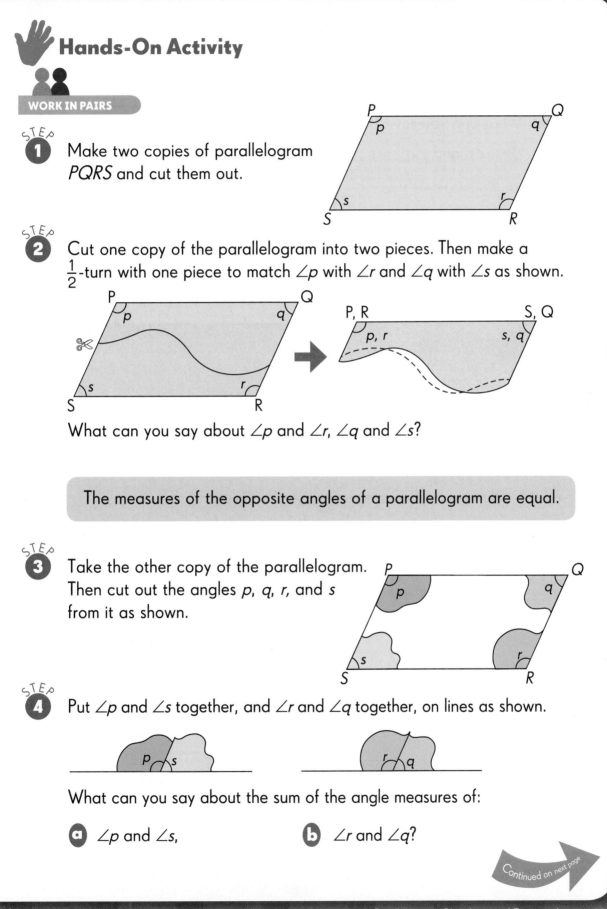

STEP 1 Make two copies of parallelogram *PQRS* and cut them out.

STEP 2 Cut one copy of the parallelogram into two pieces. Then make a $\frac{1}{2}$-turn with one piece to match ∠*p* with ∠*r* and ∠*q* with ∠*s* as shown.

What can you say about ∠*p* and ∠*r*, ∠*q* and ∠*s*?

> The measures of the opposite angles of a parallelogram are equal.

STEP 3 Take the other copy of the parallelogram. Then cut out the angles *p*, *q*, *r*, and *s* from it as shown.

STEP 4 Put ∠*p* and ∠*s* together, and ∠*r* and ∠*q* together, on lines as shown.

What can you say about the sum of the angle measures of:

a ∠*p* and ∠*s*, **b** ∠*r* and ∠*q*?

Continued on next page

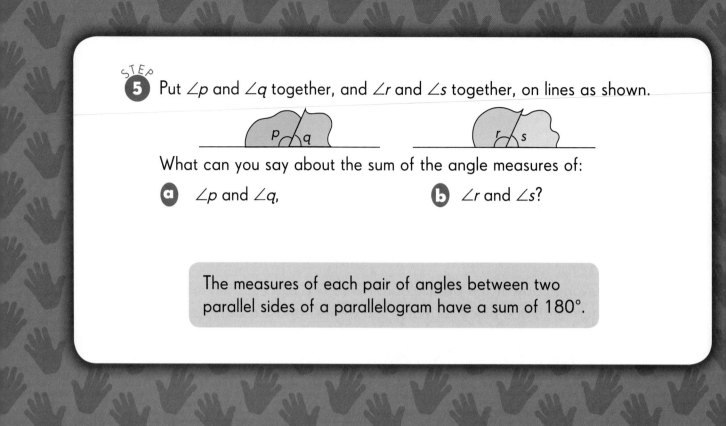

STEP
5 Put ∠p and ∠q together, and ∠r and ∠s together, on lines as shown.

What can you say about the sum of the angle measures of:

a ∠p and ∠q,   **b** ∠r and ∠s?

> The measures of each pair of angles between two parallel sides of a parallelogram have a sum of 180°.

Learn Find unknown angle measures in a parallelogram.

Find the unknown angle measures in the parallelogram *STUV*.

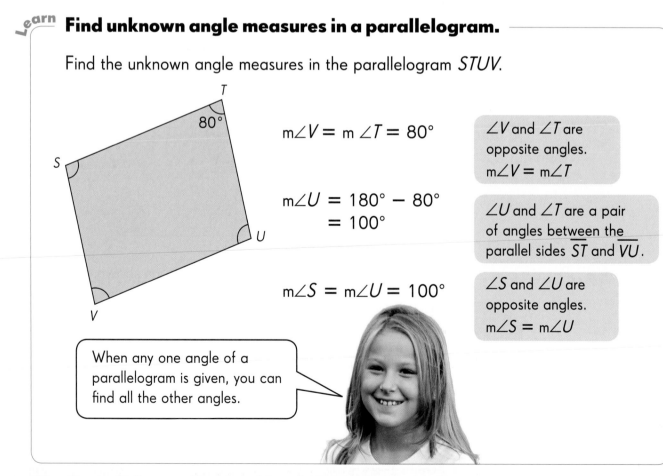

m∠V = m ∠T = 80°

> ∠V and ∠T are opposite angles.
> m∠V = m∠T

m∠U = 180° − 80°
     = 100°

> ∠U and ∠T are a pair of angles between the parallel sides $\overline{ST}$ and $\overline{VU}$.

m∠S = m∠U = 100°

> ∠S and ∠U are opposite angles.
> m∠S = m∠U

> When any one angle of a parallelogram is given, you can find all the other angles.

Guided Practice

These parallelograms are not drawn to scale. Find the unknown angle measures.

2 Find the measure of ∠S.

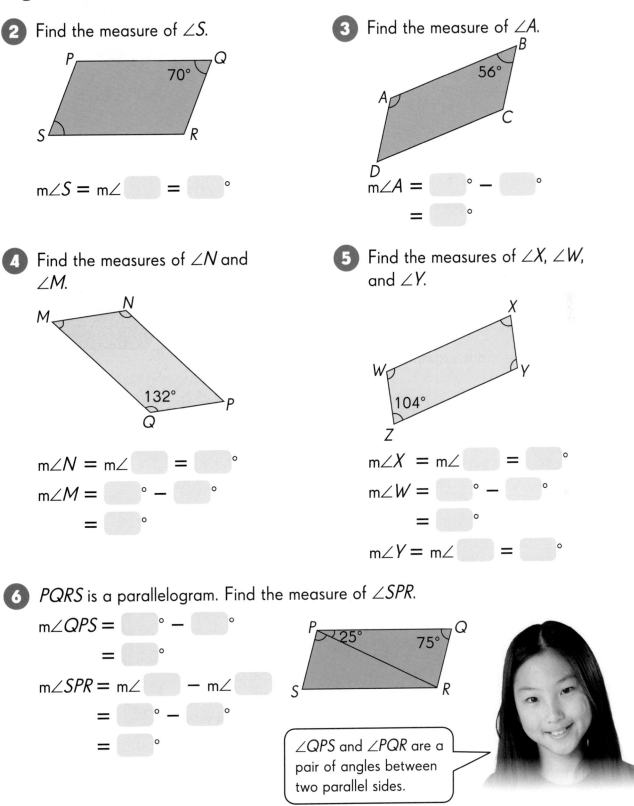

P   Q
70°
S   R

m∠S = m∠ [ ] = [ ]°

3 Find the measure of ∠A.

B
56°
A
C
D

m∠A = [ ]° − [ ]°

      = [ ]°

4 Find the measures of ∠N and ∠M.

N
M
132°
P
Q

m∠N = m∠ [ ] = [ ]°

m∠M = [ ]° − [ ]°

      = [ ]°

5 Find the measures of ∠X, ∠W, and ∠Y.

X
W   Y
104°
Z

m∠X = m∠ [ ] = [ ]°

m∠W = [ ]° − [ ]°

      = [ ]°

m∠Y = m∠ [ ] = [ ]°

6 *PQRS* is a parallelogram. Find the measure of ∠SPR.

m∠QPS = [ ]° − [ ]°

      = [ ]°

m∠SPR = m∠ [ ] − m∠ [ ]

      = [ ]° − [ ]°

      = [ ]°

P   25°   75°   Q
S   R

∠QPS and ∠PQR are a pair of angles between two parallel sides.

These parallelograms are not drawn to scale. Find the unknown angle measures.

7 ABCD is a parallelogram.
Find the measure of ∠DBC.

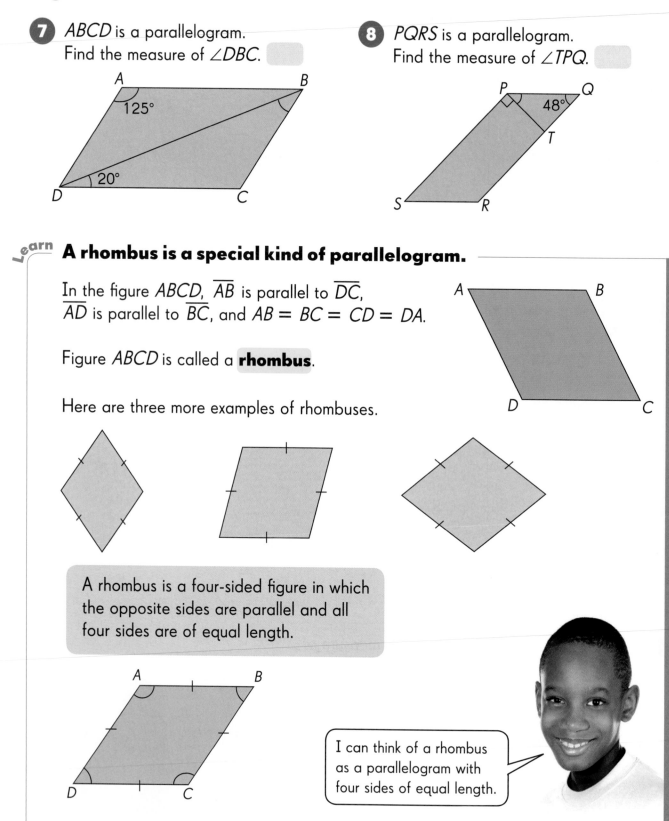

8 PQRS is a parallelogram.
Find the measure of ∠TPQ.

Learn A rhombus is a special kind of parallelogram.

In the figure ABCD, $\overline{AB}$ is parallel to $\overline{DC}$, $\overline{AD}$ is parallel to $\overline{BC}$, and AB = BC = CD = DA.

Figure ABCD is called a **rhombus**.

Here are three more examples of rhombuses.

A rhombus is a four-sided figure in which the opposite sides are parallel and all four sides are of equal length.

I can think of a rhombus as a parallelogram with four sides of equal length.

So, in the rhombus *ABCD*, m∠*A* = m∠*C* and m∠*B* = m∠*D*.

> The measures of opposite angles of a rhombus are equal.

m∠*A* + m∠*B* = 180°   m∠*A* + m∠*D* = 180°
m∠*C* + m∠*D* = 180°   m∠*B* + m ∠*C* = 180°

> The measures of each pair of angles between the parallel sides of a rhombus have a sum of 180°.

Guided Practice

Which figures are rhombuses?
Use a ruler and a drawing triangle to find out.

9

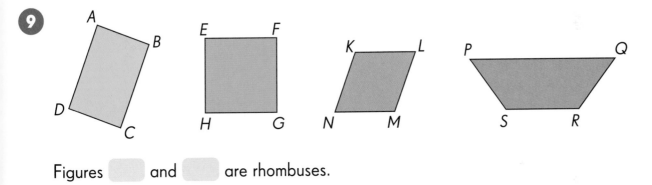

Figures ⬚ and ⬚ are rhombuses.

earn **Find unknown angle measures in a rhombus.**

Find the unknown angle measures in the rhombus *ABCD*.

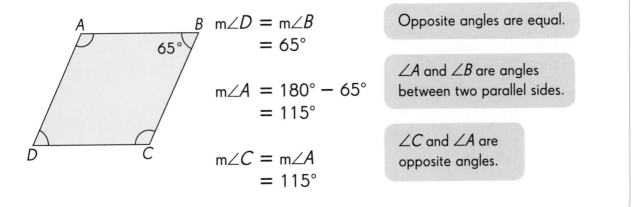

m∠*D* = m∠*B*
    = 65°

> Opposite angles are equal.

m∠*A* = 180° − 65°
    = 115°

> ∠*A* and ∠*B* are angles between two parallel sides.

m∠*C* = m∠*A*
    = 115°

> ∠*C* and ∠*A* are opposite angles.

Lesson 13.5 Parallelogram, Rhombus, and Trapezoid   **217**

Guided Practice

These rhombuses are not drawn to scale. Find the unknown angle measures.

10 Find the measure of ∠F.

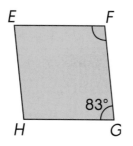

$m\angle F = \boxed{}° - \boxed{}°$

$= \boxed{}°$

11 Find the measure of ∠KML.

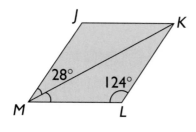

$m\angle LMJ = 180° - \boxed{}° = \boxed{}°$

$m\angle KML = \boxed{}° - 28° = \boxed{}°$

12 ABCD is a rhombus.
Find the measure of ∠DAB.

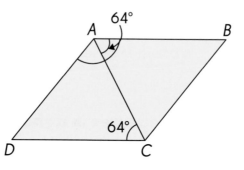

13 ABCD is a rhombus.
Find the measure of ∠ADE.

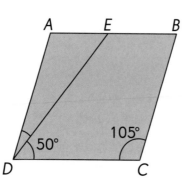

Some four-sided figures have only one pair of parallel sides.

In the figure $ABCD$, $\overline{AB} \parallel \overline{DC}$.

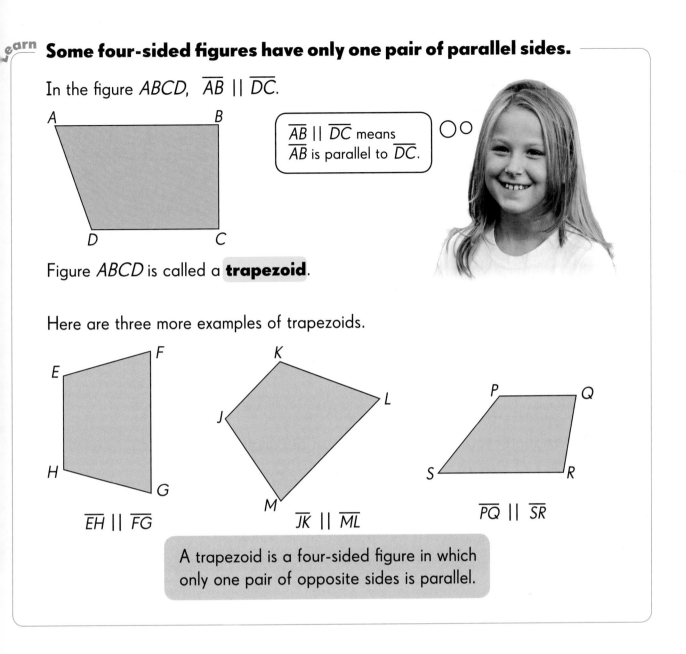

$\overline{AB} \parallel \overline{DC}$ means $\overline{AB}$ is parallel to $\overline{DC}$.

Figure $ABCD$ is called a **trapezoid**.

Here are three more examples of trapezoids.

$\overline{EH} \parallel \overline{FG}$

$\overline{JK} \parallel \overline{ML}$

$\overline{PQ} \parallel \overline{SR}$

A trapezoid is a four-sided figure in which only one pair of opposite sides is parallel.

Guided Practice

Which figure is a trapezoid?
Use a ruler and a drawing triangle to find out.

14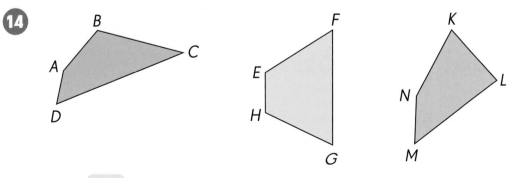

Figure _____ is a trapezoid.

Hands-On Activity

STEP 1 Make a copy of trapezoid *ABCD*. Then cut out the angles *a*, *b*, *c*, and *d* from it as shown.

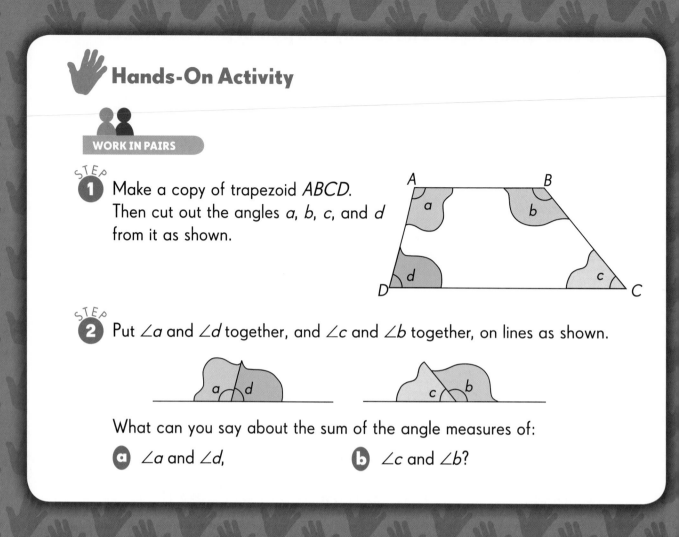

STEP 2 Put ∠*a* and ∠*d* together, and ∠*c* and ∠*b* together, on lines as shown.

What can you say about the sum of the angle measures of:

a ∠*a* and ∠*d*,

b ∠*c* and ∠*b*?

Learn **Find unknown angle measures in a trapezoid.**

In trapezoid *ABCD*, $\overline{AB} \parallel \overline{DC}$, m∠*A* = 85° and m∠*B* = 130°.
Find the measures of ∠*C* and ∠*D*.

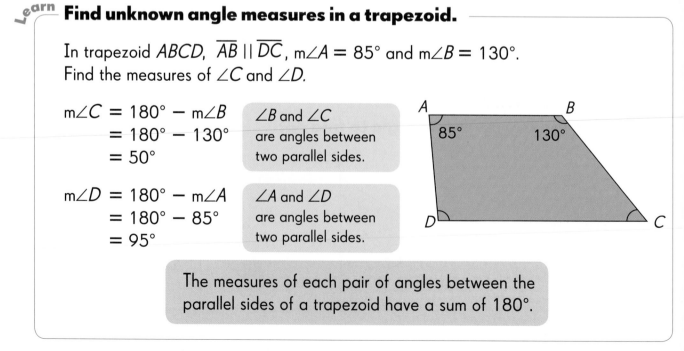

m∠*C* = 180° − m∠*B*
   = 180° − 130°
   = 50°

> ∠*B* and ∠*C* are angles between two parallel sides.

m∠*D* = 180° − m∠*A*
   = 180° − 85°
   = 95°

> ∠*A* and ∠*D* are angles between two parallel sides.

> The measures of each pair of angles between the parallel sides of a trapezoid have a sum of 180°.

Guided Practice

These trapezoids are not drawn to scale. Find the unknown angle measures.

15 In the trapezoid *ABCD*,

$$\overline{AB} \parallel \overline{DC}$$

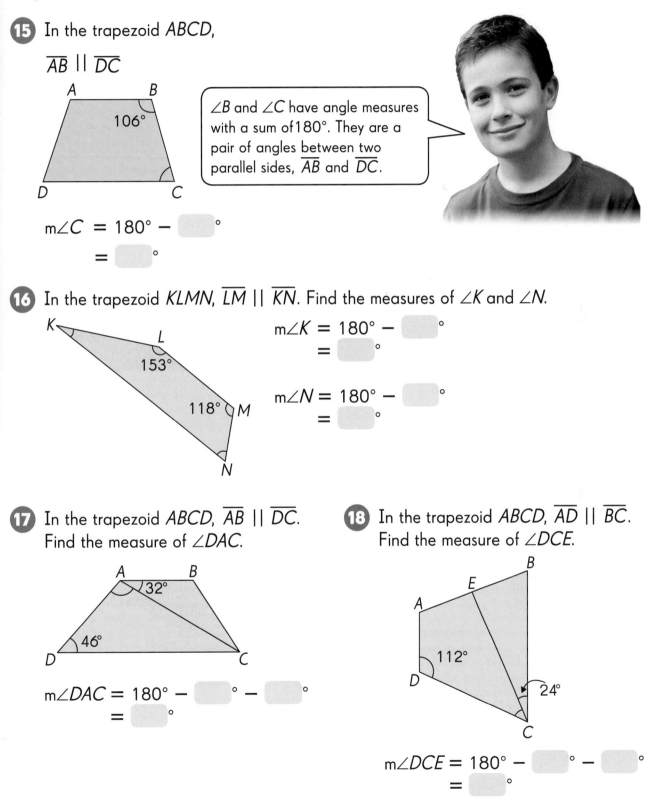

∠B and ∠C have angle measures with a sum of 180°. They are a pair of angles between two parallel sides, $\overline{AB}$ and $\overline{DC}$.

m∠C = 180° − ☐ °

= ☐ °

16 In the trapezoid *KLMN*, $\overline{LM} \parallel \overline{KN}$. Find the measures of ∠K and ∠N.

m∠K = 180° − ☐ °

= ☐ °

m∠N = 180° − ☐ °

= ☐ °

17 In the trapezoid *ABCD*, $\overline{AB} \parallel \overline{DC}$. Find the measure of ∠DAC.

m∠DAC = 180° − ☐ ° − ☐ °

= ☐ °

18 In the trapezoid *ABCD*, $\overline{AD} \parallel \overline{BC}$. Find the measure of ∠DCE.

m∠DCE = 180° − ☐ ° − ☐ °

= ☐ °

Math Journal

Work in groups of four.

List the similarities and differences between each pair of figures:

Compare	Similarities	Differences
a square and a rectangle		
a rectangle and a parallelogram		
a parallelogram and a rhombus		
a square and a rhombus		
a parallelogram and a trapezoid		

Let's Practice

The parallelograms are not drawn to scale. Find the unknown angle measures.

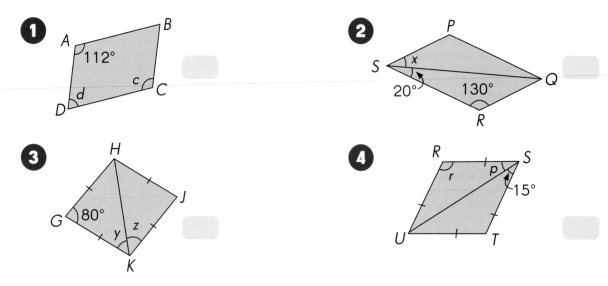

5 In the trapezoid $STUW$, $\overline{ST} \parallel \overline{WU}$.

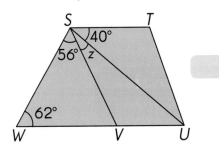

6 In the trapezoid $WXYZ$, $\overline{WX} \parallel \overline{ZY}$.

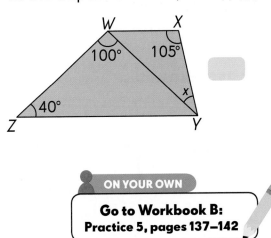

ON YOUR OWN

Go to Workbook B:
Practice 5, pages 137–142

CRITICAL THINKING SKILLS
Put On Your Thinking Cap!

PROBLEM SOLVING

1 The figure is made up of two right triangles. Find the sum of the measures of $\angle BAD$ and $\angle BCD$.

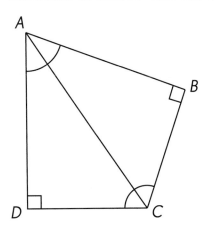

2 Find the sum of the measures of the six marked angles.

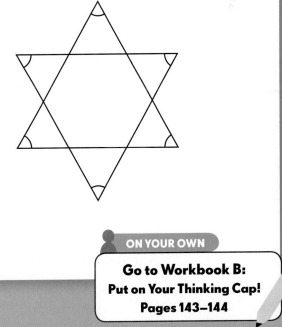

ON YOUR OWN

Go to Workbook B:
Put on Your Thinking Cap!
Pages 143–144

Chapter Wrap Up
Study Guide
You have learned...

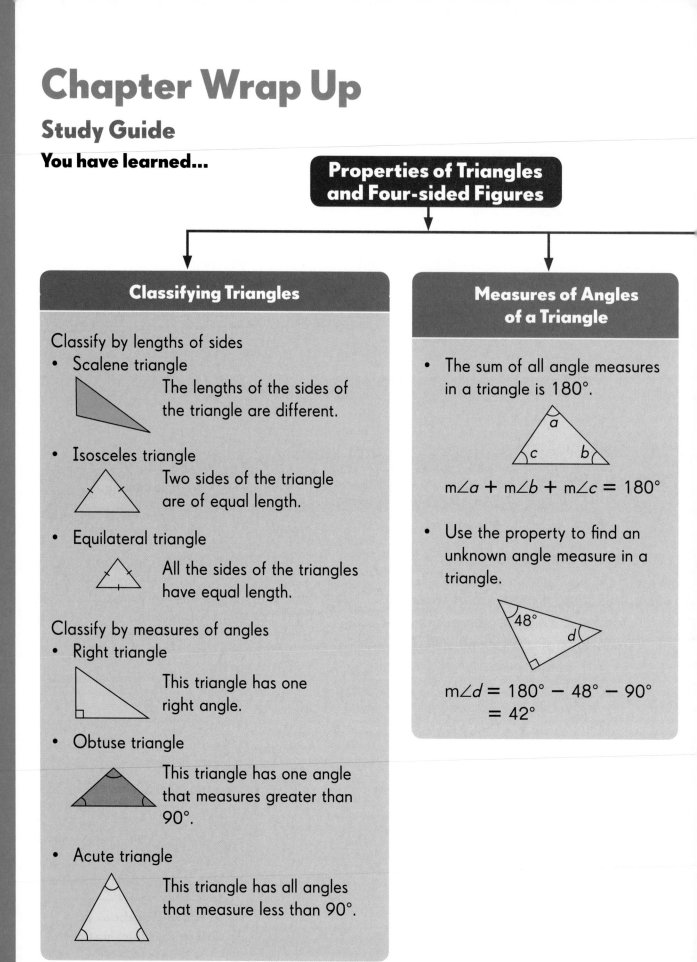

Properties of Triangles and Four-sided Figures

Classifying Triangles

Classify by lengths of sides
- Scalene triangle

  The lengths of the sides of the triangle are different.

- Isosceles triangle

  Two sides of the triangle are of equal length.

- Equilateral triangle

  All the sides of the triangles have equal length.

Classify by measures of angles
- Right triangle

  This triangle has one right angle.

- Obtuse triangle

  This triangle has one angle that measures greater than 90°.

- Acute triangle

  This triangle has all angles that measure less than 90°.

Measures of Angles of a Triangle

- The sum of all angle measures in a triangle is 180°.

  $m\angle a + m\angle b + m\angle c = 180°$

- Use the property to find an unknown angle measure in a triangle.

  $m\angle d = 180° - 48° - 90°$
  $= 42°$

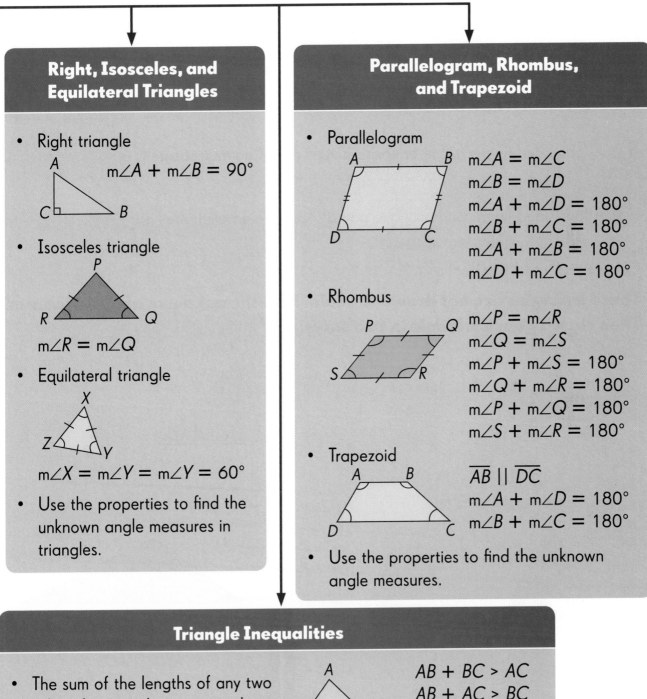

BIG IDEAS

▶ Properties of geometric figures state relationships among angles or sides of the figures.
▶ Triangles and four-sided figures have their own special properties.

Right, Isosceles, and Equilateral Triangles

• Right triangle

$m\angle A + m\angle B = 90°$

• Isosceles triangle

$m\angle R = m\angle Q$

• Equilateral triangle

$m\angle X = m\angle Y = m\angle Y = 60°$

• Use the properties to find the unknown angle measures in triangles.

Parallelogram, Rhombus, and Trapezoid

• Parallelogram

$m\angle A = m\angle C$
$m\angle B = m\angle D$
$m\angle A + m\angle D = 180°$
$m\angle B + m\angle C = 180°$
$m\angle A + m\angle B = 180°$
$m\angle D + m\angle C = 180°$

• Rhombus

$m\angle P = m\angle R$
$m\angle Q = m\angle S$
$m\angle P + m\angle S = 180°$
$m\angle Q + m\angle R = 180°$
$m\angle P + m\angle Q = 180°$
$m\angle S + m\angle R = 180°$

• Trapezoid

$\overline{AB} \parallel \overline{DC}$
$m\angle A + m\angle D = 180°$
$m\angle B + m\angle C = 180°$

• Use the properties to find the unknown angle measures.

Triangle Inequalities

• The sum of the lengths of any two sides of a triangle is greater than the length of the third side.

$AB + BC > AC$
$AB + AC > BC$
$AC + BC > AB$

Chapter Review/Test

Vocabulary

Choose the correct word.

> equilateral triangle
> isosceles triangle
> scalene triangle
> right triangle
> obtuse triangle
> acute triangle
> parallelogram
> rhombus
> trapezoid

1 A triangle with two equal sides is a/an ▢ .

2 A triangle with three equal sides is a/an ▢ .

3 A triangle with one right angle is a/an ▢ .

4 A four-sided figure whose opposite angles are of equal measure is a ▢ or a ▢ .

5 A four-sided figure with only one pair of opposite parallel sides is a ▢ .

Concepts and Skills

These triangles are not drawn to scale. Find the unknown angle measures. Then classify each triangle in two ways.

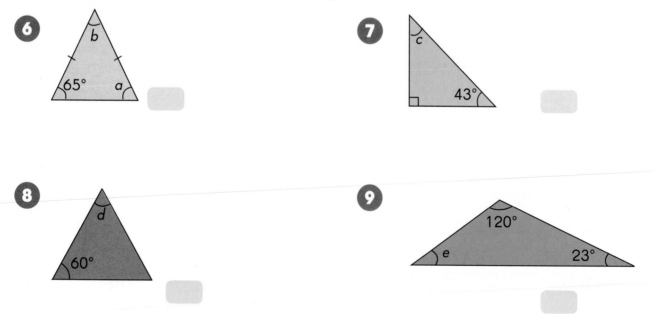

6 b, $65°$, a ▢

7 c, $43°$ ▢

8 d, $60°$ ▢

9 $120°$, e, $23°$ ▢

Measure the sides of the triangles. Use >, <, or = to compare.

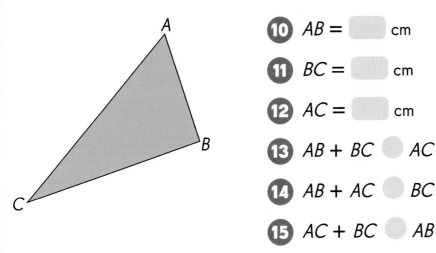

10 $AB = $ ☐ cm

11 $BC = $ ☐ cm

12 $AC = $ ☐ cm

13 $AB + BC$ ◯ AC

14 $AB + AC$ ◯ BC

15 $AC + BC$ ◯ AB

Name the figures that are rhombuses.

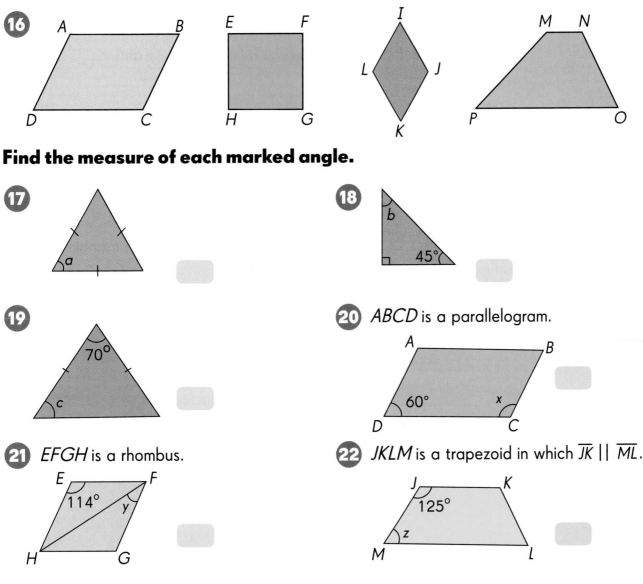

16

Find the measure of each marked angle.

17

18

19

20 $ABCD$ is a parallelogram.

21 $EFGH$ is a rhombus.

22 $JKLM$ is a trapezoid in which $\overline{JK} \parallel \overline{ML}$.

Problem Solving
Solve. Show your work.

23 The two sides of a triangle measure 10 inches and 12 inches. Find a length between 20 inches and 25 inches that is not a possible length of the third side.

24 *ABCD* is a parallelogram. Find the measure of ∠*x*.

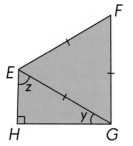

25 *EFGH* is a trapezoid where $\overline{EH} \parallel \overline{FG}$. Find the measures of ∠*y* and ∠*z*.

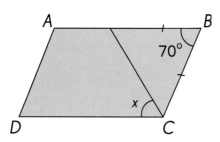

26 Triangle *ABC* is an isosceles triangle. Triangle *BDC* is an equilateral triangle. Find the measure of ∠*x*.

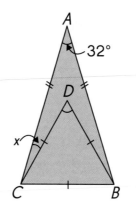

14 Three-Dimensional Shapes

My party hat is a cone.

The balls are spheres.

This looks like a square pyramid.

Lessons

14.1 Prisms and Pyramids

14.2 Cylinder, Sphere, and Cone

BIG IDEA

▶ Solid figures can be identified and classified by the number of faces, edges, and vertices.

Describing plane figures and polygons

A plane figure is a flat figure made up of line segments, curves, or both. It may be an open or closed figure.

These are examples of plane figures.

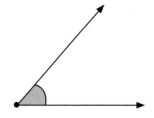

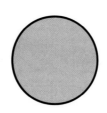

angle:
open figure
made from two
intersecting rays

circle:
closed figure
made up of a
curve

triangle:
closed figure
made up of three
line segments

Identifying sides and vertices in polygons

A polygon is a closed plane figure or shape made up of line segments only.

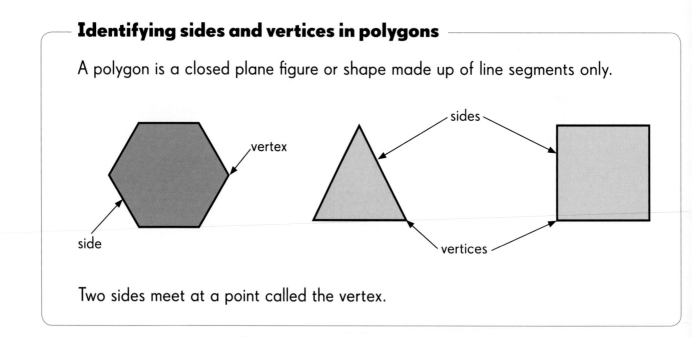

sides

vertex

side

vertices

Two sides meet at a point called the vertex.

Identifying polygons by the number of sides and vertices

A polygon has as many sides as vertices.

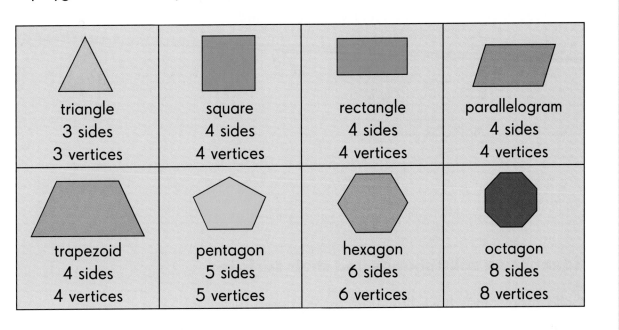

triangle 3 sides 3 vertices	square 4 sides 4 vertices	rectangle 4 sides 4 vertices	parallelogram 4 sides 4 vertices
trapezoid 4 sides 4 vertices	pentagon 5 sides 5 vertices	hexagon 6 sides 6 vertices	octagon 8 sides 8 vertices

Identifying congruent figures

Congruent figures have the same shape and size.

Congruent	Not Congruent

Identifying parallel line segments

Parallel line segments are parts of lines that are always the same distance apart. The lines never meet or intersect when extended.

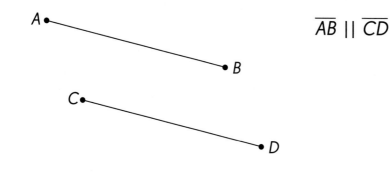

$\overline{AB} \parallel \overline{CD}$

Identifying solid shapes and their surfaces

Solid shapes may have flat surfaces or curved surfaces.

cube 6 flat surfaces 0 curved surfaces	rectangular prism 6 flat surfaces 0 curved surfaces	pyramid 5 flat surfaces 0 curved surfaces
cone 1 flat surface 1 curved surface	cylinder 2 flat surfaces 1 curved surface	sphere 0 flat surfaces 1 curved surface

Identify the plane figures. Then identify the polygons.

1
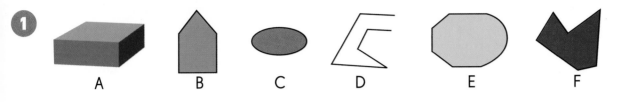

A   B   C   D   E   F

Name the parts of the polygon.

2
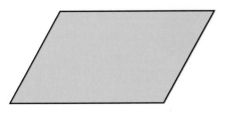

Trace the shapes. Then answer Yes or No.

3 Are these shapes congruent?

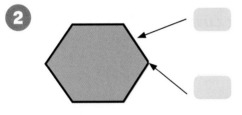
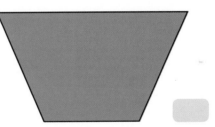

4 Are these shapes congruent?

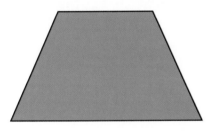
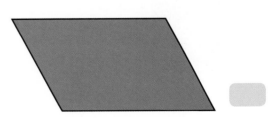

Decide which pair of line segments is parallel.

5

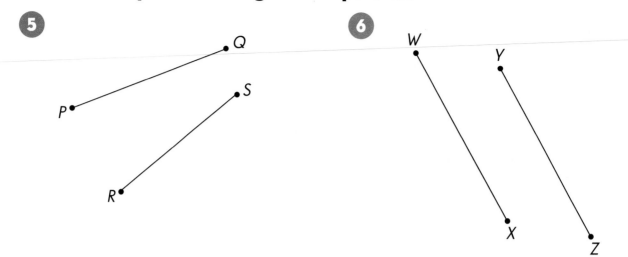

6

Decide whether each object has flat surfaces or curved surfaces, or both.

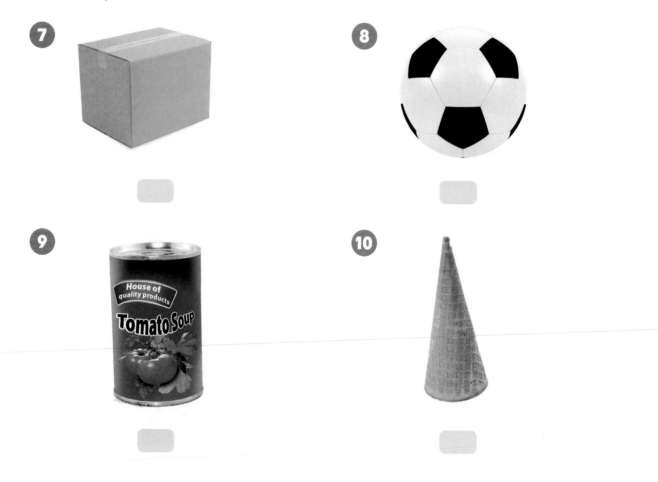

7

8

9

10

Prisms and Pyramids

Lesson Objectives

- Identify and classify prisms and pyramids.
- Identify the solid figure that can be formed from a net.

Vocabulary

face	prism	square pyramid
base	rectangular prism	triangular pyramid
edge	triangular prism	net
vertex	pyramid	

Learn   Describe a solid figure by its faces, edges, and vertices.

A plane figure is a flat or two-dimensional figure. It has only length and width. Polygons are plane figures. Most of the objects around us are solid figures or three-dimensional figures.

> A three-dimensional figure has length, width, and height.

This is a cube. Its **faces** are flat surfaces. Each face is a square formed by four sides of equal length. The sides of each square are line segments.

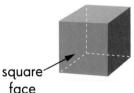
square face

A square is a special rectangle.

The top and bottom faces of a solid are called **bases**. The base of a cube is a square.

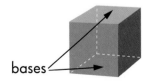
bases

Continued on next page

A cube has edges and vertices.
An **edge** of a solid figure is a line segment formed when two faces meet.
A **vertex** is the point where three or more edges meet.

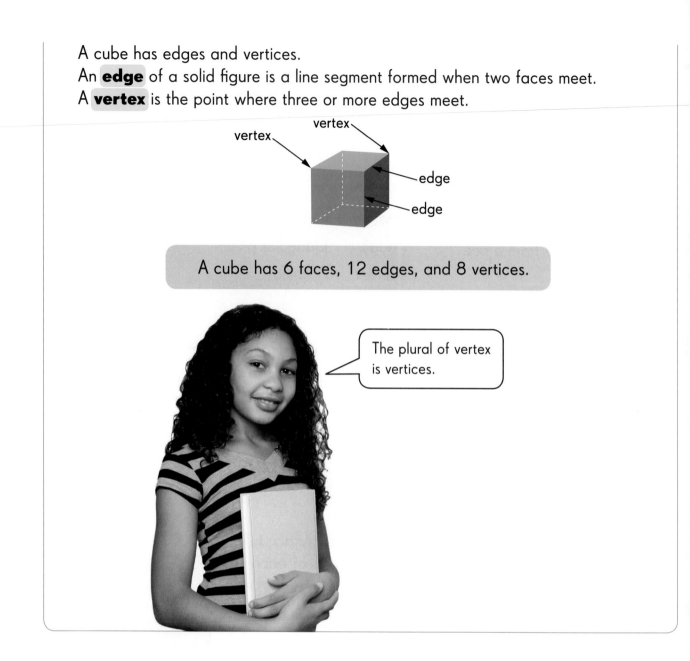

vertex

vertex

edge

edge

A cube has 6 faces, 12 edges, and 8 vertices.

The plural of vertex is vertices.

Guided Practice

Complete.

1 How many faces, vertices, and edges does a number cube have?

☐ faces

☐ vertices

☐ edges

Identify a prism.

A **prism** is a solid figure with two parallel congruent bases joined by rectangular faces. A prism is named according to the shape of its bases.

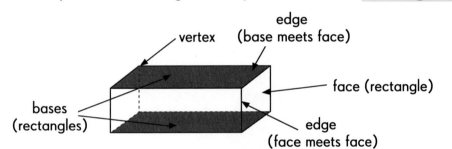

Congruent bases mean the bases have the same shape and size.

The bases of this prism are rectangles. This prism is called a **rectangular prism**.

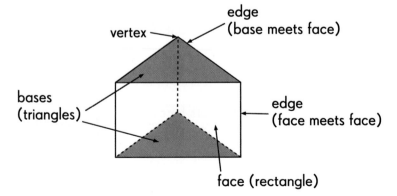

vertex
edge (base meets face)
face (rectangle)
bases (rectangles)
edge (face meets face)

Any pair of opposite faces of a rectangular prism can be the bases.

A rectangular prism has 6 faces, 12 edges, and 8 vertices.

The bases of this prism are triangles. This prism is called a **triangular prism**.

edge (base meets face)
vertex
bases (triangles)
edge (face meets face)
face (rectangle)

Can you find other pairs of bases in this triangular prism? Explain your answer.

A triangular prism has 5 faces, 9 edges, and 6 vertices.

Guided Practice

Complete.

2 Name the parts of the prism.
Identify the shapes of the faces.

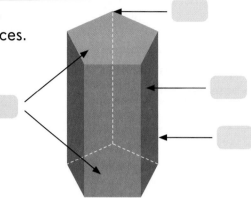

Explain.

3 Explain why this figure is not a prism.

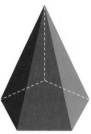

 Identify a pyramid.

A **pyramid** has one base that can be any polygon. All the other faces are triangles arising from each side of the base. The triangular faces share a common vertex. A pyramid is named according to the shape of its base.

The base of this pyramid is a square. It is called a **square pyramid**.

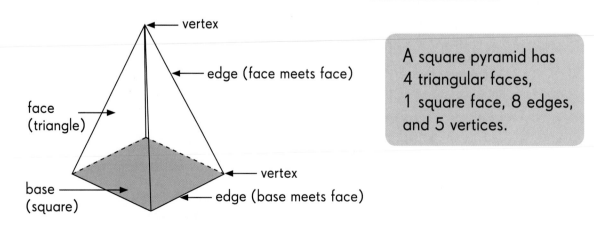

A square pyramid has 4 triangular faces, 1 square face, 8 edges, and 5 vertices.

The base of this pyramid is a triangle. It is called a **triangular pyramid**.

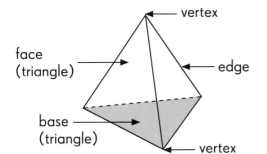

vertex

face
(triangle)

edge

base
(triangle)

vertex

The 4 triangular faces include the base.

A triangular pyramid has 4 triangular faces, 6 edges, and 4 vertices.

The faces of prisms and pyramids are polygons.

Guided Practice

Complete.

 4 Name the parts of the pyramid.
Identify the shapes of the faces.

Explain.

5 Explain why the figure is not a pyramid.

Identify solid figures from nets.

A **net** is a plane figure that can be folded to make a solid figure. More than one net may form the same solid figure.

The cube is cut along some of the edges and laid flat as shown.

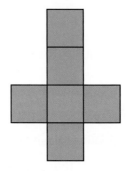

These are two more nets of a cube.

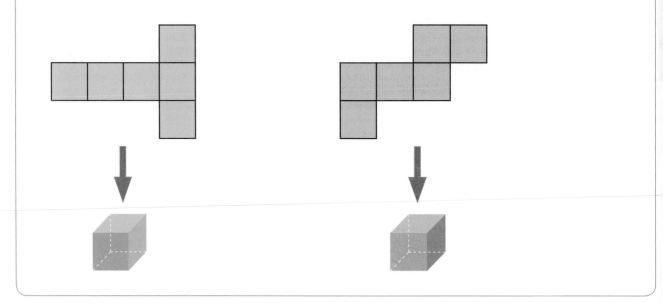

Hands-On Activity

WORK IN PAIRS

STEP 1 Trace, cut out, and fold the nets.

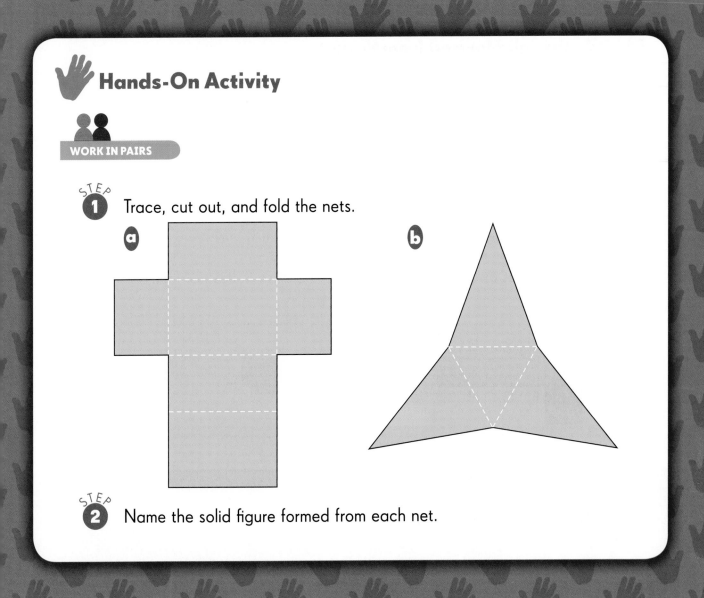

a

b

STEP 2 Name the solid figure formed from each net.

Guided Practice

Complete.

6 Copy the figure. Then draw to complete the net of a cube.

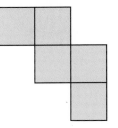

Identify the solid formed from the net.

7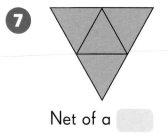

Net of a [　　]

Complete the labels for the vertices.

8 This is the net of a cube. (Hint: Locate the base in the net first.)

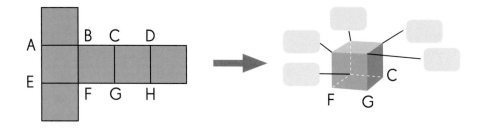

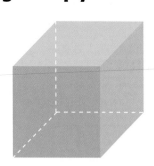

Math Journal

Answer the questions about a cube. Use the drawing to help you.

1 What shape are the faces of a cube?

2 How many bases does a cube have?

3 Are the bases parallel? Are they congruent?

4 How many faces join two bases?

5 Can a cube be called a rectangular prism?

6 Can a cube be called a square prism?

7 Can a rectangular prism be called a cube?

Let's Explore!

1 Look at these prisms.

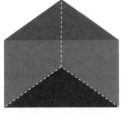 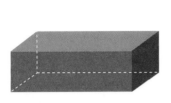  

a Copy and complete the table.

Type of Prism	Number of Sides of Each Base	Number of Rectangular Faces Connecting the Bases
triangular prism		
rectangular prism		
pentagonal prism		
hexagonal prism		

b Look at your table. What can you say about the number of sides of each base and the number of rectangular faces connecting the bases?

2 Look at these pyramids.

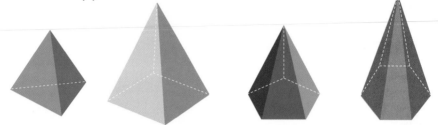

a Copy and complete the table.

Type of Pyramid	Number of Sides of the Base	Number of Triangular Faces
triangular pyramid		
square pyramid		
pentagonal pyramid		
hexagonal pyramid		

b Look at your table. What can you say about the number of sides of the base and the number of triangular faces of a pyramid?

Let's Practice

Complete.

1 Identify each polygon, prism, and pyramid.

Trace, cut out, and fold the net. Then name the solid shape formed from the net.

2

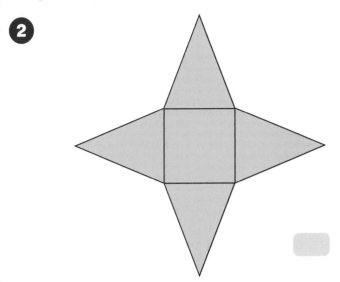

List four items found in a supermarket that are of each shape.

	Shape	Item 1	Item 2	Item 3	Item 4
3	prism				
4	not a prism				

Explain.

5 Explain the difference between a prism and a pyramid.

6 Explain why each object is not a pyramid.

a    **b**

Complete.

7 A ____ prism has 8 faces.

8 A ____ pyramid has 6 faces.

ON YOUR OWN

**Go to Workbook B:
Practice 1, pages 159–162**

Lesson 14.2 Cylinder, Sphere, and Cone

Lesson Objective

• Identify and classify cylinders, spheres, and cones.

Vocabulary
cylinder
sphere
cone

Learn Identify a cylinder.

A **cylinder** has two circular, flat surfaces, or bases, that are congruent and parallel. The bases are joined by a curved surface.

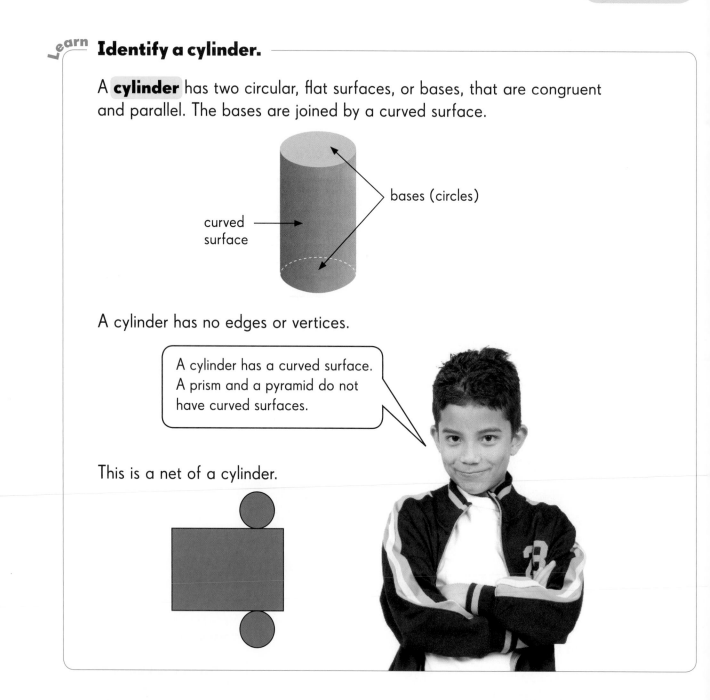

bases (circles)

curved surface

A cylinder has no edges or vertices.

A cylinder has a curved surface. A prism and a pyramid do not have curved surfaces.

This is a net of a cylinder.

This is a net of a cylinder.

Guided Practice

Complete.

1 Name the parts of the cylinder.

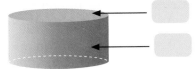

Explain.

2 Explain why the object in **1** is a cylinder.

 Identify a sphere.

A **sphere** has a smooth curved surface.
It does not have edges or vertices.

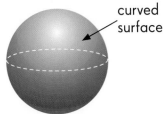

curved
surface

A sphere has no
flat surfaces.

It is the same distance across for any
line that goes through its center.

Guided Practice

Explain why each solid figure is not a sphere.

3

4

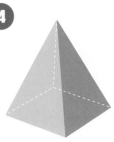

Identify a cone.

A **cone** has one circular, flat face or base and a curved surface.
It has one vertex.

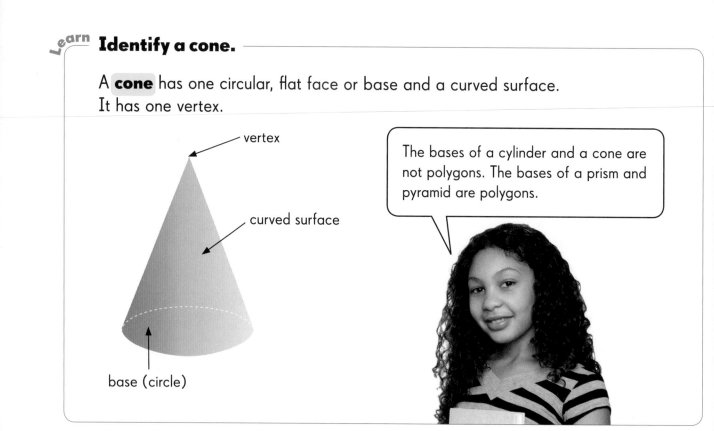

vertex

curved surface

base (circle)

The bases of a cylinder and a cone are not polygons. The bases of a prism and pyramid are polygons.

Guided Practice

Complete.

 Name the parts of the cone.

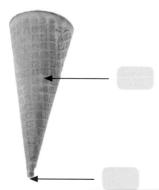

Explain why each figure is not a cone.

6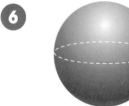

7

Hands-On Activity

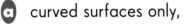

STEP 1 Look at objects around your school or in your classroom. List the objects with

a curved surfaces only,

b flat surfaces only,

c curved surfaces and flat surfaces.

STEP 2 Classify your objects in a table like the one shown here.

Prism	Pyramid	Cylinder	Cone	Sphere

Compare the faces of a pentagonal prism and a cone.

1 What polygons can you find in the pentagonal prism?
What polygons can you find in the cone?

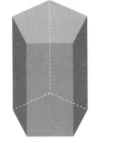

2 How many flat surfaces are in each figure in **1** ?

Identify the shape of each object.

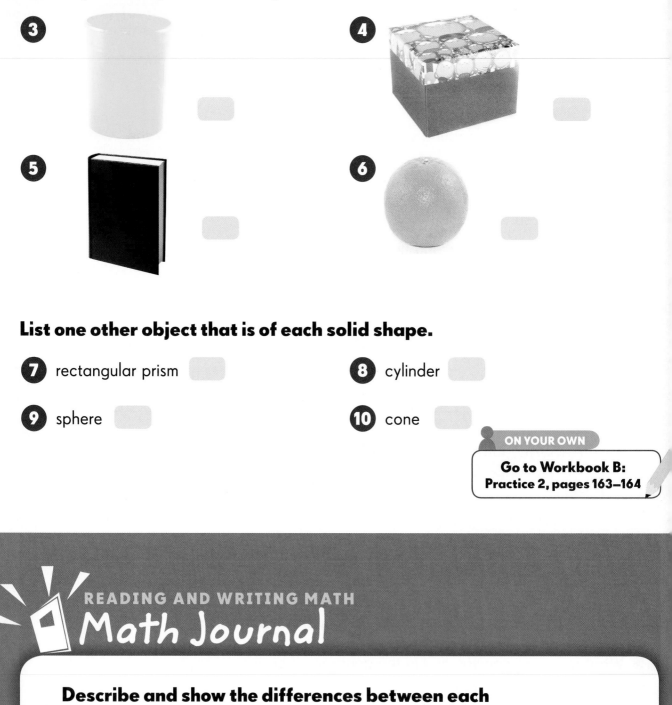

3 [ ]

4 [ ]

5 [ ]

6 [ ]

List one other object that is of each solid shape.

7 rectangular prism [ ]

8 cylinder [ ]

9 sphere [ ]

10 cone [ ]

ON YOUR OWN

Go to Workbook B:
Practice 2, pages 163–164

READING AND WRITING MATH
Math Journal

Describe and show the differences between each pair of solid shapes.

1 square prism and square pyramid

2 square prism and cylinder

3 pentagonal prism and hexagonal prism

Put On Your Thinking Cap!

PROBLEM SOLVING

Solve.

1. How many different rectangular prisms can you make using 12 identical cubes? Describe them.

2. Which of the following number of identical cubes can make prisms?
   How many prisms of different sizes can you make?
   Give the different sizes.

   (a) 8   (b) 15   (c) 23   (d) 33

3. You have a pyramid and a prism. The total number of faces of these two solids is 11. What are the solids? Explain how you solved the problem.

4. This prism is made up of two triangular prisms.
   The triangular faces are equilateral triangles.

   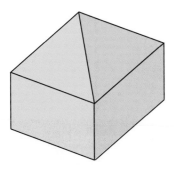

   (a) What shape is the base?

   (b) Suppose that another identical triangular prism is added on the left with its base horizontal. What shape is the base of the combined solid?

ON YOUR OWN

**Go to Workbook B:
Put on Your Thinking Cap!
pages 165– 166**

Chapter Wrap Up

Study Guide

You have learned...

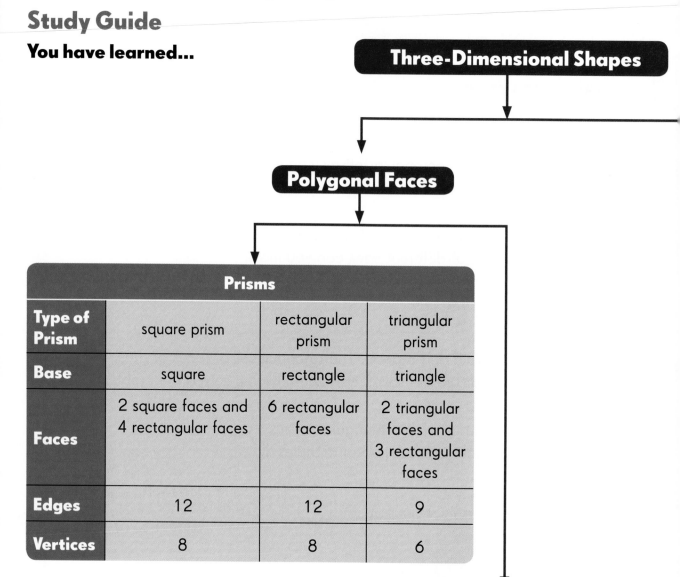

Three-Dimensional Shapes

Polygonal Faces

Prisms

Type of Prism	square prism	rectangular prism	triangular prism
Base	square	rectangle	triangle
Faces	2 square faces and 4 rectangular faces	6 rectangular faces	2 triangular faces and 3 rectangular faces
Edges	12	12	9
Vertices	8	8	6

Pyramids

Type of Pyramid	square pyramid	triangular pyramid
Base	square	triangle
Faces	4 triangular faces and 1 square face	4 triangular faces
Edges	8	6
Vertices	5	4

BIG IDEA

▶ Solid figures can be identified and classified by the number of faces, edges, and vertices.

Polygonal Faces and Curved Surfaces

Solid	cylinder	sphere	cone
Flat surfaces	2 circles	0	1 circle
Curved surfaces	1	1	1
Edges	0	0	0
Vertices	0	0	1

Nets for Solid Figures

A net is a plane figure that can be folded to form a solid figure.

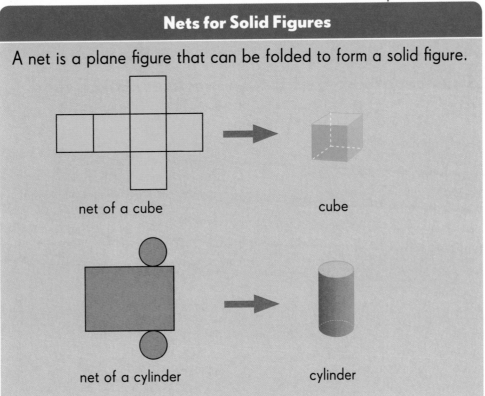

net of a cube   cube

net of a cylinder   cylinder

Chapter Review/Test

Vocabulary

Choose the correct word.

face
base
edges
vertices
prism
rectangular prism
triangular prism
pyramid
square pyramid
triangular pyramid
net
cylinder
sphere
cone

1 A solid figure with two parallel congruent bases joined by rectangular faces is a ____ .

2 A solid figure with a polygonal base and triangular faces meeting at a common vertex is a ____ .

3 A ____ is a plane figure that can be folded to form a solid figure.

4 A ____ is a solid figure with a curved surface and no flat surfaces.

5 A cylinder does not have ____ or ____ .

6 In a cone, the ____ is a circular, flat surface.

Concepts and Skills

Find the number of faces, edges, and vertices in each solid.

7

8

Name the solids formed from these nets.

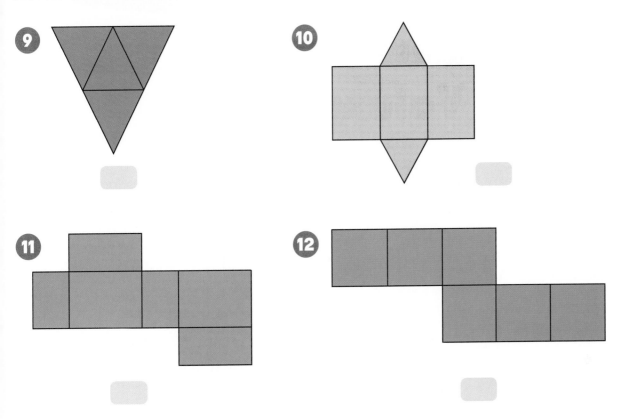

9

10

11

12

Problem Solving

Solve.

13 A solid figure has 2 circular flat surfaces and a curved surface. What is this solid figure? Sketch it.

14 These are the bases of two solid figures. What could the solid figures be? Explain.

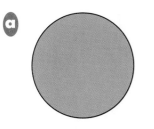

a

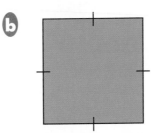

b

15 Surface Area and Volume

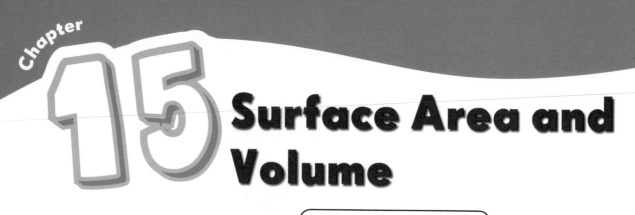

How can you find the volume of this glass box?

Lessons

BIG IDEAS

▶ The volume of cubes and rectangular prisms can be expressed as the number of cubic units they contain.

▶ The surface area of a solid is the sum of the areas of all its faces.

Recall Prior Knowledge

Identifying rectangular prisms and triangular prisms

A prism is a solid figure with two parallel congruent bases joined by rectangular faces. It is named according to the shape of its base.

Rectangular prisms

The base of each prism is a rectangle.

Triangular prisms

The base of each prism is a triangle.

Measuring capacity and volume

Some units of measure for volume are liters and milliliters.

$$1 \text{ L} = 1{,}000 \text{ mL}$$

The pitcher holds 1 liter of liquid.
The volume of liquid in the pitcher is 1 liter.

The pitcher can hold more than 1 liter of liquid.
The capacity of the pitcher is more than 1 liter.

Identify each figure.

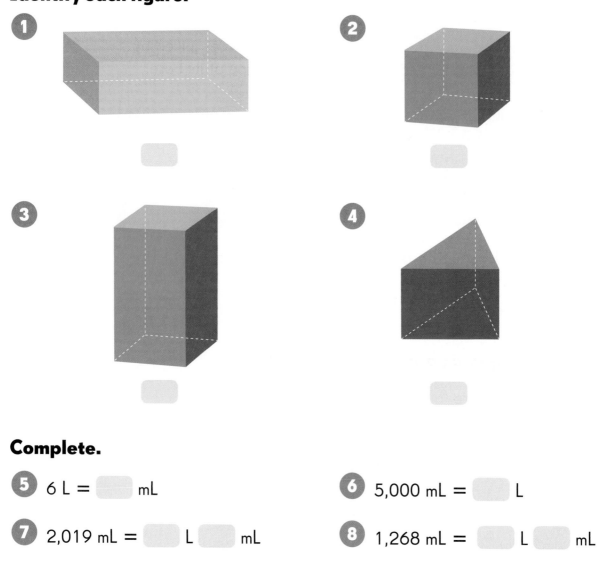

① ②

③ ④

Complete.

⑤ 6 L = [ ] mL

⑥ 5,000 mL = [ ] L

⑦ 2,019 mL = [ ] L [ ] mL

⑧ 1,268 mL = [ ] L [ ] mL

Solve.

⑨ The capacity of a pitcher is 8 liters. The pitcher is filled to the brim with water. Find the volume of water in the pitcher in milliliters.

⑩ The fuel tank of a car is half full. The volume of fuel in the tank is 25 liters. Find the capacity of the tank.

Lesson 15.1 Building Solids Using Unit Cubes

Lesson Objectives

- Build solids using unit cubes.
- Determine the number of unit cubes in an irregular solid.

Vocabulary
unit cube

Learn Build solids using unit cubes.

The solid shown is a **unit cube**.
It is a cube in which all the edges are 1 unit long.

A cube has 6 square faces.
All its faces are congruent.
It has 12 edges.
The lengths of all its edges are equal.

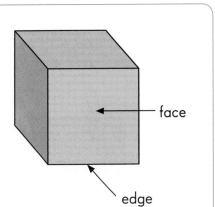

face

edge

This is another unit cube.

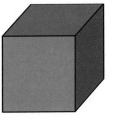

You can build solids using unit cubes.
This solid is made up of 2 unit cubes.

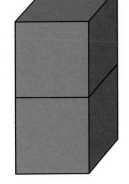

Hands-On Activity

Materials:
• 40 connecting cubes

STEP 1 Use connecting cubes to build these solids.

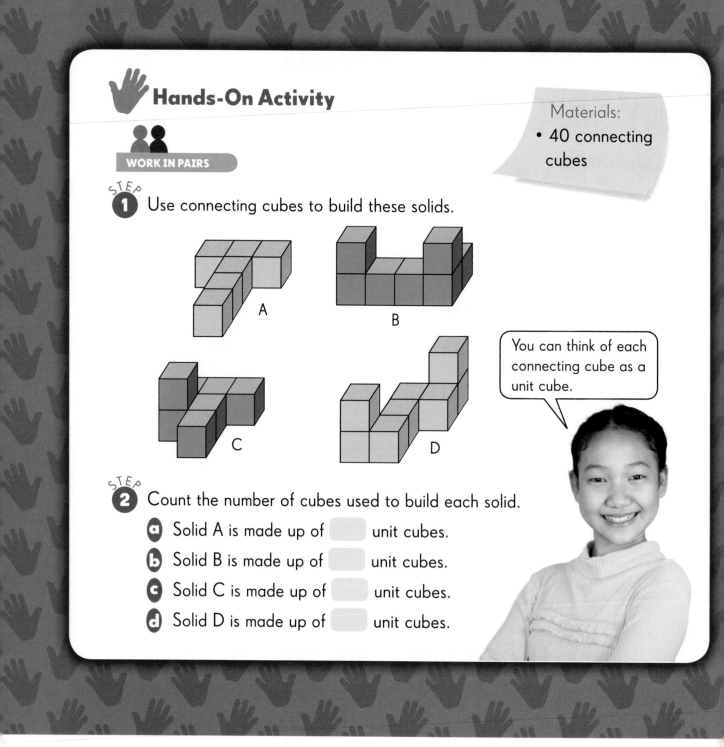

A

B

C

D

You can think of each connecting cube as a unit cube.

STEP 2 Count the number of cubes used to build each solid.

a Solid A is made up of ____ unit cubes.

b Solid B is made up of ____ unit cubes.

c Solid C is made up of ____ unit cubes.

d Solid D is made up of ____ unit cubes.

Guided Practice

Complete.

1 Each of these solids is made up of ____ unit cubes.

Complete.

2 The rectangular prism is made up of ____ unit cubes.

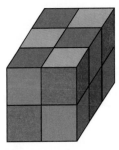

🔍 **Let's Explore!**

WORKING TOGETHER

Materials:
• 40 connecting cubes

Work in groups of four.

To build a solid using two or more connecting cubes, at least one face of a connecting cube must completely cover the face of another connecting cube.

Here are two views of the same solid built using two connecting cubes.

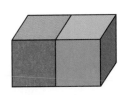

You can think of each connecting cube as a unit cube.

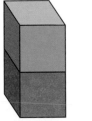

Find out how many different solids you can build.

1 Build as many different solids as you can using 3 unit cubes.

I can build ____ different solids.

2 Build as many different solids as you can using 4 unit cubes.

I can build ____ different solids.

Let's Practice

Find the number of unit cubes used to build each solid.
Some of the cubes may be hidden.

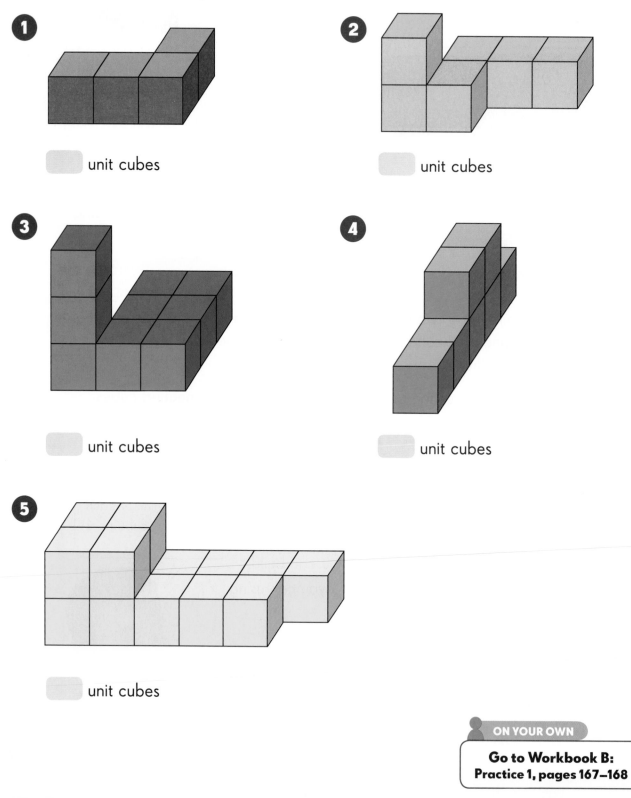

1

_____ unit cubes

2

_____ unit cubes

3

_____ unit cubes

4

_____ unit cubes

5

_____ unit cubes

ON YOUR OWN

Go to Workbook B:
Practice 1, pages 167–168

15.2 Drawing Cubes and Rectangular Prisms

Lesson Objectives

* Draw a cube and a rectangular prism on dot paper.
* Complete a partially drawn cube and rectangular prism on dot paper.

Learn **Draw cubes and rectangular prisms on dot paper.**

This is a drawing of a unit cube on dot paper.

These are drawings of rectangular prisms. These prisms are built from unit cubes.

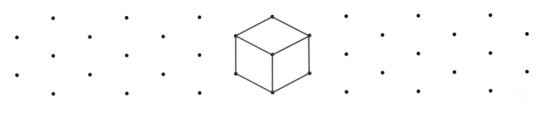

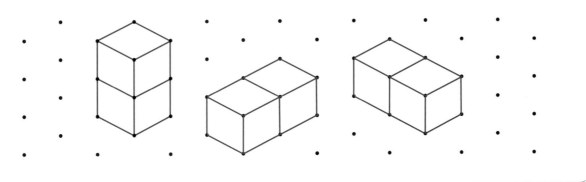

Guided Practice

Draw.

1. Copy the rectangular prisms above on dot paper. For each prism, draw one more unit cube to make a larger rectangular prism.

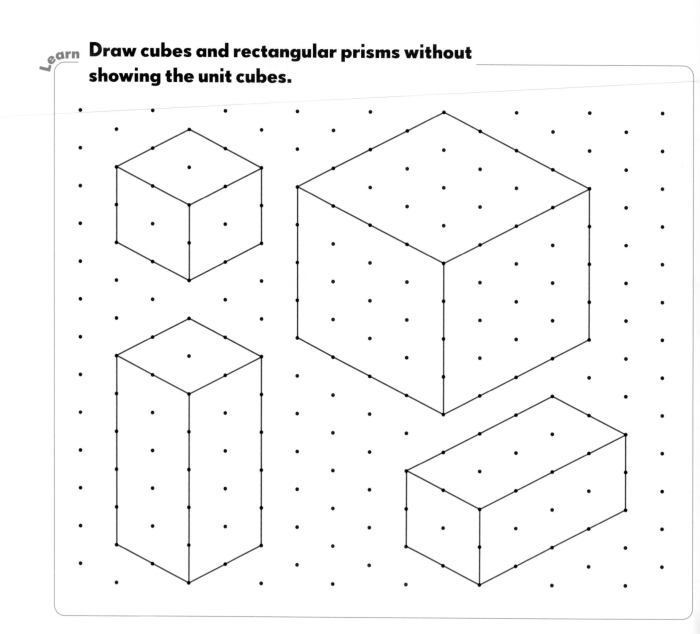

Draw cubes and rectangular prisms without showing the unit cubes.

Guided Practice

Copy and complete the drawings on dot paper.

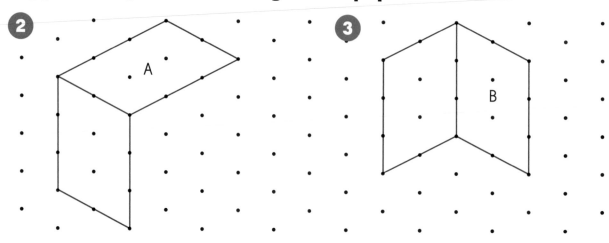

2 A

3 B

Copy and complete the drawings on dot paper.

4

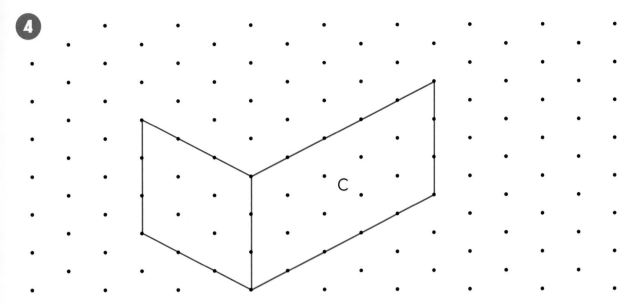

C

Draw each cube or rectangular prism on dot paper.

5

6

7

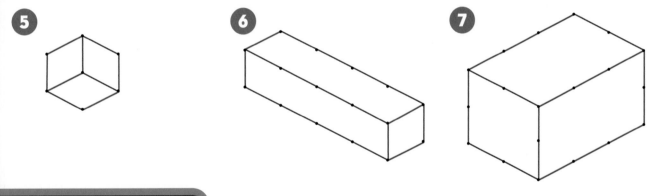

Let's Practice

Draw each rectangular prism on dot paper.

1

2

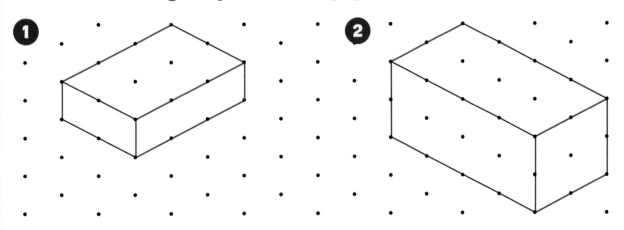

Copy and complete the drawing of each cube or rectangular prism on dot paper.

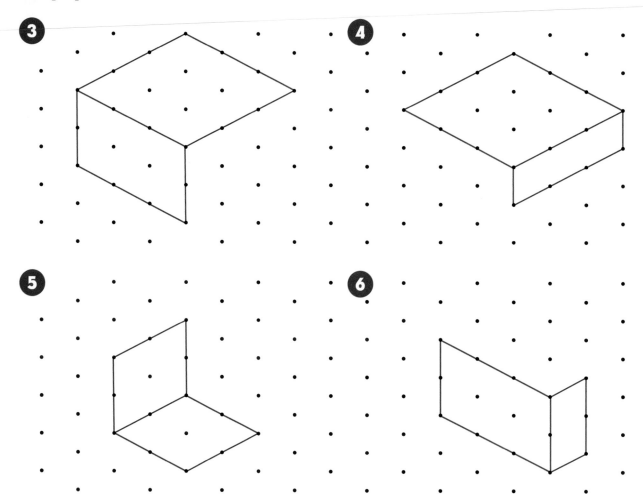

3

4

5

6

Draw on dot paper.

7 Draw a cube with edges 3 times as long as the edges of this unit cube.

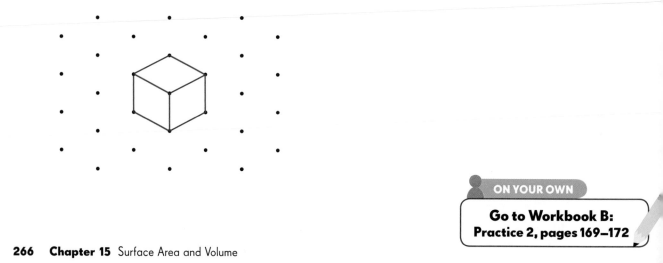

ON YOUR OWN

Go to Workbook B:
Practice 2, pages 169–172

15.3 Nets and Surface Area

Lesson Objective

• Find the surface area of a prism by adding the area of each face.

Learn Find the surface area of a cube.

A wooden box is painted red all over.

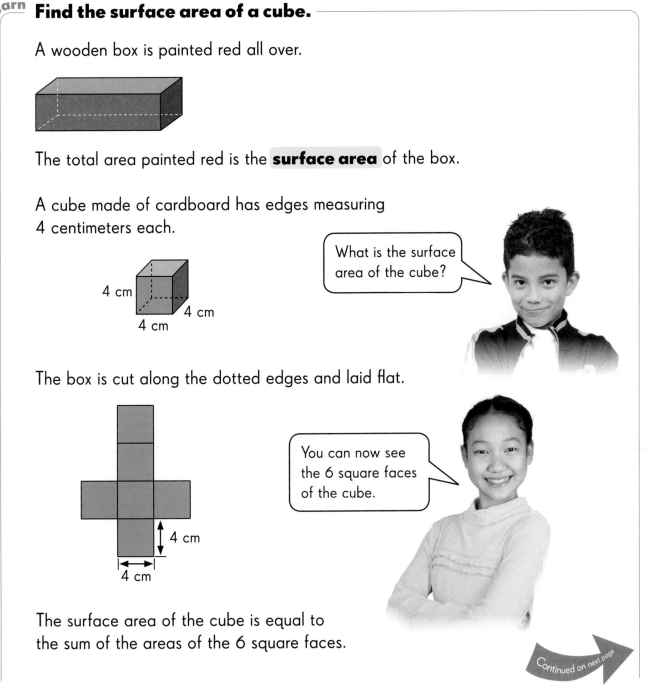

The total area painted red is the **surface area** of the box.

A cube made of cardboard has edges measuring
4 centimeters each.

4 cm
4 cm
4 cm

What is the surface
area of the cube?

The box is cut along the dotted edges and laid flat.

You can now see
the 6 square faces
of the cube.

4 cm

4 cm

The surface area of the cube is equal to
the sum of the areas of the 6 square faces.

Continued on next page

> The 6 square faces form a net of the cube.
> The area of the net is the surface area of the cube.

Area of one square face = 4 × 4
                        = 16 cm²

Surface area of the cube = 16 + 16 + 16 + 16 + 16 + 16
                         = 6 × 16
                         = 96 cm²

Guided Practice

Complete.

1 A cube has edges measuring 5 inches each. Find the surface area of the cube.

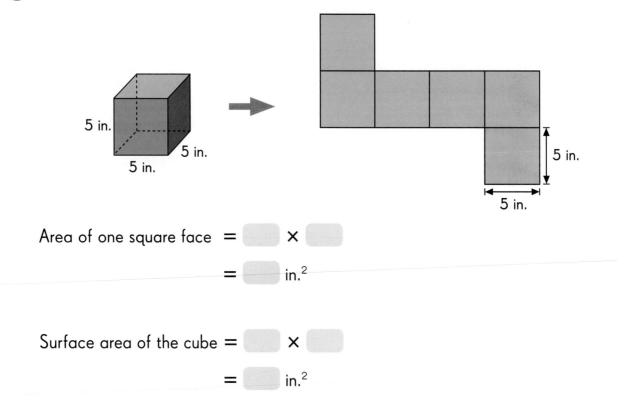

Area of one square face = ☐ × ☐

                        = ☐ in.²

Surface area of the cube = ☐ × ☐

                         = ☐ in.²

Find the surface area of a rectangular prism.

A rectangular prism is 10 inches long, 6 inches wide and 5 inches high.

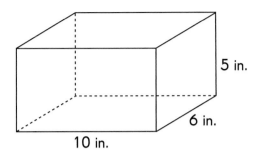

What is the surface area of the rectangular prism?

A rectangular prism has 6 faces. Its opposite faces are congruent rectangles. The 6 faces form a net of the rectangular prism.

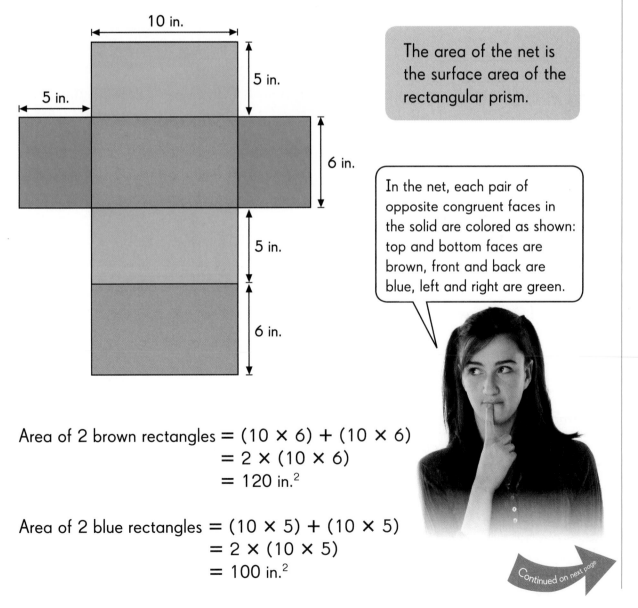

The area of the net is the surface area of the rectangular prism.

In the net, each pair of opposite congruent faces in the solid are colored as shown: top and bottom faces are brown, front and back are blue, left and right are green.

Area of 2 brown rectangles = $(10 \times 6) + (10 \times 6)$
$= 2 \times (10 \times 6)$
$= 120$ in.^{2}

Area of 2 blue rectangles = $(10 \times 5) + (10 \times 5)$
$= 2 \times (10 \times 5)$
$= 100$ in.^{2}

Continued on next page

Area of 2 green rectangles = (6 × 5) + (6 × 5)
                          = 2 × (6 × 5)
                          = 60 in.²

Surface area of the rectangular prism = 120 + 100 + 60
                                       = 280 in.²

Guided Practice

Complete.

② A rectangular prism measures 8 inches by 4 inches by 10 inches.
Find the surface area of the prism.

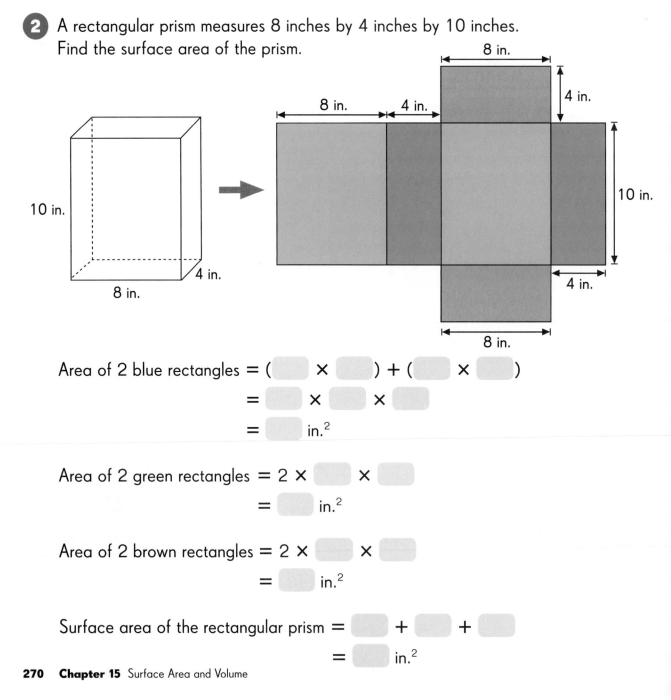

Area of 2 blue rectangles = (⬚ × ⬚) + (⬚ × ⬚)
                          = ⬚ × ⬚ × ⬚
                          = ⬚ in.²

Area of 2 green rectangles = 2 × ⬚ × ⬚
                           = ⬚ in.²

Area of 2 brown rectangles = 2 × ⬚ × ⬚
                           = ⬚ in.²

Surface area of the rectangular prism = ⬚ + ⬚ + ⬚
                                       = ⬚ in.²

Find the surface area of a triangular prism.

This is a triangular prism with its measurements shown.

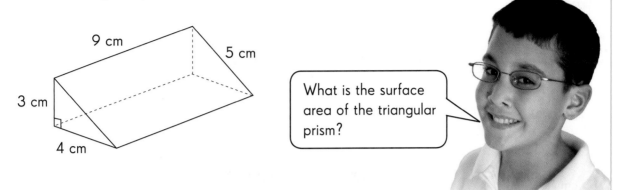

What is the surface area of the triangular prism?

This is a net of the triangular prism. Two of its faces are congruent **right triangles**. The other faces are rectangles which are not congruent.

Area of 2 brown triangles $= 2 \times (\frac{1}{2} \times 3 \times 4)$

$= 2 \times 6$

$= 12 \text{ cm}^2$

Area of the green rectangle $= 9 \times 3$

$= 27 \text{ cm}^2$

Area of the blue rectangle $= 9 \times 4$

$= 36 \text{ cm}^2$

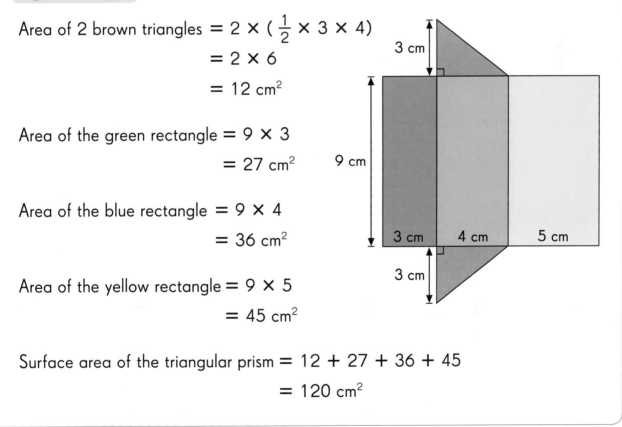

Area of the yellow rectangle $= 9 \times 5$

$= 45 \text{ cm}^2$

Surface area of the triangular prism $= 12 + 27 + 36 + 45$

$= 120 \text{ cm}^2$

Guided Practice

Complete.

3 Find the surface area of the triangular prism.

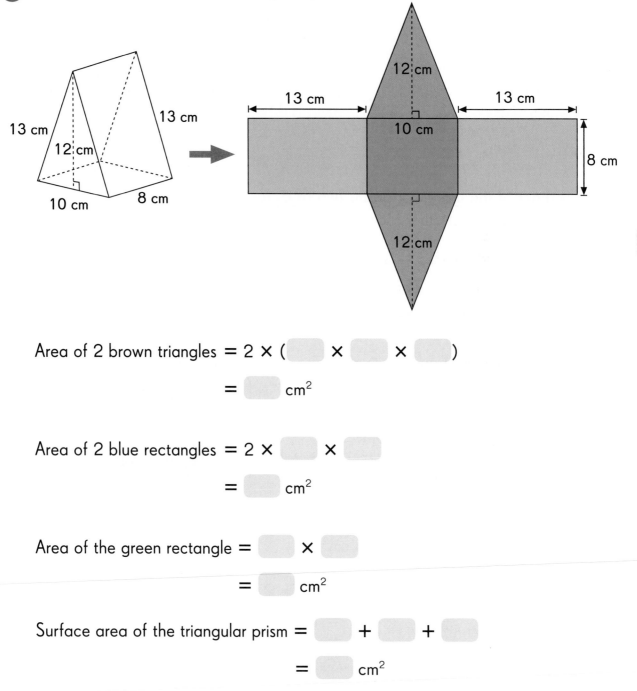

Area of 2 brown triangles = 2 × ([ ] × [ ] × [ ])

= [ ] cm²

Area of 2 blue rectangles = 2 × [ ] × [ ]

= [ ] cm²

Area of the green rectangle = [ ] × [ ]

= [ ] cm²

Surface area of the triangular prism = [ ] + [ ] + [ ]

= [ ] cm²

Let's Explore!

Copy and complete the table. Then answer the questions.

Length of Edge of Cube	Area of One Square Face	Surface Area of Cube
1 in.		
2 in.		
4 in.		
8 in.		

1 What do you observe about the surface area of a cube when the length of each edge is doubled?

When the length of each edge is doubled, the surface area is ⬜ times that of the original cube.

2 A cube has a surface area of 294 square inches. What is the surface area of the enlarged cube if the length of each edge is doubled?

The surface area of the enlarged cube is ⬜ square inches.

Let's Practice

Find the surface area of the cube.

1 This cube has edges measuring 8 inches each.

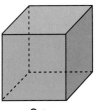

8 in.

Find the surface area of each prism.

2 This is a rectangular prism measuring 15 inches by 8 inches by 5 inches.

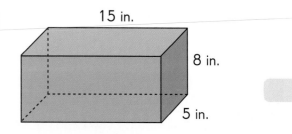

15 in.

8 in.

5 in.

3 This is a triangular prism with the measurements shown.

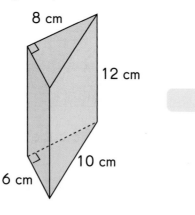

8 cm

12 cm

10 cm

6 cm

Solve.

4 A rectangular block of wood measures 6 feet by 6 feet by 10 feet. Find the surface area of the block of wood.

5 A cubical tank, made of metal, has an open top. It has edges measuring 4 feet each. Find the area of the metal sheet, in square feet, used to make the tank.

6 This net of a solid has 6 congruent squares.

a What is the solid formed from the net?

b Each square has sides measuring 5 inches each. Find the surface area of the solid.

ON YOUR OWN

**Go to Workbook B:
Practice 3, pages 173–176**

15.4 Understanding and Measuring Volume

Lesson Objectives

- Find the volumes of cubes and rectangular prisms.
- Find the volume of a solid constructed from unit cubes.
- Compare volumes of cubes, rectangular prisms, and other objects.

Learn **Compare the volumes of objects.**

The volume of an object is the amount of space it occupies.

Guided Practice

Compare the volumes of the objects.
Which object has a greater volume?

1

softball

OR

football

The ⬚ has a greater volume.

2

gift box

OR

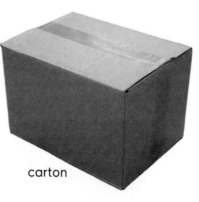

carton

The ⬚ has a greater volume.

3

OR

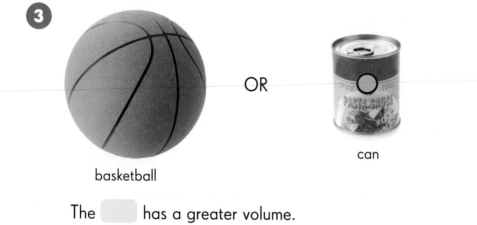

basketball

can

The ⬚ has a greater volume.

Find the volumes of cubes and rectangular prisms in cubic units.

The volume of a cube or rectangular prism is the number of cubic units needed to make it.

This is a unit cube. It has a volume of 1 cubic unit.

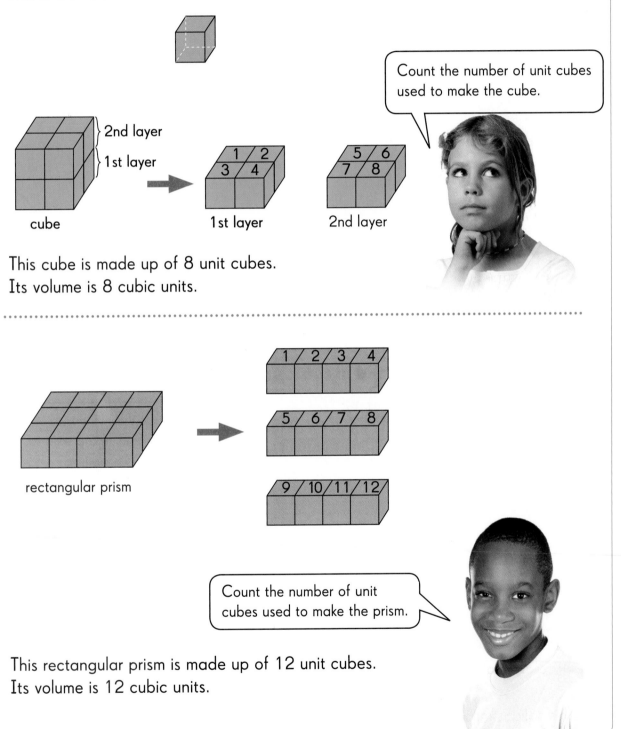

Count the number of unit cubes used to make the cube.

This cube is made up of 8 unit cubes.
Its volume is 8 cubic units.

Count the number of unit cubes used to make the prism.

This rectangular prism is made up of 12 unit cubes.
Its volume is 12 cubic units.

Guided Practice

These prisms are made up of unit cubes.
Find the volume of each prism.

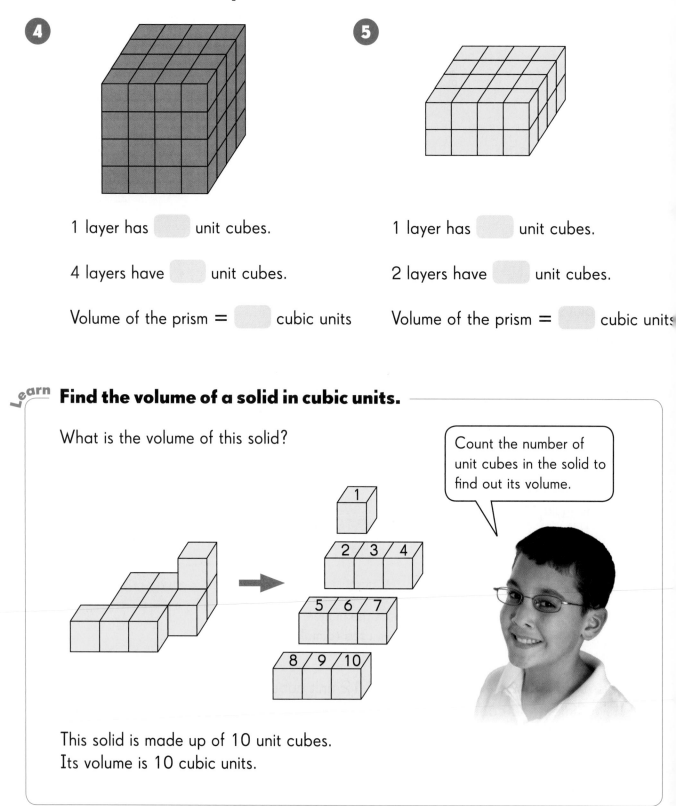

4

1 layer has ⬜ unit cubes.

4 layers have ⬜ unit cubes.

Volume of the prism = ⬜ cubic units

5

1 layer has ⬜ unit cubes.

2 layers have ⬜ unit cubes.

Volume of the prism = ⬜ cubic units

ᴸᵉᵃʳⁿ **Find the volume of a solid in cubic units.**

What is the volume of this solid?

> Count the number of unit cubes in the solid to find out its volume.

This solid is made up of 10 unit cubes.
Its volume is 10 cubic units.

Guided Practice

These solids are made up of unit cubes. Find the volume of each solid.

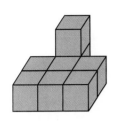

Volume of solid = ____ cubic units

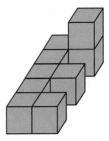 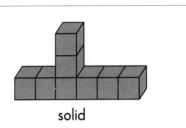

Volume of solid = ____ cubic units

Learn Compare the volumes of solids.

cube

Volume = 8 cubic units

rectangular prism

Volume = 16 cubic units

solid

Volume = 8 cubic units

The cube or solid has a **lesser** volume than the rectangular prism.
The cube has the **same** volume as the solid.
The rectangular prism has a **greater** volume than the cube or solid.

Guided Practice

Find the volume of each solid. Then compare their volumes.

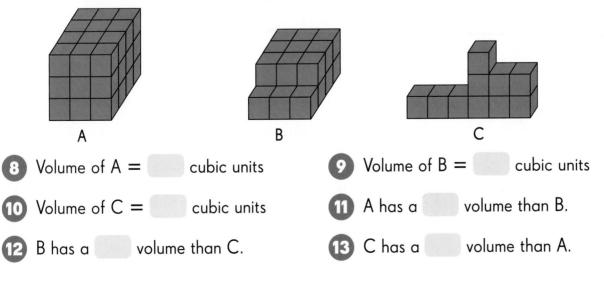

A   B   C

8 Volume of A = ____ cubic units

9 Volume of B = ____ cubic units

10 Volume of C = ____ cubic units

11 A has a ____ volume than B.

12 B has a ____ volume than C.

13 C has a ____ volume than A.

Find the volume of a solid using units of measurements.

These are some units of measurements for volume.

1 cubic centimeter (cm³)

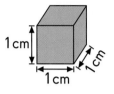

Length of each edge of the cube is 1 centimeter.
Volume of cube = 1 cm³

1 cubic inch (in.³)

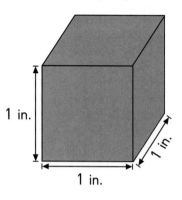

Length of each edge of the cube is 1 inch.
Volume of cube = 1 in.³

1 cubic foot (ft³)

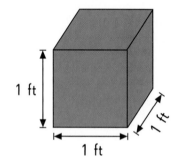

Length of each edge of the cube is 1 foot.
Volume of cube = 1 ft³

1 cubic meter (m³)

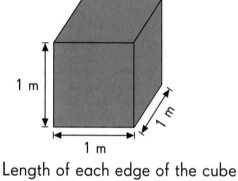

Length of each edge of the cube is 1 meter.
Volume of cube = 1 m³

This rectangular prism is made up of sixteen 1-inch cubes.

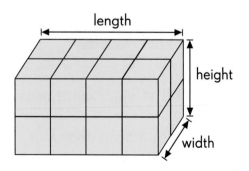

Length = 4 in.
Width = 2 in.
Height = 2 in.
Volume of rectangular prism = 16 in.³

Guided Practice

Complete.

14 This solid is made up of 1-foot cubes.

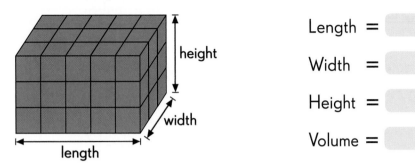

Length = ⬜ ft

Width = ⬜ ft

Height = ⬜ ft

Volume = ⬜ ft³

^{earn} **Compare the volumes of solids.**

These solids are made up of 1-centimeter cubes.

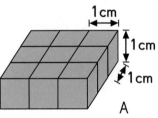

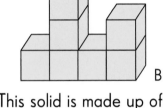

This prism is made up of nine 1-centimeter cubes.
Volume = 9 cm³

This solid is made up of seven 1-centimeter cubes.
Volume = 7 cm³

9 cm³ is greater than 7 cm³. A has a greater volume than B.

Guided Practice

**These solids are made up of 1-inch cubes.
Decide which solid has a greater volume.**

15

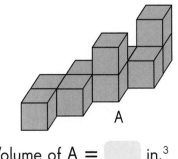

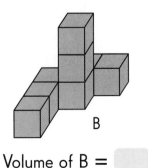

Volume of A = ⬜ in.³

Volume of B = ⬜ in.³

⬜ has a greater volume than ⬜ .

 **Hands-On Activity**

 WORK IN PAIRS

 STEP 1 Build this rectangular prism using twelve connecting cubes. The volume of the rectangular prism is [   ] cubic units.

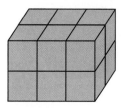

 STEP 2 Rearrange the cubes to build solid A. The volume of solid A is [   ] cubic units.

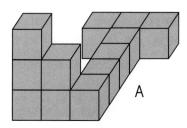

A

 STEP 3 Rearrange the cubes to build solid B. The volume of solid B is [   ] cubic units.

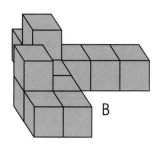

B

 STEP 4 Build two other solids using the twelve cubes.
What is the volume of each solid?
What do you notice about the volume of these different solids?
They have the [   ] volume.

Let's Explore!

WORK IN PAIRS

Materials:
• 12 connecting cubes

STEP
1 Build all the possible cubes and rectangular prisms using eight, eleven and twelve connecting cubes.

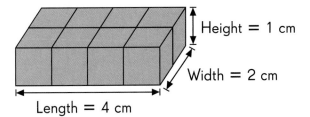

Height = 1 cm

Width = 2 cm

Length = 4 cm

STEP
2 Find the length, width, and height of the rectangular prisms you have built. Assume that the length of each edge of a cube is 1 centimeter. Record your answers in a copy of the table. Then find the volumes.

Number of 1-cm Cubes	Length (cm)	Width (cm)	Height (cm)	Volume (cm³)
8	4	2	1	8
11				
12				

What do you notice when you multiply the length, width, and height of each prism?

Let's Practice

These solids are made up of unit cubes.
Find the volume of each solid.

1

Volume = ⬚ cubic units

2

Volume = ⬚ cubic units

These solids are made up of 1-centimeter cubes.
Find the volume of each solid.

3

Volume = ⬚ cm^3

4

Volume = ⬚ cm^3

5

Volume = ⬚ cm^3

6

Volume = ⬚ cm^3

Find the volume of each solid. Then compare their volumes.

 7 These rectangular prisms are built using 1-inch cubes.

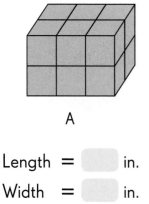

A

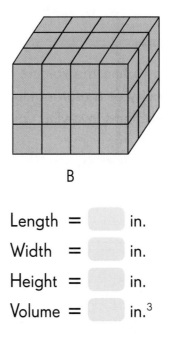

B

Length = ⬜ in.

Width = ⬜ in.

Height = ⬜ in.

Volume = ⬜ in.^{3}

A has a ⬜ volume than B.

Length = ⬜ in.

Width = ⬜ in.

Height = ⬜ in.

Volume = ⬜ in.^{3}

8 These solids are built using 1-foot cubes.

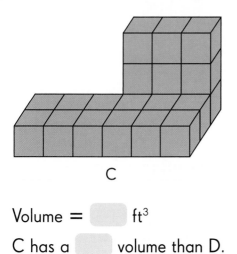

C

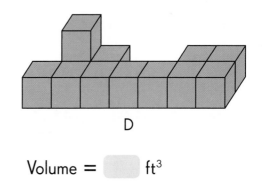

D

Volume = ⬜ ft^3

C has a ⬜ volume than D.

Volume = ⬜ ft^3

ON YOUR OWN

**Go to Workbook B:
Practice 4, pages 177–180**

15.5 Volume of a Rectangular Prism and Liquid

Lesson Objectives

- Use a formula to find the volume of a rectangular prism.
- Find the capacity of a rectangular container.
- Solve word problems involving volume of rectangular prisms and liquids.

Learn Identify the length, width, and height of a rectangular prism.

All the faces of a rectangular prism are rectangles.

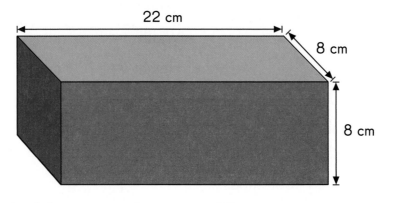

The length of this rectangular prism is 22 centimeters.

Its width is 8 centimeters.

Its height is 8 centimeters.

Guided Practice

Find the length, width, and height of each rectangular prism.

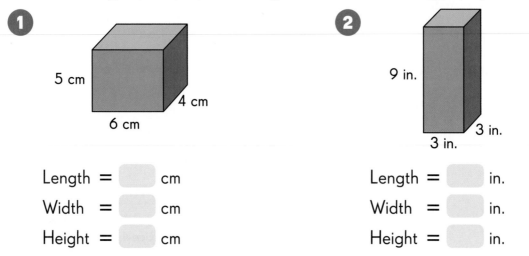

1

5 cm
4 cm
6 cm

Length = ☐ cm

Width = ☐ cm

Height = ☐ cm

2

9 in.
3 in.
3 in.

Length = ☐ in.

Width = ☐ in.

Height = ☐ in.

Find the length, width, and height of each rectangular prism.

3

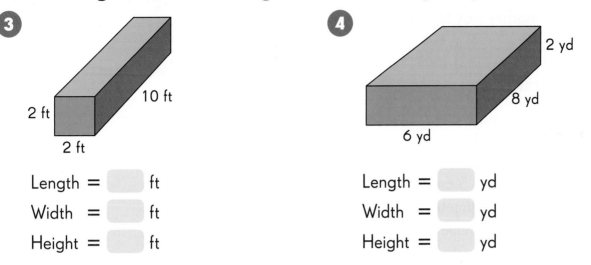

2 ft
10 ft
2 ft

Length = [ ] ft

Width = [ ] ft

Height = [ ] ft

4

2 yd
8 yd
6 yd

Length = [ ] yd

Width = [ ] yd

Height = [ ] yd

earn **Find the volume of a rectangular prism.**

This rectangular prism is made up of 1-centimeter cubes.

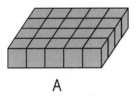

A

There are twenty 1-centimeter cubes in A.
The volume of A is 20 cubic centimeters.

Add another layer of 1-centimeter cubes to build B.

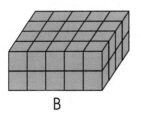

B

There are 2 layers of 1-centimeter cubes.
Each layer is made up of twenty 1-centimeter cubes.
20 + 20 = 40
There are forty 1-centimeter cubes in B.
The volume of B is 40 cubic centimeters.

Continued on next page

Here is another way to find the volume of B.

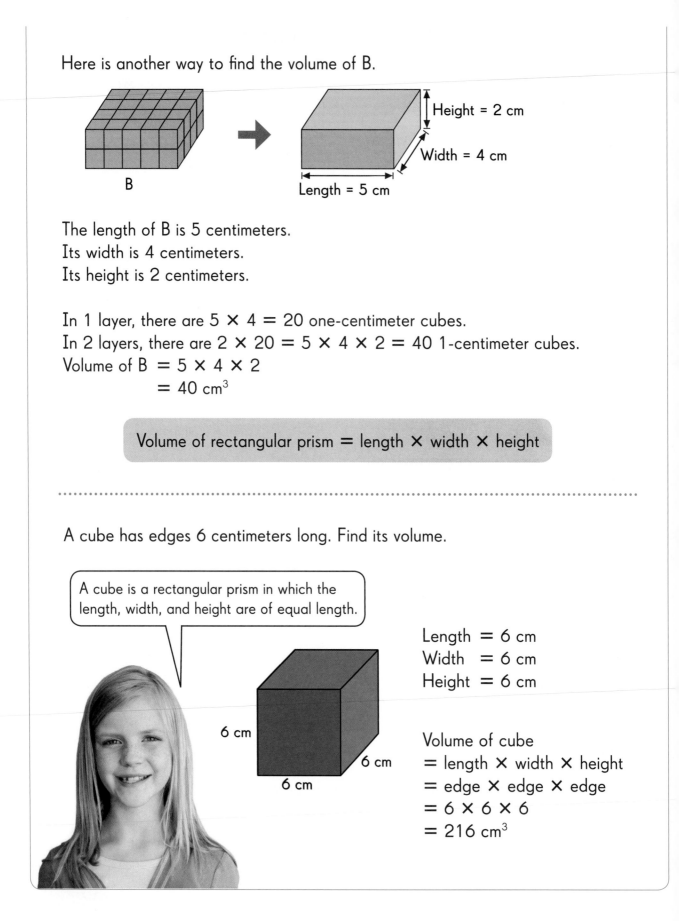

The length of B is 5 centimeters.
Its width is 4 centimeters.
Its height is 2 centimeters.

In 1 layer, there are $5 \times 4 = 20$ one-centimeter cubes.
In 2 layers, there are $2 \times 20 = 5 \times 4 \times 2 = 40$ 1-centimeter cubes.
Volume of B $= 5 \times 4 \times 2$
$\qquad\quad = 40$ cm^3

Volume of rectangular prism = length × width × height

A cube has edges 6 centimeters long. Find its volume.

A cube is a rectangular prism in which the
length, width, and height are of equal length.

6 cm
6 cm
6 cm

Length = 6 cm
Width = 6 cm
Height = 6 cm

Volume of cube
$=$ length × width × height
$=$ edge × edge × edge
$= 6 \times 6 \times 6$
$= 216$ cm^3

Guided Practice

Find the volume of each cube.

5 Edge length = 14 cm

Volume = edge × ▢ × ▢

= ▢ × ▢ × ▢

= ▢ cm³

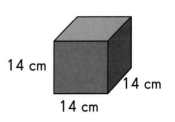

14 cm
14 cm
14 cm

6 Edge length = 22 ft

Volume = ▢ × ▢ × ▢

= ▢ ft³

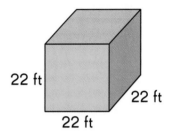

22 ft
22 ft
22 ft

Find the volume of each rectangular prism.

7 Length = 26 in.

Width = 12 in.

Height = 8 in.

Volume = length × ▢ × height

= ▢ × ▢ × ▢

= ▢ in.³

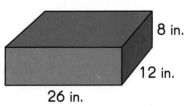

8 in.
12 in.
26 in.

8 Length = 15 m

Width = 14 m

Height = 9 m

Volume = ▢ × width × ▢

= ▢ × ▢ × ▢

= ▢ m³

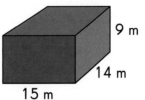

9 m
14 m
15 m

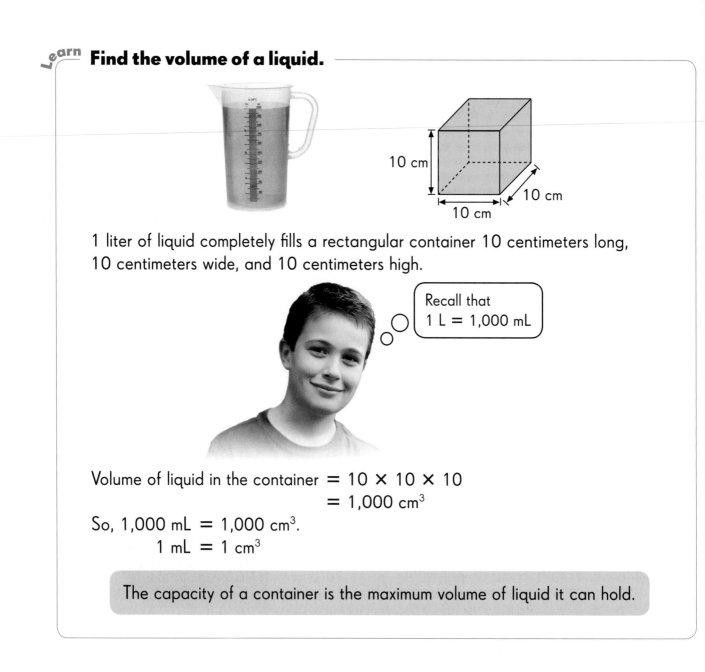

Learn Find the volume of a liquid.

10 cm

10 cm

10 cm

1 liter of liquid completely fills a rectangular container 10 centimeters long, 10 centimeters wide, and 10 centimeters high.

Recall that
1 L = 1,000 mL

Volume of liquid in the container = 10 × 10 × 10
                                               = 1,000 cm³

So, 1,000 mL = 1,000 cm³.
       1 mL = 1 cm³

The capacity of a container is the maximum volume of liquid it can hold.

Guided Practice

Write in cubic centimeters.

9 850 mL = ☐ cm³

10 2 L = ☐ cm³

11 4 L 55 mL = ☐ cm³

12 12 L 5 mL = ☐ cm³

Write in liters and milliliters.

13 530 cm³ = ☐

14 1,025 cm³ = ☐

15 7,005 cm³ = ☐

16 15,060 cm³ = ☐

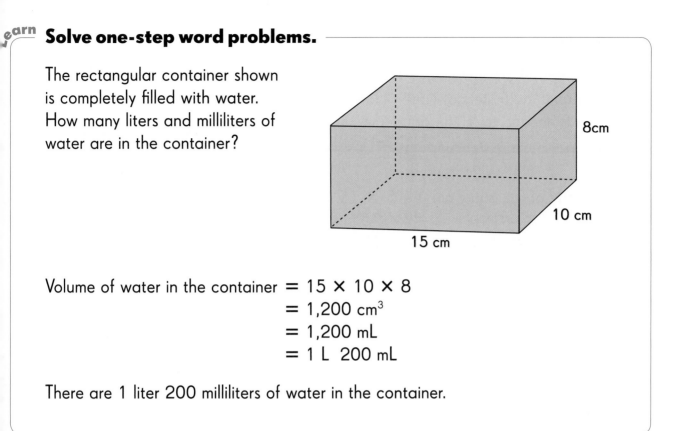

Solve one-step word problems.

The rectangular container shown is completely filled with water. How many liters and milliliters of water are in the container?

8cm

10 cm

15 cm

Volume of water in the container = 15 × 10 × 8
= 1,200 cm³
= 1,200 mL
= 1 L 200 mL

There are 1 liter 200 milliliters of water in the container.

Guided Practice

Solve.

17 Find the capacity of the box shown in liters and milliliters.

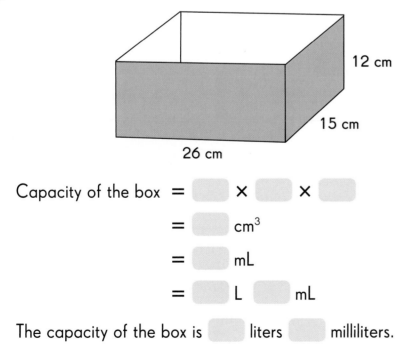

12 cm

15 cm

26 cm

Capacity of the box = ☐ × ☐ × ☐

= ☐ cm³

= ☐ mL

= ☐ L ☐ mL

The capacity of the box is ☐ liters ☐ milliliters.

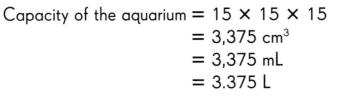

Solve two-step word problems.

Each edge of an aquarium is 15 centimeters long.
It contains 1.25 liters of water. How much more
water is needed to fill the aquarium completely?
Give your answer in liters. (1 L = 1,000 cm³)

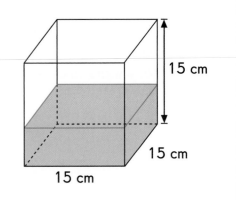

Capacity of the aquarium = 15 × 15 × 15
$$= 3,375 \text{ cm}^3$$
$$= 3,375 \text{ mL}$$
$$= 3.375 \text{ L}$$

Volume of water in the aquarium = 1.25 L

Volume of water needed to fill the aquarium completely
= 3.375 − 1.25
= 2.125 L

2.125 liters of water are needed to fill the aquarium completely.

Guided Practice

Solve.

18 There are 1.75 liters of water in the rectangular container shown.
How much more water is needed to fill the container completely?
(1 L = 1,000 cm³)

Capacity of the rectangular container

= ☐ × ☐ × ☐

= ☐ cm³

= ☐ L

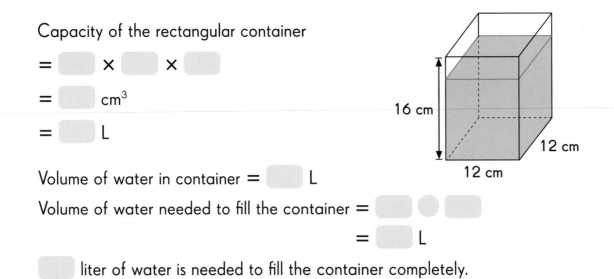

Volume of water in container = ☐ L

Volume of water needed to fill the container = ☐ ● ☐

= ☐ L

☐ liter of water is needed to fill the container completely.

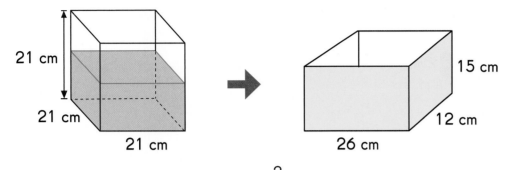

Solve three-step word problems.

The cubical tank on the left is $\frac{2}{3}$ full. The water in it is then poured into the rectangular tank on the right until it is full. How much water is left in the cubical tank? Give your answer in milliliters. (1 cm³ = 1 mL)

Volume of water in the cubical tank $= \frac{2}{3} \times 21 \times 21 \times 21$

$= 6{,}174$ cm³ $= 6{,}174$ mL

Capacity of the rectangular tank $= 26 \times 12 \times 15$

$= 4{,}680$ cm³ $= 4{,}680$ mL

Volume of water left in the cubical tank $= 6{,}174 - 4{,}680 = 1{,}494$ mL

The cubical tank has 1,494 milliliters of water left.

Guided Practice

Complete.

19 A rectangular tank shown is filled with water to $\frac{1}{4}$ of its height. Water from a tap flows into the tank at 2.5 liters a minute. How much water is in the tank after 5 minutes? Give your answer in liters. (1 L = 1000 cm³)

Volume of water in the tank

$= \boxed{} \times \boxed{} \times \boxed{} \times \boxed{}$

$= \boxed{}$ cm³

$= \boxed{}$ L

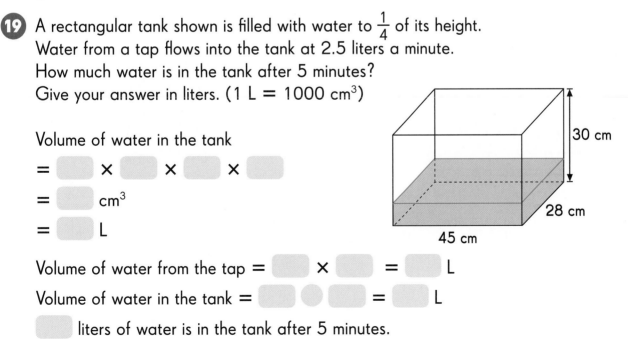

Volume of water from the tap $= \boxed{} \times \boxed{} = \boxed{}$ L

Volume of water in the tank $= \boxed{} \bigcirc \boxed{} = \boxed{}$ L

$\boxed{}$ liters of water is in the tank after 5 minutes.

Let's Practice

Find the volume of each prism.

1

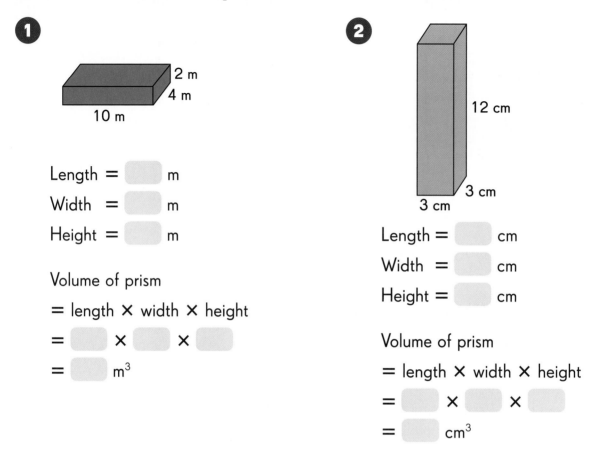

2 m
4 m
10 m

Length = [ ] m

Width = [ ] m

Height = [ ] m

Volume of prism

= length × width × height

= [ ] × [ ] × [ ]

= [ ] m³

2

12 cm

3 cm
3 cm

Length = [ ] cm

Width = [ ] cm

Height = [ ] cm

Volume of prism

= length × width × height

= [ ] × [ ] × [ ]

= [ ] cm³

Find the volume of water in each rectangular tank in milliliters.

3

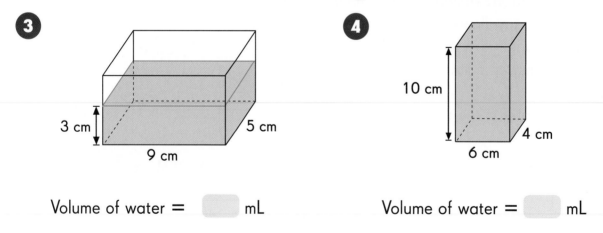

3 cm
5 cm
9 cm

Volume of water = [ ] mL

4

10 cm
4 cm
6 cm

Volume of water = [ ] mL

Find the volume of water in each rectangular tank in liters and milliliters.

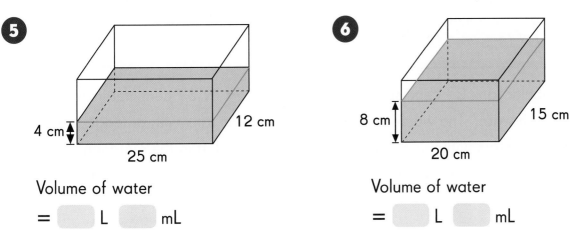

5

4 cm

25 cm

12 cm

Volume of water

= ⬚ L ⬚ mL

6

8 cm

20 cm

15 cm

Volume of water

= ⬚ L ⬚ mL

Solve.

7 A rectangular prism is 29 centimeters long, 15 centimeters wide, and 4 centimeters high. Find its volume.

8 A rectangular prism is 42 inches long, 32 inches wide, and 26 inches high. Find its volume.

9 A rectangular tub measures 15 meters by 11 meters by 5 meters. Find its capacity in cubic meters.

10 Find the volume of a cube with an edge length of 21 feet. Give your answer in cubic feet.

11 A rectangular tank 28 centimeters by 18 centimeters by 12 centimeters is filled with water completely. Then, 0.78 liter of water is drained from the tank. How much water is left in the tank? Give your answer in milliliters. (1 L = 1,000 cm^3)

12 A rectangular fish tank measures 55 centimeters by 24 centimeters by 22 centimeters. It contains 6.75 liters of water. How much water is needed to fill the tank completely? Give your answer in liters. (1 L = 1,000 cm^3)

13 A rectangular tank with a square base of side 60 centimeters and a height of 45 centimeters is $\frac{1}{3}$ filled with water. Water from a tap flows into the tank at 6 liters per minute. How long will it take to fill the tank completely? (1 L = 1,000 cm³)

14 A rectangular tank 27 centimeters by 20 centimeters by 37 centimeters is $\frac{1}{2}$ filled with water. The water is poured into a cubical tank with an edge length of 16 centimeters until it is $\frac{3}{4}$ full. How much water is left in the rectangular tank? Give your answer in liters rounded to one decimal place. (1 L = 1,000 cm³)

ON YOUR OWN

Go to Workbook B:
Practice 5 and 6, pages 181–192

CRITICAL THINKING SKILLS
Put On Your Thinking Cap!

PROBLEM SOLVING

1 These rectangular prisms are built using 4 and 6 one-centimeter cubes.

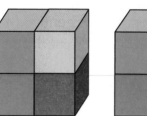 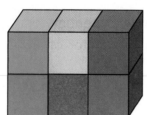

a How many different rectangular prisms can you build using 5, 6, 7, 8, and 9 one-centimeter cubes?

b List the length, width, and height of each rectangular prism you have built.

Put On Your Thinking Cap!

PROBLEM SOLVING

2

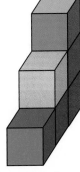

Staircase 1   Staircase 2   Staircase 3

a Look at the pattern of staircases formed using unit cubes.
Build staircases 4 and 5 using unit cubes.
Record your answers in a table like this:

Staircase	Number of Unit Cubes
1	1
2	1 + 2 = 3
3	1 + 2 + 3 = 6
4	
5	

b Without building Staircase 6, find the number of unit cubes it would take to build it.

c Find the number of unit cubes in Staircase 8.

d If each unit cube has an edge length of 1 centimeter, what are the volumes of staircases 9 and 10?

ON YOUR OWN

**Go to Workbook B:
Put on Your Thinking Cap!
pages 193 – 194**

Chapter Wrap Up

Study Guide

You have learned...

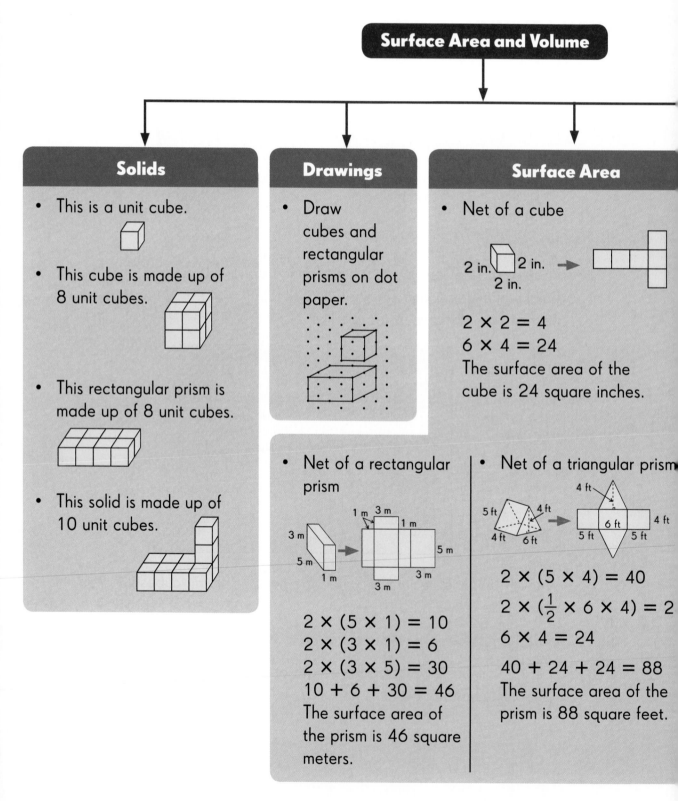

Surface Area and Volume

Solids

- This is a unit cube.

- This cube is made up of 8 unit cubes.

- This rectangular prism is made up of 8 unit cubes.

- This solid is made up of 10 unit cubes.

Drawings

- Draw cubes and rectangular prisms on dot paper.

Surface Area

- Net of a cube

  2 in. 2 in.
  2 in.

  $2 \times 2 = 4$
  $6 \times 4 = 24$
  The surface area of the cube is 24 square inches.

- Net of a rectangular prism

  3 m
  5 m
  1 m
  1 m 3 m
  1 m
  5 m
  3 m
  3 m

  $2 \times (5 \times 1) = 10$
  $2 \times (3 \times 1) = 6$
  $2 \times (3 \times 5) = 30$
  $10 + 6 + 30 = 46$
  The surface area of the prism is 46 square meters.

- Net of a triangular prism

  5 ft   4 ft
  4 ft
  4 ft   6 ft

  4 ft
  6 ft
  5 ft 5 ft
  4 ft

  $2 \times (5 \times 4) = 40$
  $2 \times (\frac{1}{2} \times 6 \times 4) = 2$
  $6 \times 4 = 24$

  $40 + 24 + 24 = 88$
  The surface area of the prism is 88 square feet.

BIG IDEAS

▶ The volume of cubes and rectangular prisms can be expressed as the number of cubic units they contain.

▶ The surface area of a solid is the sum of the areas of all its faces.

Volume of Solid

- The volume of an object is the amount of space it occupies.

A   B

A has a lesser volume than B.

Volume = 12 cubic units

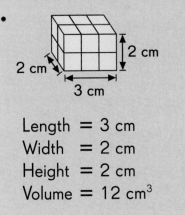

Length = 3 cm
Width = 2 cm
Height = 2 cm
Volume = 12 cm³

Volume of Rectangular Prism and of Liquid

- Volume of rectangular prism

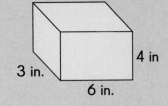

Volume of prism = length × width × height
= 6 × 3 × 4
= 72 in.³

- Conversion of measurement units
1 mL = 1 cm³
1 L = 1,000 mL

- Volume of liquid in a rectangular container

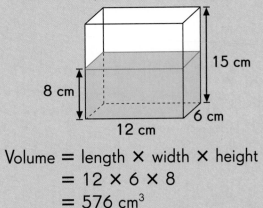

Volume = length × width × height
= 12 × 6 × 8
= 576 cm³

Chapter Review/Test

Vocabulary

Choose the correct word.

1 The [____] of a rectangular prism is the sum of the areas of all its faces.

2 A [____] is a cube in which all the edges are 1 unit long.

> unit cube
> surface area
> right triangle

Concepts and Skills

These solids are made up of unit cubes.
Find the volume of each solid.

3

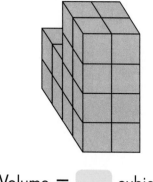

Volume = [____] cubic units

4

Volume = [____] cubic units

Draw on dot paper.

5 Copy this rectangular prism on dot paper.

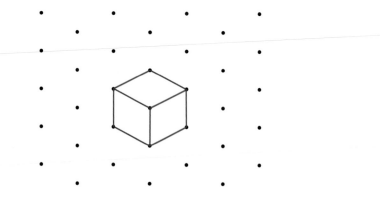

Find the surface area of each prism.

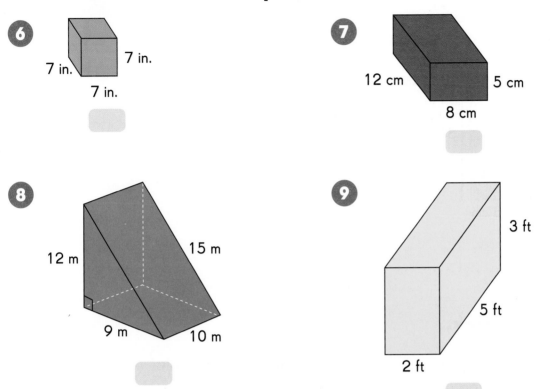

6 7 in.   7 in.   7 in.

7 12 cm   5 cm   8 cm

8 12 m   15 m   9 m   10 m

9 3 ft   5 ft   2 ft

Find the volume of each rectangular prism.

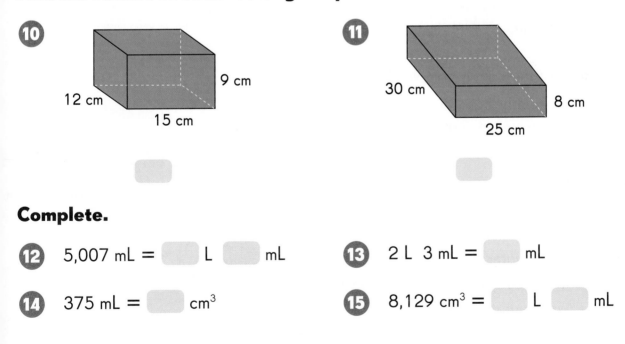

10 12 cm   9 cm   15 cm

11 30 cm   8 cm   25 cm

Complete.

12 5,007 mL = ___ L ___ mL

13 2 L 3 mL = ___ mL

14 375 mL = ___ cm³

15 8,129 cm³ = ___ L ___ mL

Find the volume of water in each rectangular container.

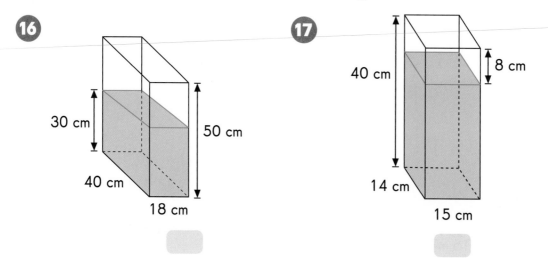

16 30 cm   50 cm   40 cm   18 cm

17 40 cm   8 cm   14 cm   15 cm

Problem Solving

Solve. Show your work.

18 A carton is 15 inches long, 10 inches wide and 12 inches high. Mindy wants to wrap up the carton. What is the minimum area of wrapping paper needed to cover the carton?

19 A rectangular container measures 8 feet by 6 feet by 4 feet. Find its volume.

20 The tank at the right is completely filled with water. If $\frac{2}{5}$ of the water from the tank is poured into another container, how much water is left in the tank?

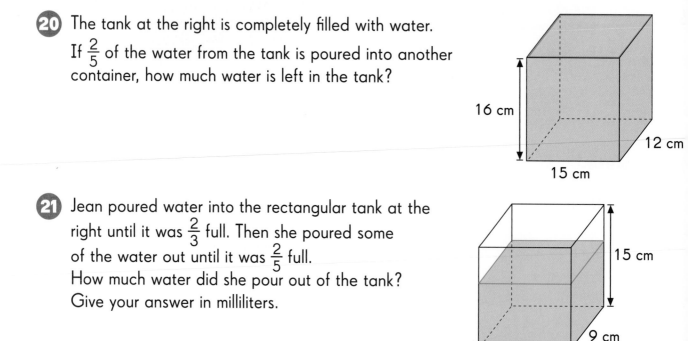

16 cm   12 cm   15 cm

21 Jean poured water into the rectangular tank at the right until it was $\frac{2}{3}$ full. Then she poured some of the water out until it was $\frac{2}{5}$ full. How much water did she pour out of the tank? Give your answer in milliliters.

15 cm   9 cm   13 cm

 **Focus Lessons**

9.2.a Multiplying Decimals by Powers of Ten

COMMON CORE

5.NBT.2 Explain patterns in the number of zeros of the product when multiplying a number by powers of 10, and **explain patterns in the placement of the decimal point when a decimal is multiplied** or divided **by a power of 10. Use whole-number exponents to denote powers of 10.**

Lesson Objective

- Multiply decimals by 10 squared or 10 cubed.

Learn **Multiply decimals by 10^2 or 10^3.**

Think about the rules you learned for multiplying whole numbers by 10^2 or 10^3. You can use these rules to help you multiply decimals by 10^2 or 10^3.

> Multiplying by 10 squared is the same as multiplying by 100. Multiplying by 10 cubed is the same as multiplying by 1,000.

a Find 0.125×10^2.

	Thousands	Hundreds	Tens	Ones		Tenths	Hundredths	Thousandths
0.125				0	.	1	2	5
0.125 × 10²		0	1	2	.	5		

$$0.125 \times 10^2 = 0.125 \times (10 \times 10)$$
$$= 0.125 \times 100$$
$$= 12.5$$

> When you multiply a decimal by 10^2 or 100, each digit of the decimal moves 2 places to the left in the place-value chart.

b Find 3.006×10^3.

	Thousands	Hundreds	Tens	Ones	Tenths	Hundredths	Thousandths
3.006				3 .	0	0	6
3.006 × 10²	3	0	0	6			

$$3.006 \times 10^3 = 3.006 \times (10 \times 10 \times 10)$$
$$= 3.006 \times 1,000$$
$$= 3,006$$

When you multiply a decimal by 10^3 or 1,000, each digit of the decimal moves 3 places to the left in the place-value chart.

Let's Practice

Multiply.

1 0.6×10^2

2 3.09×10^2

3 5.3×10^3

4 0.421×10^3

11.1.a Making and Interpreting Line Plots

COMMON CORE

5.MD.2. Make a line plot to display a data set of measurements in fractions of a unit 1/2, 1/4, 1/8. Use operations on fractions for this grade to solve problems involving information presented in line plots.

Lesson Objectives

- Make a line plot to represent data given in fractions of a unit.
- Use operations on fractions to solve problems from the information presented.

Learn **Use line plots to organize data.**

Emma carried out a science experiment. She measured the different volumes of colored water in ten identical beakers and recorded her data in a table.

Volume of Colored Water in Beakers

Volume (qt)	$\frac{1}{8}$	$\frac{1}{4}$	$\frac{3}{8}$	$\frac{1}{2}$
Number of Beakers	2	4	2	2

$\frac{2}{8} = \frac{1}{4}$ and $\frac{4}{8} = \frac{1}{2}$.

Emma then made a line plot to show the results of her experiment. Each ✗ represents 1 beaker.

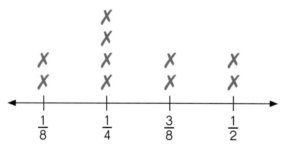

Volume of Colored Water in Beakers (qt)

ⓐ What is the total volume of the colored water in the ten beakers?

$$2 \times \frac{1}{8} + 4 \times \frac{1}{4} + 2 \times \frac{3}{8} + 2 \times \frac{1}{2} = 3$$

The total volume of the colored water in the ten beakers is 3 quarts.

ⓑ The total volume of the colored water in the ten beakers is redistributed equally into each beaker. What is the volume of colored water in each beaker now?

$$3 \div 10 = \frac{3}{10}$$

The volume of colored water in each beaker is now $\frac{3}{10}$ quart.

Jacob recorded the weights of ten slabs of cheese in the table below.

Weight of Slabs of Cheese

Weight (lb)	$\frac{1}{8}$	$\frac{1}{4}$	$\frac{3}{8}$	$\frac{1}{2}$
Number of Slabs	3	3	1	3

Make a line plot to show the data in the table.

Use the data in the line plot to answer the questions.

2 What is the total weight of the ten slabs of cheese?

3 The ten slabs of cheese are mixed together and redivided into equal portions. What is the weight of each portion?

The table shows the lengths of 15 sticks of clay.

Length of Sticks of Clay

Length (ft)	$\frac{1}{10}$	$\frac{1}{5}$	$\frac{3}{10}$	$\frac{2}{5}$	$\frac{1}{2}$
Number of Sticks	2	4	1	3	5

Make a line plot to show the data in the table.

Use the data in the line plot to answer the questions.

 What is the total length of the 15 sticks of clay?

6 The 15 sticks of clay are joined together and redivided into sticks of the same length. What is the length of each stick of clay now?

15.5.a Volume of a Rectangular Prism

COMMON CORE

5.MD.5.a. Apply the formulas
$V = l \times w \times h$ and $V = b \times h$ **for**
rectangular prisms to find volumes
of right rectangular prisms with
whole-number edge lengths in the
context of solving real world and
mathematical problems.

Lesson Objective

- Use a formula to find the volume of a rectangular prism.

Learn **Find the volume of a rectangular prism.**

This is a rectangular prism. The bases of a rectangular prism are rectangles.

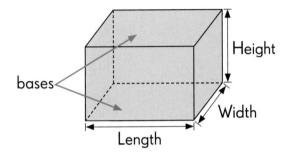

You have learned that the volume of a rectangular prism
= length × width × height.

> Volume = $\ell \times w \times h$

Since length × width = area of base, the volume of a rectangular prism
= area of base × height.

> Volume = $B \times h$

A rectangular tissue box has a height of 5 centimeters.
The area of its base is 105 square centimeters.
Find the volume of the tissue box.

$V = B \times h$
$\quad = 105 \times 5$
$\quad = 525 \text{ cm}^3$

5 cm

105 cm^2

The volume of the tissue box is 525 cubic centimeters.

Find the volume of each prism.

1

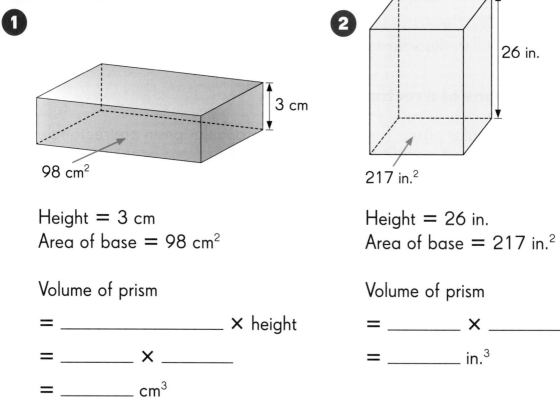

98 cm²

Height = 3 cm
Area of base = 98 cm²

Volume of prism

= _____ × height

= _____ × _____

= _____ cm³

2

26 in.

217 in.²

Height = 26 in.
Area of base = 217 in.²

Volume of prism

= _____ × _____

= _____ in.³

Solve.

3 A rectangular fish tank has a height of 12 feet. The area of its base is 169 square feet. Find the volume of the fish tank.

4 A rectangular container has a height of 34 centimeters. The area of its base is 399 square centimeters. Find the volume of the container.

15.5.b Volume of Solid Figures

COMMON CORE

5.MD.5.c. Recognize volume as additive. Find volumes of solid figures composed of two non-overlapping right rectangular prisms by adding the volumes of the non-overlapping parts, applying this technique to solve real world problems.

Lesson Objectives

- Find the volume of a solid figure composed of two rectangular prisms.
- Solve real-world problems involving the volume of a solid figure composed of two rectanglar prisms.

Learn **Find the volume of a solid figure composed of two rectangular prisms.**

This solid is made up of two rectangular prisms.

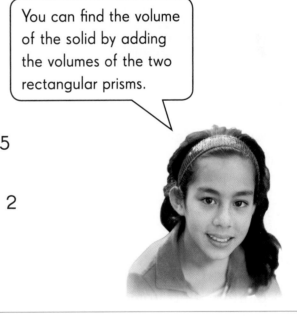

5 cm

2 cm

3 cm

4 cm

5 cm

> You can find the volume of the solid by adding the volumes of the two rectangular prisms.

Volume of yellow prism = 4 × 3 × 5
$$= 60 \text{ cm}^3$$

Volume of orange prism = 5 × 3 × 2
$$= 30 \text{ cm}^3$$

Volume of solid = 60 + 30
$$= 90 \text{ cm}^3$$

Let's Practice

Find the volume of each solid.

1

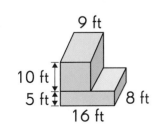

9 ft

10 ft

5 ft

8 ft

16 ft

2

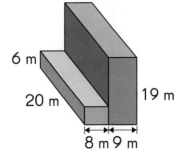

6 m

20 m

19 m

8 m 9 m

ᴸᵉᵃʳⁿ Find the volume of solid figures to solve real-world problems.

Kathleen buys a pet stairs for her dog. The stairs are made up of two rectangular wooden blocks. Find the volume of the pet stairs.

Total volume of the two rectangular blocks
$$= (18 \times 8 \times 12) + (18 \times 9 \times 7)$$
$$= 1{,}728 + 1{,}134$$
$$= 2{,}862 \text{ in.}^3$$

The volume of the pet stairs is 2,862 cubic inches.

12 in. 7 in. 18 in. 8 in. 9 in.

Let's Practice

Solve.

1 Jason has an eraser that is made up of two rectangular pieces of different colors. Find the volume of the eraser.

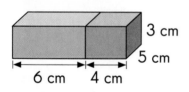

3 cm
5 cm
6 cm   4 cm

2 A platform bed frame is made up of two rectangular wooden blocks. Find the total volume of the wooden blocks.

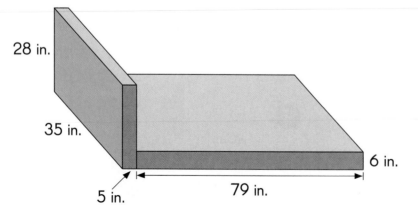

28 in.
35 in.
5 in.
79 in.
6 in.

Glossary

A ⎯⎯⎯⎯⎯⎯

- **acute triangle**

  A triangle with all angle
  measures less than 90°.

  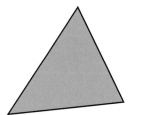

- **angles at a point**

  The sum of angle measures
  at a point is 360°.

  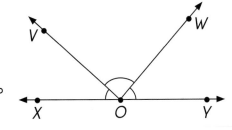

  $m\angle AOD + m\angle DOC + m\angle COB + m\angle AOB = 360°$

- **angles on a line**

  The sum of angle measures on
  a line is 180°.

  $m\angle XOV + m\angle VOW + m\angle WOY = 180°$

B

- ## base (of a solid figure)
  A special face of a solid figure.

C

- ## combinations
  A grouping of items or events. Placing these items or events in a different order does not create a new combination.

- ## cone
  A solid figure with one circular base, a curved surface, and a vertex.

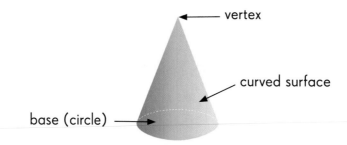

coordinate grid

A coordinate grid is used to locate points in a plane.
It has a horizontal number line and a vertical number line.

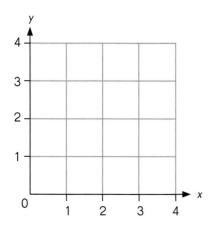

coordinate plane

See *coordinate grid*.

coordinates

An ordered pair of numbers that give the location of a point in the coordinate grid.

The coordinates of point *A* are (2, 3).

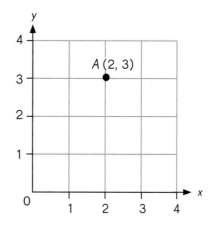

- **cylinder**

  A solid figure with two circular bases that are parallel and congruent, joined by a curved surface.

  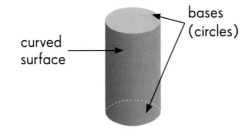

  curved surface

  bases (circles)

D

- **discount**

  A discount is the difference between the regular price and the selling price. It is the amount you save.

- **dividend**

  The number that is being divided. $5\overline{)7.75}$

  dividend

- **divisor**

  The number the dividend is being divided by. $5\overline{)7.75}$

  divisor

- ## double bar graph

  A bar graph that presents two sets of data for comparison.

  This graph compares the favorite yogurt flavor of students in Class 5A and Class 5B.

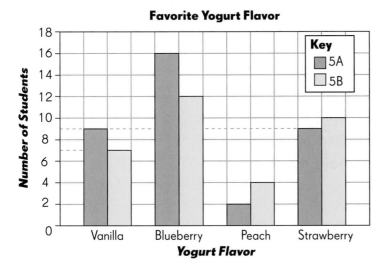

  Favorite Yogurt Flavor

- E ———————

- ## edge

  The line segment where two faces of a solid figure meet.

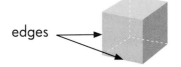

- ## equation

  A statement that joins two equal expressions by an '=.'
  In the equation $y = 2x$, the expression $2x$ is joined to the expression y.

- **equilateral triangle**

  A triangle with all sides of equal length.

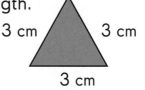

  3 cm   3 cm

  3 cm

- **equivalent**

  Having the same value.

  0.001 is equivalent to $\frac{1}{1000}$.

- **estimate**

  A number close to the exact number.
  You can estimate the sum of 6.75 and 15.45
  by rounding to the nearest whole number.
  6.75 is about 7.
  15.45 is about 15.
  7 + 15 = 22
  The estimate of 6.75 + 15.45 is 22.

- **experimental probability**

  The probability of an event that is based on
  the actual results of trials.

  $$\text{Experimental probability} = \frac{\text{Number of favorable outcomes in an actual experiment}}{\text{Total number of trials}}$$

F————————

- **face**

  A flat surface on a solid figure.

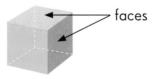

  faces

favorable outcome

A favorable outcome is a desired result.

Anne wants the spinner to land on yellow.
Yellow is a favorable outcome.

---

interest

Amount that a bank pays you for depositing your money with them.

intersecting lines

Lines that meet or cross.
$\overleftrightarrow{AB}$ and $\overleftrightarrow{CD}$ are intersecting lines.

isosceles triangle

A triangle with two sides of equal length.

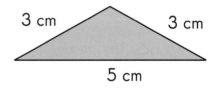

K

- **key**

  The key in a double bar graph shows what data set each color represents.

  The green bars show the Class 5A data and the yellow bars show the Class 5B data.

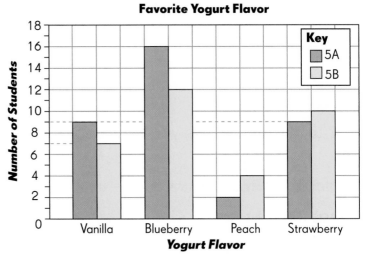

M

- **meals tax**

  Tax to pay for meals in a restaurant.

N

- **net**

  A plane figure that can be folded to make a solid figure.

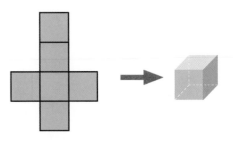

O

- ## obtuse triangle

  A triangle with one angle measure greater than 90°.

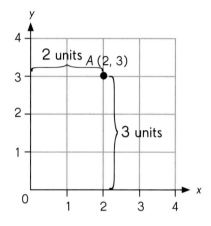

- ## ordered pair

  A pair of numbers used to name a location on a grid.
  The first number tells the distance from the vertical axis.
  The second number tells the distance from the horizontal axis.

  (2, 3) is the ordered pair for point A.

- ## organized list

  An organized list helps you to record combinations in a systematic order.

- ## origin

  The point where the x- and y-axes intersect at right angles in the coordinate plane. The coordinates are (0, 0).

P _____

- **parallelogram**

  A four-sided figure in which both pairs of opposite sides are parallel and congruent.

  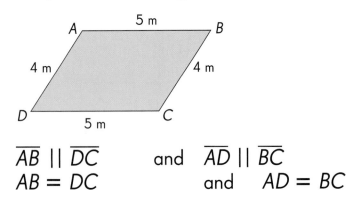

  $\overline{AB} \parallel \overline{DC}$ and $\overline{AD} \parallel \overline{BC}$
  $AB = DC$ and $AD = BC$

- **percent**

  Percent means 'out of 100'.
  The symbol for percent is %.
  75% means 75 out of 100.
  Percent can be expressed as a fraction and a decimal.
  $75\% = \dfrac{75}{100} = 0.75$

- **per unit**

  For each unit.
  Used in talking about rates. The price *per* foot of jump rope means the price of 1 foot of jump rope.

- **prism**

  A solid figure with two parallel congruent faces joined by rectangular faces.

  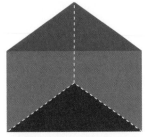 

- **pyramid**

  A solid figure whose base is a polygon and whose other faces are triangles that share a common vertex.

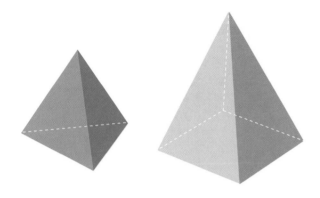

- **rectangular prism**

  A prism with six rectangular faces.

- **rhombus**

  A four-sided figure in which the opposite sides are parallel and the four sides are congruent.

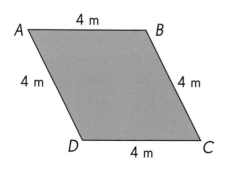

$\overline{AB} \parallel \overline{DC}$ and $\overline{AD} \parallel \overline{BC}$

$AB = BC = CD = DA$

- **right triangle**

  A triangle that has one 90° angle.

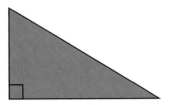

S ────────────

- **sales tax**

  Tax to pay upon buying products.

- **scalene triangle**

  A triangle with three sides of different lengths.

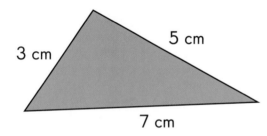

3 cm 5 cm 7 cm

- **sphere**

  A sphere is a solid figure with a smooth curved surface, and no edges or vertices.

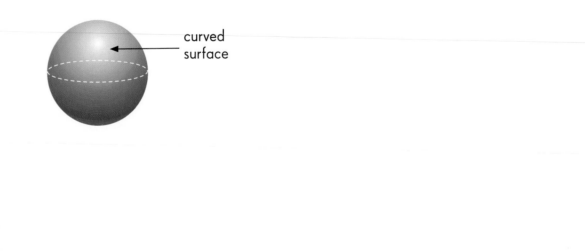

curved surface

- **square pyramid**

  A pyramid with a square base.

  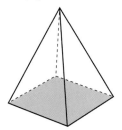

- **straight line graph**

  A graph in which all the points fall on a straight line.

  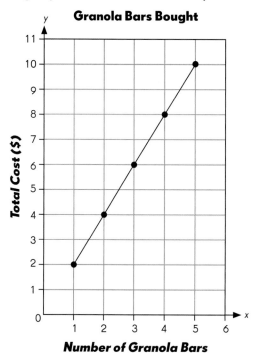

- **surface area**

  The total area of the faces (including bases) and curved surfaces of a solid figure.

T

- **theoretical probability**

  If each outcome is equally likely, the theoretical probability of an event is

  $$\frac{\text{Number of favorable outcomes}}{\text{Total number of possible outcomes}}$$

- **thousandth**

  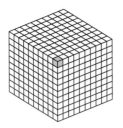
  One part out of thousand is $\frac{1}{1,000}$ (one thousandth).

- **trapezoid**

  A four-sided figure with only one pair of parallel sides.

  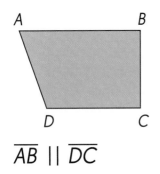

  $\overline{AB} \parallel \overline{DC}$

- **tree diagram**

  A diagram that shows all possible combinations
  of outcomes of an event.

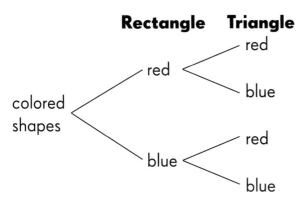

- **triangular prism**

  A prism with triangular bases.

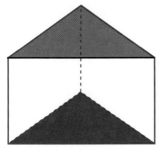

- **triangular pyramid**

  A pyramid with a triangular base.

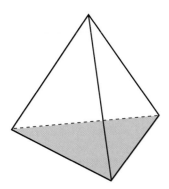

U

- **unit cube**

  A cube in which all the edges are 1 unit long.

V

- **vertex (of a solid figure)**

  The point where three or more edges meet.

  vertices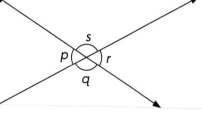

- **vertical angles**

  The congruent angles formed when two lines intersect.

  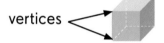

  $\angle p$ and $\angle r$ are vertical angles. So are $\angle s$ and $\angle q$.

  Vertical angles have equal measures.

  $m\angle p = m\angle r$

  $m\angle s = m\angle q$

X

- ## x-axis

  The horizontal axis on a coordinate grid.

  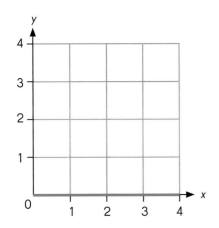

- ## x-coordinate

  In an ordered pair, the number that is written first.
  It tells the distance along the x-axis.
  In (2, 3), 2 is the x-coordinate.

Y ――――――

- **y-axis**

  The vertical axis on a coordinate grid.

  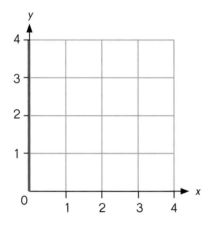

- **y-coordinate**

  In an ordered pair, the number that is written second.
  It tells the distance along the y-axis.
  In (2, 3), 3 is the y-coordinate.

Index

A

Acute triangle, *throughout, see for example* **257**, 264

Addition
    estimating sums,
        with fractions, **124**–126, 156, 158; *WB 98*
        with mixed numbers, **142**–144, 156, 159;
            WB 112
        with whole numbers, 3–4, 27–28, 30, 34–38;
            WB 17, 19
        with decimals, 68–69, 72–74, 82–83; *WB 37, 39*
    expressions involving, *throughout, see for example*
        208–209; *WB 175–176*
    properties, 205, 223
    sum, *throughout, see for example* 48
    using a calculator, *throughout, see for example*
        48–49, 100, 113; *WB 27–28*
    with fractions,
        like denominators, 118, 121; *WB 97*
        unlike denominators, 118, 121–123, 125–126,
            152–154, 156, 158; *WB 95–97*
            modeling, **122**–123; *WB 95–97*
    with like terms, *throughout, see for example* **220**
    with mixed numbers,
        unlike denominators, 140–142, 144, 156, 159;
            WB 109–111
            modeling, 140–142; *WB 109–111*
    with whole numbers, *throughout, see for example* 42

Algebra
    equations, *See* Equations
    coordinate graphs of, **133**–135, 138, 156;
        WB 87–88, 97
    with two variables, 133–135, 156; *WB 87, 97–98*
    expressions, *See* Algebraic expression
    formulas, 248, 256–259, 263
    inequalities, **226**–228, 235, 238–239,
        243–244; 207–212, 227, 229; *WB 133–134*
    inverse operations, 206
    order of operations, **90**–95, 111–112, 206, 222;
        WB 55–62
    properties, *See* Properties
    variables, *throughout, see for example* **209**–245

Algebraic expressions
    comparing, 227; *WB 187*
    evaluating, **211**, 213, 215–216, 218, 242, 244;
        WB 176, 178, 181–182
    forming, **208**–210, 212–218, 244; *WB 175–181*
    in inequalities and equations, **226**–241, 243, 245
    involving addition and subtraction, *throughout, see for*
        example **208**–209; *WB 175–176*
    involving multiplication and division, *throughout, see for*
        example **212**, 214–217, 237, 242, 244;
            WB 175, 181–182
    like terms, *throughout, see for example* **220**
    simplifying, **219**–225, 242, 244–245;
        WB 183–184
    terms, *throughout, see for example* **220**

Algebraic thinking
    angle sums (on a line or at a point), 163–173, 180;
        WB 101–105, 107–108
    bar models, *throughout, see for example* 42–43,
        103–106, 109, 151–152
    functions. *See* Input-output machines, Straight line graphs
    input-output machines (functions), 204
    patterns on a place-value chart, 52–53, 57–58,
        71–72, 75–76, 81

Angle
    acute, 189, 195–196; *WB 122*
    at a point, **169**–173, 178, 180–181;
        WB 105–119, 151–152
    between the parallel sides, 213–218, 220–223, 225,
        227–228; *WB 137–142, 158*
    classifying triangles by, 182–183, 188–190,
        224–226; *WB 122, 125, 127, 130*
    congruent, 186, 190, 198–204, 213–218, 222,
        224–228; *WB 127–131*
    degrees, 159
    equal measures, 174–181; *WB 109*
    form, 158–160, 167–168, 170
    identifying, 158, 160, 168, 172–173, 178
    intersect, 175
    measuring, 159
    measure of an, 159–160, 162–181
    naming of an, 159, 161, 170, 179, 184
    obtuse, 188–190, 193–194, 203–204, 224, 226
    of an acute triangle, 189–190, 192, 194, 199–204,
        224–227; *WB 122*
    of an equilateral triangle, 201–204, 225–226, 228;
        WB 121, 129–132
    of an isosceles triangle, 198–200, 203–204, 225–228;
        WB 127–128, 130–131, 144
    of an obtuse triangle, 188–190, 192–194, 204, 224,
        226; *WB 122*
    of a right triangle, 195–197, 200, 224–227;
        WB 125–126
    of a scalene triangle, 188–190

Pages listed in black regular type refer to Student Book A.
Pages in blue type refer to Student Book B pages.
Pages in *italic* type refer to Workbook (WB) A.
Pages in *blue italic* type refer to Workbook (WB) B pages.
Pages in **boldface** type show where a term is introduced.

D

Pages listed in black regular type refer to Student Book A.
Pages in blue type refer to Student Book B pages.
Pages in *italic* type refer to Workbook (WB) A.
Pages in *blue italic* type refer to Workbook (WB) B pages.
Pages in **boldface** type show where a term is introduced.

Organized list
    to find the greatest common factor, 267
    to find the least common multiple, **122**, 127, 156
    to find the number of combinations, 139–140, 143, 154–155, *WB 89*
    to solve problems, *See* Problem-Solving, Strategies

Origin, **132**

Outcome, 144
    equally likely, 144
    experiment, 148–149
    favorable, 144

Parallelogram, **183**, 211–218, 222, 225–228; *WB 137–138, 144*

Parentheses, order of operations and, 92, 93

Part of a whole
    as a decimal, 88–89
    as a fraction, 88–89
    as a percent, 88–89

Pattern, find a, strategy, *See* Problem-Solving, Strategies

Patterns
    division, 70–72, 74–77, 81
    multiplication, **51**–54, 56–59, 63

Per unit, **59**

Percents, **88**, 95, 117; *WB 55*
    decimals as, 91, 94, 117; *WB 56*
    denominator of 100, 86
    equivalent fraction, 92, 98; *WB 59*
    expressing
        as decimals, 89, 93, 95, 117; *WB 57*
        as fractions, 88–89, 92, 94, 117; *WB 56*
        as fractions in simplest form, 92; *WB 57*
        fraction as, 80, 90, 94, 96–97, 99, 117–118; *WB 59–61*
    model, 89–94
    number line, 91, 93, 95–97; *WB 58, 60*
    of a number, 86, 118; *WB 63–66*
    parts of a whole, 88–90, 106
    real-world problems, *See* real world problems as percent
    involving discount, 110–111, 113–115, 118; *WB 68–69, 82*
    involving interest, 112–113, 115, 119; *WB 67, 69*
    involving meals tax, 109, 115; *WB 69–70*
    involving sales tax, 108, 113–115, 119; *WB 67, 81*
    of a number, 101–104, 106–107, 118; *WB 63–66, 80*

Perimeter, *WB 87*

Period of a number, **8**, 10, 13, 38; *WB 2*

Perpendicular line segments, 247; 160, 162, 160, 163, 167–168, 177, 179

Place value
    charts,
        for decimals, 3, 5–6, 8–13, 16–19, 21–22, 36–39, 51, 53–55; *WB 1–2, 5, 21, 33*
        through hundreds, 52
        through thousands, 71–72, 81
        through ten thousands, 2, 57, 75–76
        through hundred thousands, 5–8, 16, 20–21, 53; *WB 1–3, 7, 11*
        through millions 9–10, 12–13, 18, 20, 36, 38–39, 58; *WB 5–6, 9, 12*
    meaning of, **16**,18

Positive numbers, 14, 15

Practice
    Guided Practice, 6–8, 10, 12–13, 16–18, 21–23, 25–28, 30–34, 53–56, 59–63, 65–69, 72, 74, 77, 79–80, 82, 84–88, 90–93, 96–98, 100–101, 104–105, 107, 123–124, 128–129, 132–133, 135–138, 141–143, 145–148, 150–152, 166, 170, 172–173, 176, 178, 181–183, 186–187, 191, 194–196, 210–211, 213, 215, 220–223, 227–228, 231, 234, 236 –237, 239, 253, 260, 270, 272–273, 278–279, 281, 283–286, 288, 291–293, 297, 299–300, 303–306, 308; 8–10, 12–14, 19, 21, 24–25, 37–38, 41, 44–45, 48–49, 52, 54, 56–58, 61–63, 65–66, 69–73, 76–78, 89–93, 97–98, 102, 104, 109, 111–112, 127, 132, 135, 140–142, 145, 147, 164, 166, 170–171, 175–177, 187, 189, 192, 197, 200, 202, 207, 209–210, 215–219, 221, 236, 238–239, 241, 247–248, 260–261, 268, 270, 272, 276, 278–279, 281, 289–293

Pages listed in black regular type refer to Student Book A.
Pages in blue type refer to Student Book B pages.
Pages in *italic* type refer to Workbook (WB) A.
Pages in *blue italic* type refer to Workbook (WB) B pages.
Pages in **boldface** type show where a term is introduced.

associative properties, 205
commutative properties, 205, 223
distributive property, 205
equality properties, 228–230
identity properties, 205
special properties of four-sided figures, 183, 211–217, 219–221, 226
triangle properties, 186–189, 203, 224–226
zero property, 205

Protractor, 159, 162–164, 167, 170, 172, 175

Put on Your Thinking Cap!, *See* Problem Solving

Pyramid, **235**, 238–239, 241–242, 244–245, 252, 254–255; *WB 160–161, 195*

Quick Check *See* Assessment

Quotients
computing, *throughout, see for example* 50, 99–100, 102, 104, 108, 113; *WB 27*
decimals, 51–67; *WB 25–36*
estimating, **33**, 34, 37, 40, 44, 46, 79–81, 83–85, 111, 113; *WB 22, 48, 50–51*
rounding to the nearest hundredth, 57–58; *WB 7–8, 13*
rounding to the nearest tenth, 56, 58; *WB 7, 13*

Rates, 59

Ratios
as comparison of relative size, 271
different forms of, **269**–270, 290, 313
equivalent, **276**–289, 296–304, 311, 313–315; *WB 215–216, 227–228*
in fraction form, 290–295; *WB 221–226*
part-whole models and, 273; *WB 213 –214*
reading, **269**–270
simplifying, *throughout, see for example,* **279**, 296–297
terms of, **269**
using to compare,
two quantities, **269**–275; *WB 209–214*
three quantities, 296–301; *WB 227–228*
writing, 269–270, 290, 292, 313

Rays, 247; 158–159, 161, 169–170; *WB 105, 120*

Reasoning, 125, 129, 143, 168; *WB 75, 195*

Real-World problems
algebra, 236–240; *WB 189–192*
decimals
addition, 68, 77, 80, 84; *WB 49*
division, 51, 54, 76–78, 80, 84; *WB 41–46, 48–51*
multiplication, 39–40, 76–78, 80, 84; *WB 40–49, 51–52, 54*
subtraction, 78, 80, 84; *WB 42–43, 45, 47–48, 51–52, 54*
multiplication and division with fractions, 190–197; *WB 147–148*
multiplication with fractions, 169–174; *WB 133–138*
multiplication with mixed numbers, 181–184; *WB 153 – 157*
percents
of a number, 101–104, 106–107, 118; *WB 63–69, 71*
involving discount, 110–111, 113–115, 118; *WB 68–69*
involving interest, 112–113, 115, 118; *WB 67*
involving meals tax, 109, 115; *WB 69–70*
involving sales tax, 108, 113–115, 118; *WB 67*
ratios and more ratios, 283–289, 302–310; *WB 217–220, 229–234*
use fractions and mixed numbers, 150–153, *WB 117–127*
use multiplication and division, 96–108; *WB 63–72*

Recall Prior Knowledge, *See* Prerequisite skills

Reciprocals
using to divide, **185**–187, 189; *WB 149–152*

Rectangles
area of, *throughout, see for example* 248
perimeter of, 205

Rectangular prism, **237**, 257–258, 263–266, 269–270, 274–275, 277, 279–280, 282–283, 286–288, 296, 299–301; *WB 159, 165, 169–177, 180–184, 186–193*

Pages listed in black regular type refer to Student Book A.
Pages in blue type refer to Student Book B pages.
Pages in *italic* type refer to Workbook (WB) A.
Pages in *blue italic* type refer to Workbook (WB) B pages.
Pages in **boldface** type show where a term is introduced.

volume of, 286–288, 296–301; *WB 199*

ainder
  divide decimals, 53–57
  interpreting, 96, 97, 102

resentation, *See* Models, Number lines, Variables.

ources
  technology,
    calculator, 47–50, 55, 60, 73, 78, 98–100, 102, 104,
      108; *WB 27–28, 36, 63, 65–66, 72, 207*
    computer drawing tool, 123, 128, *196*
    internet, 11, 15
  non-technology, *See* Manipulatives

iew
  Chapter Review/Test, *See* Assessment
  Chapter Wrap Up 36–37, 110–111, 156–157,
    200–201, 242–243, 263, 313; *26–27, 82, 116,*
    154, 180–181, 224–225, 252–253, 298–299

mbus, **183**, 185, 216–218, 222, 225–227;
  WB 139–140, 143

ht angle, 247

ht triangle, *throughout, see for example* **257**

nding
  decimals, 4, 6, 20–22, 27–29, 56–58, 68–80, 82–83;
    WB 7–8, 13
  whole numbers, 3–4, 25–27, 34, 39, 43,
    46; *WB 15–16*
  to estimate 3–4, 27–28, 32–36, 39, 43, 46,
    61–63; *WB 17–18, 22, 35*

es tax, **108**, 113–116, 118; *WB 67, 69*

ere, **232**, 247–250, 253–254; *WB 163–164*

es of figures, **251**

plest form of fractions, *throughout, see for example* 267

plest form of ratios, **276**, 278, 301

Skip counting, **5**, 6, 9, 10; *WB 1*

Square pyramid, **238**, 244–245, 250, 252; *WB 161*

Squares,
  area of, *throughout, see for example* 248

Standard form, 2, 4, 6, 7, 10, 12, 14, 36, 38; *7–8, 10–12;*
  WB 1–3, 5–6; WB 1–2

Straight line graph (on a coordinate grid), 133–136, 138,
  156; *WB 87–88, 97*

Strategies, *See* Problem Solving

Subtraction
  difference, *throughout, see for example* 48
  estimating differences
    with fractions, 129–130, 156, 158; *WB 101*
    with mixed numbers, 147–149, 156, 159;
      WB 116
    with whole numbers, 3, 4, 27–29, 31–32, 34–37,
      39; *WB 18, 20–21*
  expressions involving, *throughout, see for example*
    208–209; *WB 175–176*
  using a calculator, *throughout, see for example*
    48–49, 102, 108, 113; *WB 27*
  with decimals, 69, 72–74, 82–83; *WB 37, 39*
  with fractions,
    like denominators *throughout, see for example,*
      118, 121
    unlike denominators, *throughout, see for example*
      118, 121, 127–128, 130, 151, 156, 158;
      WB 99–100
    modeling, 127–128; *WB 99–100*
  with like terms, *throughout, see for example,* 221
  with mixed numbers,
    unlike denominators, **145**–149, 156, 159;
      WB 113–115
    modeling, 145–147; *WB 113–115*
  with percents, 103–104, 107, 110–111, 115, 118;
    WB 65–66, 69
  with whole numbers, *throughout, see for example* 42

Surface area, **267**–274, 298, 300–301; *WB 173–176,*
  198, 213

T

Table,
  Using data from, 40, 101–102, 274; *120, 124, 127–130, 133–134*; *WB 68, 209–210*

Tally chart, 120, 146–148, 150–152; *WB 96*

Tangram, 182

Terms of a ratio, **269**

Theoretical probability, **144**–145, 147–155,

Three-dimensional shapes, 235
  cylinder, sphere, and cone, 246–250, 253–255;
    WB 163–164
  describing by its faces, edges, and vertices, 235–239,
    243–248, 252–254; *WB 159–161, 163–164*
  nets, 240–242, 246, 253–255; *WB 162, 164, 166*
    243–248, 252–254;
  prisms and pyramids, 235–245, 251–252, 254;
    WB 159–161, 165

Thousandths, 7–14, 17–21, 24–26, 28, 44, 63–64

Trapezoid, **183,** 211, 219–221, 223, 225–227;
  WB 141–142, 144

Tree diagram, **140**–143, 145, 154–156; *WB 90–91*

Triangles,
  acute, *throughout, see for example* **257**, 264; *189–192, 194, 199–204, 224–227*
  angles, *See* Angles
  area of, **256**–265
  base of, **251**–259, 262–264; *WB 197*
  equal, 183, 185–190, 194–195, 198–204, 224–228
  equilateral, 186–187, 189–190, 201–204, 223–228;
    WB 121, 129–132
  height of, **252**–259, 262–264; *WB 197–198*
  inequalities
    compare lengths of sides, 205–210, 225
    form, 208–210; *WB 133–136, 154*
    greater than, 205–210, 225
    less than, 209–210
    possible lengths, 209–210, 228
  isosceles, 186–188, 190, 198–200, 203–204,
    224–228; *WB 122, 127–128, 130–131, 144*

measurement
  of angles, 189–190, 196; *WB 123, 125, 129*
  of sides, 187, 190, 206; *WB 129*
obtuse, *throughout, see for example* **257**; *186*
opposite, 198–199
parts of, **251**
right, *throughout, see for example* **257**; *186, 188*
scalene, 186, 188–190, 203–204, 224, 246; *WB 121*
side, **251**
vertex, **251**

Triangular prism, **237**, 239, 241, 244, 251–252, 255,
  257–258, 271–272, 274; *WB 159, 165*

Triangular pyramid, **239**, 241, 244, 252, 254–255;
  WB 160, 165

U

Unit cube, **259**–265, 275–282, 284, 296–298, 300;
  WB 167–168, 197, 212

Use dot paper to draw
  cubes and rectangular, 264–266, 298, 300,
    WB 169–172, 198

V

Values of digits in numbers, 2, 5–7, 9–10, 12, 16–21,
  36, 39; *WB 7–10, 14*

Variables, *throughout, see for example* **209**–245

Vertex
  of angles, 247; *158–162*
  of cone, 248, 253
  of prisms, 235–238, 252
  of pyramids, 238–239, 252
  of a solid figure, 236–239, 254
  of triangles, **251**; *230–231*

Pages listed in black regular type refer to Student Book A.
Pages in blue type refer to Student Book B pages.
Pages in *italic* type refer to Workbook (WB) A.
Pages in *blue italic* type refer to Workbook (WB) B pages.
Pages in **boldface** type show where a term is introduced.

Photo Credits

Blank

Blank